SPECTRUM MACHINE LANGUAGE FOR THE ABSOLUTE BEGINNER

Edited by
William Tang

Melbourne House Publishers

Published in the United Kingdom by:
Melbourne House (Publishers) Ltd.,
Church Yard,
Tring, Hertfordshire HP23 5LU
ISBN 0 86161 110 1

Published in Australia by:
Melbourne House (Australia) Pty. Ltd.,
Suite 4, 75 Palmerston Crescent,
South Melbourne, Victoria 3205.

Published in the United States of America by:
Melbourne House Software Inc.,
347 Reedwood Drive,
Nashville TN 37217.

Printed in Hong Kong by Colorcraft Ltd.

D C B A 9 8 7 6 5 4 3 2 1 0

Contents

The Beginning

This book is designed as an introduction to the field of machine and assembly language programming for the "Sinclair ZX Spectrum."

It may be that you are coming to this book with no clear idea of what machine language programming is all about.

You may not even know what machine language is. You may not even be aware that there is a difference between machine language and assembly language, nor indeed how they differ from programming in BASIC.

Don't worry, and don't be frightened by the jargon - we will explain everything step by step.

First, let us look at the way a computer operates:

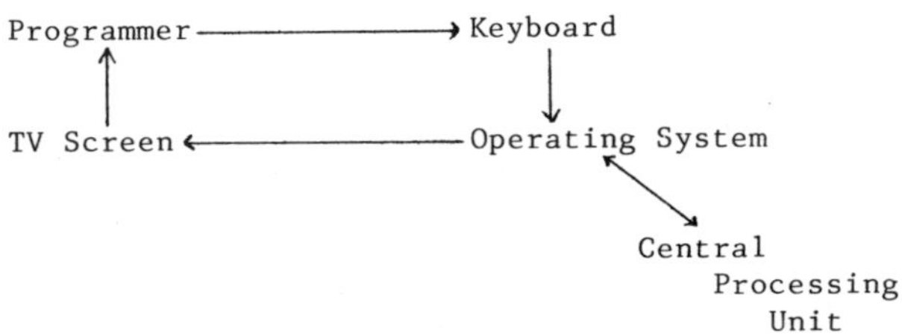

What this diagram aims to show is that there is a barrier between the programmer and the brain of the Spectrum, the Central Processing Unit. It is not possible under normal processing for the programmmer to tell the Central Processing Unit - usually referred to as the CPU - what to do.

In the Sinclair machines, the CPU chosen is the Z80A chip, which is a faster version of the popular Z80 chip. There are 4 chips - Z80, 6502, 6809, and 8088 - which have become widely accepted as CPUs for microcomputers. The Z80 is by far the most popular chip.

I am sure it comes as no surprise to learn that the Z80A does not understand a word of 'BASIC'! Indeed no CPU has been designed so that we can communicate directly with the brain of the computer.

If you think about it for long enough, you will realise that it would be very difficult, if not impossible, in any case to give a chip in a computer an instruction that would make any sense to a human. Take the top off your Sinclair (if you dare!) and have a look at the chip nearest to the speaker - this is the Z80A CPU. Obviously this chip in your computer can only respond to electrical signals that are passed on to it by the rest of the circuitry!

What is Machine Language?

The Z80 chip has been designed in such a way that it can accept signals simultaneously from eight of the pins connected to it.

The designers of the Z80 chip constructed it in such a way that different combinations of signals to the Z80 chip along these eight pins would 'instruct' the Z80 to perform different functions.

Keeping in mind that what is really happening are electrical signals, let's adopt a convention to represent these signals - for example showing a '1' if there is a signal to one of the pins, or a '0'if there is no signal.

A typical instruction might therefore look something like:

0 0 1 1 1 1 0 0

Quite a long way from something like
'Let A = A + 1',
for example, isn't it!

Nonetheless, this is what machine language is all about. The name says it all! It is a language for machines. Each manufacturer of the different chips has designed a different 'language' for its products!

At this stage you may be asking yourself - if this is what machine language is all about, why bother? Why not accept the benefits of someone else's work which allows me to program the computer in a language I can easily understand, such as BASIC or COBOL?

The reason is because of the main benefits of machine language which are:

* FASTER EXECUTION OF THE PROGRAM
* MORE EFFICIENT USE OF MEMORY
* SHORTER PROGRAMS (in memory)
* FREEDOM FROM THE OPERATING SYSTEM

All of the above benefits are a direct result of programming in a language that the CPU can understand without having to have it translated first. When you program in BASIC, the operating system is the machine language program that is really being run by the machine. The program is something like:

```
Next          Look at next instruction
              Translate it into a series of
                 machine language instructions
              Perform each instruction
              Store the result if required
              Go to Next again
```

If you are wondering where the computer finds this program, the operating system, it is in the ROM. In other words, it is built into the Spectrum. (ROM is the abbreviation for Read Only Memory, memory locations whose content you cannot change, but can only be read/PEEKed.)

Programming in BASIC can be up to 60 times slower than a program written directly in machine language!

This is because translation takes time, and also the resulting machine language instructions generated usually are less efficient. Similarly, it is usually faster to drive yourself than to take public transport; you can take shortcuts you know, instead of following the public transport route which needs to cater for the GENERAL public CASE.

Nonetheless, we would have to be among the first to admit that programming in machine language does have drawbacks.

The main disadvantage of machine language are:

* PROGRAMS ARE DIFFICULT TO READ AND DEBUG
* IMPOSSIBLE TO ADAPT TO OTHER COMPUTERS
* LONGER PROGRAMS (in instructions)
* ARITHMETIC CALCULATIONS DIFFICULT

This means that you must make a very conscious decision of which programming method you should use for each particular application.

A very long program for financial applications should be written in a language designed to deal with numbers and one in which programs can be easily modified if required.

On the other hand there is nothing quite so bad as an arcade game written in BASIC - when you get down to it, it is just too slow.

Your own needs, the amount of memory in your computer, the response time required, the time available for development, and so on will determine your choice of programming language.

Thus, in summary, machine language is a series of commands which the CPU can understand and which can be represented by numbers.

What is Assembly Language?

Quite obviously if machine language could only be represented by numbers, very few people would be able to write programs in machine language.

After all, who could make sense of a program which looked like

```
0 0 1 0 0 0 0 1
0 0 0 0 0 0 0 0
0 1 0 0 0 0 0 0
etc ...
```

Fortunately, we can invent a series of names for each of these numbers. Assembly Language is just such a representation of Machine Language so that it can be read by humans in a form that is easier to understand than

0 1 1 1 0 1 1 1.

There is only one difference between Assembly Language and Machine Language: Assembly Language is one level higher than Machine Language. It is more easily read by humans than Machine Language, but on the other hand, computers can't read Assembly Language.

It is not an adaptation of Machine Language such as BASIC. For each Assembly Language instruction there is an identical (in function) Machine Language instruction, and vise versa. ie. there is a ONE-TO-ONE relationship between them. We can therefore say that Assembly Language is EQUIVALENT to Machine Language.

Assembly Language makes use of mnemomics (or abbreviations) to enhance readability. For example at this stage, the instruction

```
INC    HL
```

may not mean much to you, but at least you can read it. If you were told that 'INC' is a standard abbreviation (or mnemonic) for INCrease and that HL is a 'variable', then by simply looking at that instruction you can get a feel for what is happening.

The same instruction in Machine Language is

```
0 0 1 0  0 0 1 1
```

Now obviously you can also "read" that instruction in the sense that you can read the number, but it isn't going to mean much to you unless you have a table to look up or when your brain is functioning almost like a computer.

Assembly Language can be converted directly to machine code by a program or by you. Such a program is called an ASSEMBLER. You can see this as a program which performs the rather boring task of translating your assembly language program into a sequence of machine language instructions that the Spectrum will understand. And we understand that an ASSEMBLER for the ZX Spectrum is already available.

Nonetheless, such assemblers typically require 6K of memory, and are therefore of limited use on a 16K machine. The Spectrum display takes up 7K of memory, and after loading the Assembler you may have only 4K of memory left for your assembly language program. (This will means about 1/2 K of machine language program).

The alternative to an Assembler program is for you to do the translation of the assembly language mnemonics into machine language by hand, using the tables provided in this book.

It's hard, it's frustrating at first, it's inconvenient, but it's wonderful practice and gives you a great insight into the way the Spectrum CPU works.

We would in fact recommend that you try writing short machine language programs in this way - ie writing them in assembly language and translating it into machine language by hand - before buying an Assembler program.

SUMMARY

CPU

The central processing unit of the computer. This is the chip that does the controlling and calculating work in the computer.

Machine Language

The language understood by the CPU. For the Spectrum's CPU, this is the Z80 machine language which is made up of about 200 'instructions'.

BASIC language

A computer language designed to be intelligible to humans. When a computer executes a command in BASIC, it needs to translate this command into a series of machine language commands. BASIC programs are therefore considerably slower than machine language programs but easier to write.

Assembly Language

The human shorthand representation of the machine language instructions so that each of the latter instructions can be understood more easily. For example, HALT is the assembly language equivalent of the machine language instruction 0 1 1 1 0 1 1 0.

Assembler Program

A program that translates assembly language instructions (easily read and understood by human) into machine language instructions (which can be understood by the computer eg the Spectrum).

Read Only Memory (ROM)

A long machine language program usually known as FIRMWARE; a program that has been FIRMLY built into the hardware of the computer; it will remain there even when the power is off. For the Spectrum, the ROM is in Z80 machine code, and was written specifically for it. The ROM of Spectrum occupies from memory locations 0 to 16383. You can only refer to the contents of these locations, unlike the rest of memory which you can refer to and change as desired.

BASIC Machine Language Concepts

WHAT IS THE CPU?

If we want to communicate with the computer we have to know what sort of commands it will accept and what language the brains of the machine (the CPU) talks.

Unless we know what sort of information the CPU understands we can't really instruct the computer to perform remarkable tasks from being a chess partner to an accountant looking after our accounts.

The CPU is no big mystery. I like to think of the CPU as a lonely little fellow, sitting in the middle of your Spectrum, being ask to do things all the time.

Especially calculations.

But the poor fellow doesn't even have a piece of paper and pencil to keep track of what is happening. How does he do it?

The design of the CPU:

At this stage, I should probably tell you about the way that the designers of the Z80 see things, and how the CPU is supposed to handle them. The CPU has been designed to do extremely simple tasks only, but he is able to do those tasks very quickly.

We mentioned above that the CPU doesn't even have pencil and paper, and that is part of the design of the CPU. Any number he can't remember or keep track of has to go in a box for safe keeping.

Let us look at one example - say you want the CPU to work out the time in NEW YORK, knowing the time in LONDON.

Now given that the CPU doesn't know anything, first of all you have to tell it what the time in London is: say 10 o'clock. The CPU has nowhere to keep this information and doesn't know what you will ask it to do next, so it puts that information away in a box, say box #1.

Then you have to tell it the time difference between New York and London, say five hours earlier, and it puts that away in box #2.

Comes the time for calculations, it races across to box #1, gets the number, goes to box #2, performs the calculation, and puts the result away, say in box #3.

$$10 - 5 = 5$$

The answer of course is 5 o'clock.

All of this racing between boxes, adding, substracting and so on would be extremely tedious if the CPU had to do it all in its head, so it does exactly what you or I would do - it counts on its fingers and toes.

The CPU's hands and feet are called Registers.

The Z80 chip in your Spectrum is remarkable in that it has a lot of hands and toes - but we will get to that later.

To illustrate how exactly the CPU calculates the time difference in the above exercise, let's call one of the CPU's hands "HAND A". How does the CPU manipulate the contents of the box #1 and box #2?

The following sequence is pretty close to what the CPU would actually do given the above instructions

* Count out the value of box #1 on the fingers of Hand A;

* Subtract the contents of box #2 from what he has already on his fingers;

* Look at the value on the fingers of Hand A and store it in box #3.

Now if this is what truly happens, there are some pretty phenomenal conclusions to be drawn from this:

1. The CPU would not be able to deal with a number like 11.53 - it could only deal in whole numbers.

2. The CPU would be limited in its calculations to whatever number it could count on its fingers.

This is indeed true.

The main consolation however is that the CPU has a lot of hands and feet and can count on each of them separately, and that it can count to 255 using only the 8 fingers of Hand A.

We will deal in the next chapter with the details of how the CPU can count up to more than 8 on each hand while we can only manage 10 using two hands! Suffice it to say that each hand can count to 255 and each foot can be used to count to over 64,000!

The time difference exercise above has still not been represented in anything like the language the CPU understands - all we have done is describe the processes.

To let you have an early look into the exciting part of machine language programming, let's now use mnemonics (Abbreviations) to instruct the CPU at each step:

```
SETTING UP:
        LD      (BOX #1),    10       ;Load box 1 with 10
        LD      (BOX #2),    5        ;load box 2 with 5

CALCULATIONS:
        LD      A,   (BOX #1)         ;load A with box 1 contents
        SUB     A,   (BOX #2)         ;subtract contents of box 2

STORING THE RESULT:
        LD      (BOX #3),    A        ;load box 3 with A value
```

These instructions may seem a little terse at first, but after all, mnemonics are mnemonics.
"LD" is an abbreviation for LOAD so that

```
        LD  A,1
```

for example, would mean load A with 1: that is count off 'one' on the fingers of hand A.

We also use a rather clever image in these mnemonics by the use of brackets: THE BRACKETS ARE USED TO INDICATE WE WISH TO DEAL WITH THE CONTENTS OF WHATEVER IS INSIDE THE BRACKETS.

It should be fairly easy to remember this on a visual basis because brackets do look like they are meant to indicate a container.

So running through the mnemonics above, we load the contents of Box #1 and #2 with 10 and 5, ...etc... to get the final result of 5 in box #3.

All of this is fairly simple to follow and I am sure you can understand that while you are doing this calculation, the numbers on Hand "A" are used to represent the time in New York. A minute later they may be used to represent the number of employees in a company, and at some other time how much money you have.

If you are used to the concept of variables from your BASIC programming, you must leave that behind in machine language programming.

The fingers of Hand "A" are not a variable in the same sense as in a BASIC program. They are merely what the CPU uses to count with.

ONE OF THE BIG DIFFERENCES IN PROGRAMMING IN MACHINE LANGUAGE AND PROGRAMMING IN BASIC IS THIS LACK OF VARIABLES.

You may realise that you can think of the BOXES we use to store information as being similar to BASIC variables if we gave each one a name.

Yes, you are absolutely correct, but these are not variables either. They can be immensely useful and perform similar storage purposes to variables, but bear in mind that these boxes are no more than memory locations set aside for a specific purpose.

The way the CPU copes with negative numbers is different, and we will look into that later.

What if the CPU runs out of hands?:

I should mention here that you would probably find the CPU a very strange looking fellow were you to meet him in the street.

His hands have eight fingers each, and he has eight hands! He only has two feet, but each foot has 16 toes, and he is extremely agile with his toes!

He is therefore well suited for the large number of calculations he is required to do, keeping track of all the numbers on his fingers and toes.

Nonetheless, it is possible that in some cases the CPU will not have enough hands to do the calculation it wishes to perform, or that for one reason or other the programmer will wish the CPU to stop in the middle of calculation to do something else.

The CPU can't just put the information away in boxes, because then it would have to keep some hands free just to keep track of which boxes it put the information in!

The Z80 CPU gets away with using a stack, which is one of those tall spiky things that some people keep on their desks to store bills, spare notes, etc. I am sure you have seen those stacks, where you spike one piece of paper on, and then the next one, and so on. It's a great filing system if you want the top piece of paper only, but very inconvenient if you want one in the middle, because you have to riffle through all the pieces of paper on the stack.

As it happens, it's a very convenient system for the CPU because it ever only needs to look at the top piece of information.

Whenever an interruption causes the CPU to stop doing its calculations, it PUSHes all the information it has on its hands onto the STACK, and as soon as the interruption is over, it POPs the top bits off, and continues with its work.

In computer terminology, we call this spike a "STACK". When we put a piece of information on the stack, we "PUSH" it on, and when we get it off, we "POP" it off.

All kinds of information can be "PUSH"ed and "POP"ed on and off the stack - for example in the middle of a complex calculation the CPU may wish to save all the information on its many hands and feet, and this would then involve many separate "PUSH"es. To retrieve the information, there then needs to be many separate "POP"s.

For reasons best know to the designers of the Z80, our CPU likes to keep the stack stuck to the ceiling. This means that the more information is "PUSH"ed onto the stack, the further the stack grows downwards.

The main advantage of using the stack to store temporary bits of information is that the CPU does not need to remember which box the information is in - it knows it is the last piece of information "PUSH"ed on the stack. Naturally it needs to be a little bit organised if there are many bits of information to be PUSHed and POPed.

What can the CPU do?:

I think it's worth considering at this stage the type of instructions that the designers thought it would be useful to have built into the Z80 chip.

Because the CPU has to be able to keep track of all its calculations on its fingers and toes, there are only two kinds of numbers the CPU can deal with:

* one handed numbers - ie numbers you can count on one hand
* two handed numbers - ie numbers you can count off on two hands.

You may find this difficult to believe, but the CPU cannot deal with numbers larger than those it can count on two hands!

The types of instructions the CPU can perform are also very limited:

* counting off numbers on one hand
* counting off numbers on two hands
* adding, subtracting, increasing, decreasing, or comparing one handed numbers
* adding, subtracting, increasing or decreasing two handed numbers
* various manipulations on one handed numbers - eg making the number negative
* making the CPU skip to another part of the program
* trying to communicate one handed numbers to and from the outside world.

I am sure you will agree that this is a very limited set of instructions, and yet using only such limited instructions you can get the CPU to play chess, or to work out your wages!

Note that even such simple instructions as multiplication do not exist! If you need to multiply two numbers in machine language you have to write a program to do so.

This is why writing programs in machine language is so much slower than writing programs in BASIC - you can only do things in tiny little steps.

SUMMARY:

Registers

The CPU has a number of registers it can use for calculations. Eight of these can be thought of as the CPU's hands, and two of these can be thought of as the CPU's feet. Each 'hand' has eight 'fingers', while each 'foot' has 16 'fingers'.

Memory Locations

The CPU can transfer information from its hands into or from any other other hand, and into or from memory.

Specific memory locations can be set aside by the programmer to represent specific information.

The Stack

The CPU can use the stack to transfer information the programmer may wish to store temporarily. Information is transferred to the stack by PUSHing the information on, and is retrieved by POPping the information off.

Possible Instructions

The kinds of instructions the CPU is able to perform are only the simplest type of information transfer and simple arithmetic calculations. All programs must be made up of series of these simple instructions.

The Way Computers Count

We mentioned previously that the CPU was able to count to 255 using only eight fingers. How can this be when with 10 fingers we can only manage to count to 10?

It is certainly not because computers are smarter (they aren't) but because the CPU is more organised in its information than we are: why should raising your index finger have the same value (= '1') as having your little finger raised?

It seems obvious that if you so wished you could represent two different numbers in this way.

It is very much the same sort of thing as realising that the number 001 is different from the number 100. The plain truth is that humans are not very efficient in the use of fingers for counting.

The CPU understands that not having a finger is of some information and that which finger is raised is a valuable piece of information.

With only two fingers it is possible to devise a way to count from 0 to 3, as follows:

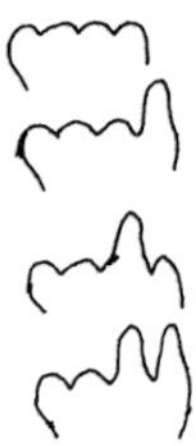

00 = 0 We can indicate not having a finger raised as '0',

01 = 1 and having a finger raised as '1'.

10 = 2 This does not mean 11 = 3

11 = 3 It means we chose to let the representation 11 (or two fingers) have the value 3.

We could just as easily have chosen a different representation.

There is a direct relationship between this and binary Representation. The CPU"s fingers are locations in memory and they can be made to indicate on an off (or '0' and '1' as convention dictates).

If we added a third finger to our example above we could represent all the numbers from 0 to 7. Three fingers for all the numbers from 0 - 7!

Four fingers would be able to represent all the numbers from 0 to 15! If you don't believe it, it would be a good exercise to write out all the possibilities for four fingers being raised.

In order to simplify the notation of such numbers, and to avoid confusion in trying to write down the number eleven as opposed to indicating that two bits were set, a universal convention has been adopted:

The numbers 10 - 15 are indicated by the letters A - F.

Decimal	10 =		A
	11 =		B
	12 =		C
	13 =		D
	14 =		E
	15 =		F

This means we write the numbers from 0 to 15 decimal as

0 1 2 3 4 5 6 7 8 9 A B C D E F

Simple, isn't it?

This way of treating numbers is called the HEXADECIMAL FORMAT.

To prevent confusion, some people write "H" after a hexadecimal number (eg. 10H). The "H" has no value, but serves to remind the user of the hexadecimal convention.

In machine language programming, it is CONVENIENT to deal with numbers in hexadecimal format.

This is only a convention and if you so wished you could write all your instruction in normal decimal format. It is convenient for us to use the hexadecimal format because:

1. It is easy to convert from this form to binary, which tells us which bit (or finger) is doing what.

2. It gives us an easy means of seeing whether numbers are one handed or two handed - ie 8-bit or 16-bit.

3. It standardises all numbers to sets of 2-digit numbers. (We will elaborate on this)

4. It is the common convention and familiarity with hexadecimal will allow you to read other books and manuals more easily.

5. As the CPU is designed to process information represented by binary numbers which are cubersome for humans to read, we need a representation which is more easily readable.

But it is only a convention and not a sacred rule.

The hexadecimal system, as we mentioned earlier, lets us represent the numbers 0 to 15 using only 4 bits. Any 8-bit memory location or 8-bit register can therefore be described by two sets of 4 bits.

(This is the same as saying that any combination of 10 fingers can be represented by two hands of 5 fingers each.)

THE REASON WE ARE CONCERNED WITH 8-BIT MEMORY LOCATIONS AND 8-BIT REGISTERS IS THAT THIS IS THE STRUCTURE OF THE ZX SPECTRUM.

All memory locations and all single registers have 8 bits. This is not hard to understand - it's like saying all humans have 5 fingers on each hand.

Taking things one step at a time, let us become familiar with 4 fingers first:

```
1 1 1 1 = 2**3 + 2**2 + 2**1 + 2**0
        = 8 + 4 + 2 + 1
        = Decimal 15
        = F (in hexadecimal notation)
```

For those of you with a mathematical bent, you may notice that the number each finger represents is multiplied by 2 as you go to the left. If we number the fingers:

then the value of each finger is '2 to the power N' where N is the finger number. Let's call a 4-finger hand a "handlet" (just as a small cigar is a cigarette?)

Exercise:

What decimal and hexadecimal value do the following arrangement of bits (or fingers) represent?

	Decimal	Hexadecimal
0010	2	2
0110	6	6
1001	9	9
1010	10	A
1100	12	C

It is important for you to become familiar with the hexadecimal convention, and if you had difficulty with the concept, do read the last few pages again before going on.

Let us examine what happens if we want a number greater than 15? Say 16? We would use the next finger on the left, as:

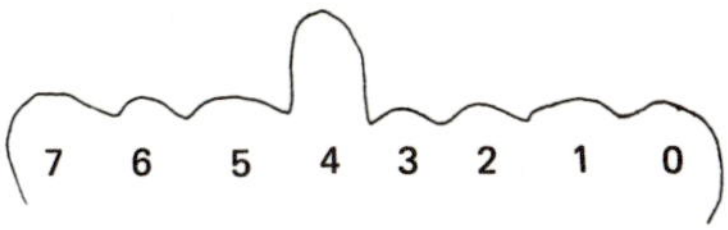

= 16 decimal = 10H (Hexadecimal)

The reason we write the number as 10H is that we divide the hand into two "4-bit handlets". We can therefore easily denote each handlet by one of the hexadecimal numbers representing 0 to 15 (0-9 & A-F).

In this way any 8-bit hand can be written as exactly two hexadecimal handlets:

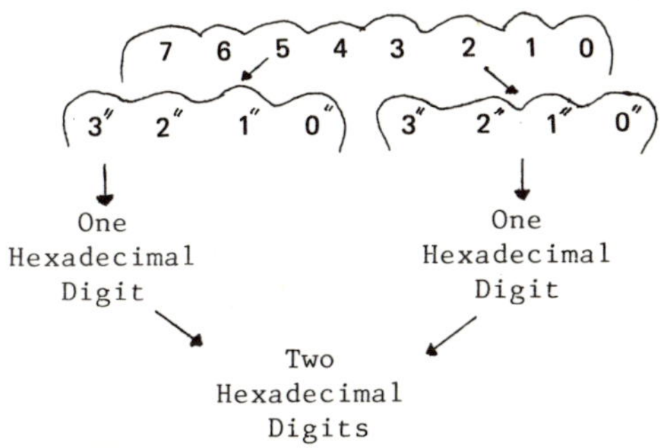

The "handlet" on the left indicates 16 times as much as the "handlet" on the right. This is much the same way as in decimal notation, the digit in the "tens" column is worth ten times as much as the digit in the "ones" column.

We convert numbers in decimal format such as 15 automatically to:

15 = (1*10) + 5

This is so automatic that we don't even think about it.

It is exactly the same thing in hexadecimal notation. To convert back from hexadecimal notation to decimal notation, we multiply the hexadecimal number on the left "handlet" by 16. Using the example above:

10H = (1*16) + 0
= 16 Decimal

This is how we are able to count to 255 using only 8 fingers. The maximum is obtained when all fingers are held up:

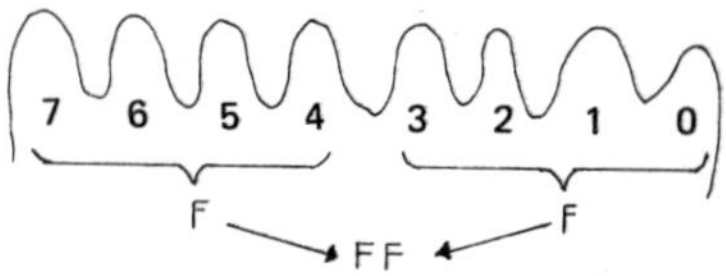

FFH = (F*16) + F
    = (15*16) + 15 (in decimal)
    = 255 (Decimal)

The smallest number is when no fingers are held up:

OOH = 0 Decimal

Note that all numbers, from the smallest to the largest require 2 and only 2 digits to define the number.

Try out for yourself any combination of 8 digits and see if you can convert it to hexadecimal notation, and then into decimal notation.

It may seem a little strange and awkward at first, but you will soon get the hang of it.

Also that when you count in hexadecimal, you do the same as in decimal:

Decimal: 26 27 28 29 30 etc.

Hexadecimal: 26 27 28 29 2A 2B 2C 2D 2E 2F 30 etc.....

The values of the numbers in the decimal and hexadecimal series above have different values of course. Note that after 29H you get 2AH, not 30H!

The following BASIC program will enable you to input to your Spectrum a decimal number and convert it to a hexadecimal value.

```
100 REM decimal to hexadecimal conversion
110 PRINT "Please input decimal value."
120 INPUT n : PRINT n
130 LET S$ = "" 135  LET n2 = INT (n/16)
140 LET n1 = INT (n - n2*16)
150 LET S$ = CHR$ ((n1 (= 9) * (n1 + 48) +
        (n1 )9)*(55 + n1)) + S$
160 IF n2 = 0 THEN PRINT : PRINT "HEXADECIMAL = 0"; S$
        ; " H": FOR I = 1 TO 200: NEXT I: RUN
170 LET n = n2: GO TO 135
```

Try converting the following numbers to theirs hexadecimal value and use the BASIC program to test your answer.

i.	16384	memory address of the start of Spectrum display file
ii.	22528	memory address of the start of Spectrum attribute file
iii.	15360	memory address of the start of Spectrum character set
iv.	15616	address of the start of ASCII characters in Spectrum

SUMMARY:

Decimal

The decimal notation is a convention of counting numbers in groups of ten units at a time. These are represented by 0, 1, 2, 3, 4, 5, 6, 7, 8, and 9.

Hexadecimal

The hexadecimal notation is a convention of counting numbers in groups of 16 units at a time. These are represented by 0, 1, 2, 3, 4, 5, 6, 7, 8, 9, A, B, C, D, E, and F.

Sometimes an H is added at the end of a hexadecimal number to remind us it is written in this format. For example, 1800H.

8-Bit Memory Locations

The ZX Spectrum is designed so that each memory location has 8 bits ('fingers'). Each memory location can store a number from 0 to 255 decimal. This is conveniently represented in the hexadecimal format as a two digit number.

How Information is Represented

There is a big difference in information representation between human and computer. Human information is mainly composed of numbers and characters (alphanumeric information), whereas all information in a computer is stored as groups of bits.

A bit stands for Binary digIT ("0" or "1"); in the Z80A microprocessor, these bits are structured in groups of eight. A group of eight bits is called a BYTE.

This way of representing information using binary digits is called the BINARY FORMAT. This is the structure of the language which the Z80 and most microcomputer CPUs talk.

Basically, there are two types of information represented inside the Spectrum. The first one is the PROGRAM. The second one is the DATA on which the program will operate, which may include numbers or alphanumeric text. We will thus discuss below these three representations: PROGRAM, NUMBERS, and ALPHANUMERICS.

Program Representation

A PROGRAM is a sequence of instructions to the CPU to perform a particular task which can be broken down into a number of "sub-tasks".

In the Z80, all instructions are represented internally as single or multiple bytes. Instructions represented by one byte are called the "SHORT instructions". Longer instructions are represented by two or more bytes.

Because the Z80 is an eight-bit microprocessor, it can only deal with one byte at a time, and if it requires more than one, it fetches bytes successively from memory. Therefore, a single-byte instruction will generally be executed more quickly than a two- or three-byte instruction. Thus, as a general rule, it is always more efficient to write your machine language program using single-byte instructions where possible.

You can turn to the instruction set table in the Appendix and have a look at the SHORT and LONG instructions. Don't worry if you can't understand them, we will discuss each instruction in depth later on.

Numeric Data Representation

* Integer Representation

We discussed earlier that because of the way the Z80 is designed we cannot have a number such as 11.53. The CPU can only deal in whole numbers. Also, by using only 8 fingers (ie an 8-bit number), we could represent all the numbers in the range 0 to 255.

e.g. decimal 255 is represented by OFFH
    the binary representation of which is 1 1 1 1 1 1 1 1

But what about negative numbers?

* Signed Integer Representation

Remember one byte is a HAND with eight fingers and a number is represented by holding different fingers up.

Obviously, to represent signed integer in Binary Format, we have to have some way of representing a positive or negative numbers. Let's say that in order to represent a negative number, we adopt the following convention (signed representation):

A NUMBER ON THE CPU'S HAND WILL BE CONSIDERED TO BE A NEGATIVE NUMBER IF THE CPU HOLDS HIS THUMB UP. (in computer terminology, the highest bit - bit 7 is on.)

So we have only seven fingers (bits) left to represent the value of the number. That means the highest number we can have is no longer 255. In fact, half of the numbers which can be held on a single HAND (a single byte) will be negative and half of them will be positive (depending on whether the thumb is up or not).

The total number range possible on one hand if we allow negative numbers will therefore be from -128 to +127. (Note that the total number range that can be represented will still be 256 numbers).

Now comes the crunch: When is a number with the thumb up a large positive number and when is it a negative number?

The answer is whenever you feel like it; You have to make a choice: numbers can either be in the range of 0 to 255 or in the range -128 to +127. They can't be both at the same time! It is up to you, the programmer, to decide which convention you are using at a particular time.

All the instructions will work equally well, whether you choose to let the number contained in the registers or memory be all positive or positive and negative.

* Choosing a Representation for negative numbers:

We have already decided that holding the thumb up will mean the number is negative, and not holding the thumb up means it is positive. Is this enough?

No. We need to decide which of the 127 possibilities of the remaining 7 fingers will denote -1, which one -2, and so on.

We need a representation of negative numbers, such that when a number is added to its negative we get zero. As an execise, let's think about the number which when added to 1 gives us zero: (This will obviously be -1, and we already know that the thumb - bit 7 - will be up)

```
      0 0 0 0  0 0 0 1                        0 0 0 0  0 0 0 1
      1 ? ? ?  ? ? ? ?   could it be=)?       1 0 0 0  0 0 0 1
     -----------------                       -----------------
      0 0 0 0  0 0 0 0                        1 0 0 0  0 0 1 0
```

Let's try 1 0 0 0 0 0 0 1 - in other words, the same as +1, but with the thumb up. To test if that is -1, let's try adding this value to +1. From above the sum 10000010 is obviously not the right answer! If it was right, the answer would have been 0 0 0 0 0 0 0 0. Obviously, we need a number that will take that carry from Bit 0, and convert it to zeros all along.

You can try to do it yourself, and you will see that the only number which will give us the right answer is

```
      1 1 1 1  1 1 1 1    (FFH in hexadecimal)
```

To confirm this:

```
           0 0 0 0  0 0 0 1
           1 1 1 1  1 1 1 1
      <--  ----------------
(carry)    0 0 0 0  0 0 0 0
```

Is there a way that we can work out a general rule for the negative of any number from this example? It looks as if though we might have to get the opposite of the number and add one at the end.

Let's try this rule on another number, such as 3, say:

```
3=         0 0 0 0  0 0 1 1
opposite   1 1 1 1  1 1 0 0
add 1 =)   1 1 1 1  1 1 0 1      (FDH)
```

Let's add to this number to 3 and see what happens:

```
          0 0 0 0  0 0 1 1
          1 1 1 1  1 1 0 1
    <-    ----------------
(carry)   0 0 0 0  0 0 0 0        It works!
```

We have found a way to represent negative numbers!

```
          -01 =)  FF
          -02 =)  FE
          -03 =)  FD and so on.
```

The largest positive number is

```
          0 1 1 1  1 1 1 1  =  7F  =)  127 Decimal
```

and the negative of this is

```
          1 0 0 0  0 0 0 1  =  81  =) -127 Decimal
```

The real test of this rule is to see if by applying the rule to a negative number we get back the positive again!

Let's try it out on -3 which we worked out above is FDH.

```
Number     1 1 1 1  1 1 0 1
Opposite   0 0 0 0  0 0 1 0
Add 1=)    0 0 0 0  0 0 1 1     =) 3
```

This is therefore a representation that works! We can apply it to get the negative of any number.

16 - bit Negatives

Exactly the same reasoning applies to two handed numbers (16-bit numbers), except that the thumb of only one hand needs to be shown as 'ON' to indicate if the number is negative or not. (ie. bit 7 of the high byte).

Convention:

The computer terminology for this convention is called TWO's COMPLEMENT. You can find 2's complement tables for negative decimal numbers at the Appendix of this book.

Remember that this is only a convention! You still have to decide at all times whether the numbers you are using are meant to designate numbers in the range 0 to 255 or numbers in the range -128 to +127.

Exercise:

i. If 127 (0 1 1 1 1 1 1 1) is the highest positive

number which can be represented in this convention, how would you represent -128?

ii. Find the highest positive 16-bits (TWO HANDS/BYTES) and the highest 16-bits negative number? iii. Find the 2's complement of the smallest 16-bit negative number 8000H. Why is it 8000H?

Alphanumeric Data Representation

Sometimes, in machine language we do not want the numbers to be instructions for the computer, nor do we want them to be numbers for calculations. we may just want them to represent characters of letters and numbers - eg. the title of your latest program, perhaps called "THE WORLD'S NUMBER 1 PROGRAM".

Our convention to represent alphanumeric data, ie. characters is pretty straightforward: all characters and numbers can be represented on a single hand (ie in an eight-bit code).

In the computer world, there are two standards for alphanumeric characters representation: The ASCII Code, and the EBCDIC Code.

ASCII stands for "American Standard Code for Information Interchange" and is universally used in the microcomputer industry. EBCDIC is a variation of ASCII used by IBM.

In the ZX Spectrum, alphanumeric characters conform to the ASCII standard except for the pound (61H) and copyright (7FH) characters. You can find an ASCII conversion Table in the Appendix. Compare it with the character set table in appendix A of your Spectrum manual pp 183-186.

Try this : PRINT CHR$ 33
and you will get a "!"; because "!" is represented internally by 21H.

HELP!: We have just shown that the CPU's hand can be said to show a variety of things:

It could be
- a program instruction to the CPU
- a number in the range 0 to 255
- a number in the range - 128 to + 127
- part of a two handed number
- an alphanumeric character

This is all true, and it is up to you, the programmer, to remember just what it is the CPU's hand is supposed to be holding.

SUMMARY:

Memory Contents

The Spectrum's memory can store programs, numbers, or text, as we desire. There is no way of telling which is which just by examining the contents of a single memory location.

Programs

Program instructions are stored in memory as sequences of bytes. Some instructions require only one byte, while others require up to four bytes.

Numbers

Each memory location can be used to store either positive integer numbers or signed integer numbers (numbers which can be positive or negative), as we choose. The range of numbers is either from 0 to 255 or -128 to +127.

Negative Numbers

A convention has been adopted that when we choose to have memory store a signed (+ or -) number, the following rule shall apply:

If bit 7 is on, the number is negative

If bit 7 is not on, the number is positive

To obtain the negative of any number, get the "2's complement" and add 1.

2's Complement

The 2's complement of any number is its opposite in binary form. Any bit that is on becomes off, and vice versa.

A Look into the CPU

Introduction

We have said that the brain of the Spectrum is the CPU, the Z80A processor. This is a faster version of the Z80 processor produced under a licence from Zilog Inc.

The only difference between the Z80 and Z80A processors is that the former processor is running at a clock speed of 2 Mhz/s (Megahertz per second) while the later processor is running at a clock speed of 3.5 Mhz/s. 'Clock speed' is merely a measure of how fast the CPU is performing its calculations. In the Spectrum, 3.5 million clock pulse signals are generated per second, ie one clock pulse every 0.000000286 of a second.

The fastest instruction the CPU can perform takes up 4 clock pulses, while the slowest requires 21 clock pulses. That means, that even if all instructions performed are the slowest ones, about 160,000 instructions can be performed each second!

A Physical View of The Brain

The processor in the Spectrum is a silicon chip with forty pins numbered from 1 to 40. These pins are the communication lines between the processor and the rest of the computer. For example, the processor draws its power from the power supply through pin 11, gets its clock signals from pin 6, sends addresses in or out through pins 1 to 5 and pins 30 to 40, and sends data in or out through pins 7 to 15 except pin 11. The rest of pins are for control signals communication.

You may find yourself totally lost at this stage. But no need to puzzle, it's really to our advantage that we don't know the internal structure of the machine, and we don't need to know it to use its capabilities. It's just the same as with a calculator. The physical structure of the machine is 'transparent' to the users (in other words we don't see it!). We are only interested in the logical structure of the calculator, or in this case the Z80 chip, and how we can use it to our purposes.

Logical View of The Brain

Logically, the Z80 can be divided into five functional parts.

They are
- i. the CONTROL UNIT
- ii. the INSTRUCTION REGISTER
- iii. the PROGRAM COUNTER
- iv. the ARITHMETIC-LOGIC UNIT
- v. the 24 USER-REGISTERS (the usable HANDS and FEET of the CPU)

* CONTROL UNIT

We can see the CONTROL UNIT as a supervisor for the CPU's processing. Its task is to time and coordinate the Input, Processing, and Output of the particular job that the CPU is being asked to perform, whether the instructions come from the ROM program, or from your program.

* INSTRUCTION REGISTER

This is a HAND that the CPU uses to hold the current instruction that it is going to perform. The whole task which comprises a program must reside somewhere in memory - either in the ROM or in the RAM (Random Access Memory). You may recall that a program is a sequence of instructions. Thus, to perform the task, the CONTROL UNIT has to fetch each instruction in turn from the memory (either ROM or RAM) and place it in the INSTRUCTION REGISTER HAND.

* PROGRAM COUNTER

This is really one of the Z80's FEET which tell the CPU where the next part of the program is (the address of the next memory location from which the CONTROL UNIT is going to fetch an instruction). It is like an instructions warehouse manager keeping track of the location of the next instruction to fetch out.

* ARITHMETIC and LOGIC UNIT

This is the calculator inside the CPU. It can perform both arithmetic and logical operations. Out of all the basic arithmetic functions as you and I know them, this unit can only perform simple addition and subtraction, incrementation (adding 1) and decrementation (subtracting 1), but not multiplication or division. The unit can also compare one handed numbers, or perform 'bit' operations such as rotating fingers around, holding specific fingers up or down, etc.

As a byproduct of the calculations the ALU is asked to perform, the calculations usually affect the status of the various FLAGS in the FLAG register. This is discussed in more detail further on.

* USER-REGISTERS

These are the CPU's Hands and Feet, which you, the programmer, can control.

There are twenty four User-registers within the Z80 microprocessor - some are HANDs, and some are FEET.

The images we have been building up of hands, feet and boxes make the processes easy to visualise and are a good representation of what is going on, but computer buffs tend to look askance if you say things like "...and then the computer shifted its information from its right hand to its left hand."

We will now give you the proper names for the CPU's hands and feet, so that when faced with that situation, you will be able to say:

"LD B,A"

To start off with, computer buffs refer to the hands and feet of the CPU as "registers".

We mentioned earlier that the CPU has eight hands: these are called A, B, C, D, E, F, ...In our world, the definition of a hand is something with eight fingers.

The CPU has two feet: these are named IX and IY. The definition of a foot is anything with 16 toes!

The naming of hands and feet is fairly easy to follow because if a register has only one letter in its name then it must be a hand (that is, contains 8 bits), while if it has two letters in its name then it must be a foot (that is, have 16 bits).

Did you notice the smooth transition from fingers and toes to bits? We will have you used to computer terminology in no time.

Actually the remaining two hands for the CPU after D, E, F, ...are not named "G" and "H" as one would expect but "H" and "L".

The conventional way to represent all these registers is as follows:

A	F
B	C
D	E
H	L
IX	
IY	

Notice that "F" is paired with "A", but after that the rest follow fairly naturally. The reason that registers are paired in this way is that it is sometimes possible to make a foot out of two hands!

After all, if the definition of a foot is something with 16 bits, then maybe we can fake it from time to time and use two 8-bit hands to do the work of a foot. We therefore talk about "register pairs" such as BC, DE, and HL.

The reason the register pair "HL" was called "HL" instead of something like "GH" was to help people remember which of the two registers had the high number and which had the low number.

It's as if though you wished to represent the numbers 0 to 100 on your hands and toes. You can easily set up your fingers to represent the numbers 0 through 10, and similarly with your toes (assuming that you are agile enough). One way you could denote the number 37 in this way would be to count off 3 on your fingers and 7 on your toes. But there has to be some agreement on which is the high number and which is the low number otherwise someone else might think you meant to represent the number 73.

The "H" in "HL" stands for HIGH and the "L" stands for LOW, so there is no chance of confusion - right?

This diagram of register pairs also serves to indicate which register in the other register pairs contains the high number:

B in BC
D in DE

because all the highs and lows are treated in the same order.

The feet (IX and IY) also have a special name: they are called "index registers". This has a lot to do with the fact that they can be used to organise information in much the same way as a book index is organised. Alternatively, you can view them as table pointers.

OK, now that you understand the terminology, here are some special points:

THE ACCUMULATOR (A register)

This 8-bits (single byte) register is the most important register of the Z80. Its name dates back to the early generation of computers when there was only a single register that could be used to 'accumulate' a result.

So, as we have advanced from the early generations of computers, the accumulator continued to be used extensively for logical and arithmetic operations. In fact, most computers are still designed in such a way that many operations can only be performed using the A register.

This is true of the Z80 chip, and the A register is a favoured register. You can think of the A register as being like the CPU's right hand, in the same way that most people can perform some tasks more easily with their right hand than with the left hand.

The Flags:

Please note that "AF" is not usually treated as a register pair. The "F" in this case is used to denote "Flag Register". This is a hand with 8 fingers such that each finger indicates whether a certain condition is met or not met and we will be dealing with this in a separate chapter.

The HL Register Pair:

Of the three register pairs (BC, DE, HL), the HL pair is probably the most important one. Besides giving the user the option of using it as two single registers or as a register pair, the Z80 is designed in such a way that there are certain 16-bit arithmetic operations that can only be performed using the HL register pair.

Because of this particular hardware privilege, general register pair operations usually will be faster using the HL register. This makes HL preferable to use in machine language programming.

Maybe the HL register is the CPU's right foot?

An Alternate Register Set:

I thought that this might be a nice place to mention that the CPU also has a spare set of hands!

Not really so much a spare set of hands (all right, alternate register set, if you want the proper terminology), as a spare set of work gloves.

It's like you had a set of stiff plastic gloves, so stiff in fact that they retained the shape of your hand when you took them off. If you had counted off the number 3 on your hand for example and took off your gloves, then the glove would still retain the shape of a hand with the number 3 counted off!

You can no doubt think of uses for such gloves immediately - you could make a note of a number while wearing one set of gloves, swap gloves and the old number would still be there when you needed it on the other set of gloves!

The other glove is there if you want to use it and it won't forget the impression of your hand when you took it off. Unfortunately you can't just glance down and see what was the number you had retained there. Nor, naturally, can the glove perform any calculations without a hand inside the glove!

You actually have to swap gloves again to be able to use whatever information the gloves retain.

The CPU has a spare set of gloves for each pair of hands (but not for feet - who ever heard of gloves for feet?) but they are not interchangeable between hands, just as you can't put a left glove on a right hand.

The representation of all the registers is now therefore:

```
A - F   (===)   A' - F'
B - C   (===)   B' - C'
D - E   (===)   D' - E'
H - L   (===)   H' - L'
          IX
          IY
```

Note that the set of gloves you are wearing has the same name as the hand it is for, while the spare set is always indicated with the dash symbol.

The instructions still relate to what the hands are doing, not to which pair of gloves you have on. So although we show the spare set with a dash, there are no instructions such as LD A',1. The CPU only works on your HANDS, not your gloves.

The only instructions involving the alternate register set are of the "swap gloves now" type. For example:

```
1.  LD A, (Box #1)        ;Load A with contents of
                          ;Box #1
2.  EX AF, AF'            ;Short for exchange -
                          ; ie. swap gloves on AF
                          ;with those of AF'
3.  LD A,(Box #2)         ;
4.  EX AF,AF'             ; Another exchange
5.  LD A,(Box #3)         ;
```

You will note that in the above 5 instructions there are no instructions which have specifically affected the alternate register set but we have without doubt altered their contents.

This example is designed to illustrate the concept of the alternate register set. Try to work out what is happening.
Do you know what will be in register "A" after each instruction?

For simplicity's sake, let's assume that the contents of the three boxes are as follows:

(Box #1) = 1
(Box #2) = 2
(Box #3) = 3

Then the following is what happens after each instruction:

	Register A	Register A'
1.	1	Not known
2.	Not known	1
3.	2	1
4.	1	2
5.	3	2

Really quite simple, isn't it?

You will find that these EXCHANGE registers are particularly useful when you run out of HANDs, run out of registers and you don't want to spare your hands/feet by storing what is on them onto the STACK or into MEMory. We will follow through this point later.

Even More Registers?

Yes, there are even more registers, but you will probably not be using these to any great extent.

The STACK POINTER

The STACK POINTER is another foot the CPU has (2-byte addressing register).

It always points to where the pile on the stack has got to. As the stack grows, it grows downward from high memory locations to lower memory locations.

You do not usually have to do anything about the Stack Pointer in Machine Language programming. The CPU looks after it, and updates it every time you do a PUSH or POP.

Note that it is a common mistake to forget to POP back a value that you PUSHed on to the stack. You can be sure that this will cause your program to "CRASH".

The I Register

This is the Interrupt Vector register. In Z80 based systems other than the SPECTRUM this register would normally be used to hold the base address of a table of addresses for handling different responses to an interrupt, for example, Input/Output requests.

However in the SPECTRUM this facility is not used and the I register is involved in generating T.V frame signals. It is unlikely you will ever have to use this register.

The R Register

The R register is the memory-refresh register. It is provided in the Z80 to refresh dynamic memories automatically. As the Z80 processor is doing its job, the information stored in those parts of dynamic memory which haven't been accessed recently will 'leak' away because of a drop of voltage through time. Unless these memory locations are refreshed (recharged), information stored originally will disappear!

The R register serves as a simple counter that is incremented every time a 'memory information retrieval cycle' occurs. The value in the R register thus cycles over and over from 0 to 255.

This can be used by the hardware to ensure that all parts of the memory are 'refreshed'. But don't worry - you never need to know about it. That is something that Mr. Sinclair had to worry about when he designed the Spectrum. We can just make use of his computer without ever worrying about refreshes, etc.

From a programming point of view, you can think of the R register as relating only to hardware and system usage. But sometimes you can use it as a mean of obtaining a random number between 0 and 255. We will demonstrate this usage later.

SUMMARY:

User's Registers

There are eight main 8-bit registers in the CPU (A, F, B, C, D, E, H, L), and two 16-bit registers (IX and IY). Eight-bit registers have only one letter in their name, while 16-bit registers have two letters.

Register Pairs

Six of the eight 8-bit registers can in some circumstances be used in pairs to operate on 16-bit numbers.

These are the BC, DE and HL register pairs. The name HL can serve to remind us which is the High order byte and which the Low order byte.

Preferred Registers

The Z80 CPU is designed in such a way that some 8-bit instructions can only be performed by the A register, while some 16-bit instructions can only be performed by the HL register pair.

Alternate Register Set

The eight main 8-bit registers can be swapped with another 'alternate' set of registers.

The values stored in the main registers are retained by the CPU while the alternate set is being used, but cannot be accessed.

Exchanging the register sets again allows us to operate on the original values again.

This is all very well...

BUT . . . HOW DO I RUN A MACHINE LANGUAGE PROGRAM?

You have probably heard enough about the CPU and hexadecimal notation, and it all seems so irrelevant. It doesn't explain how you actually RUN a machine language program.

The ZX Spectrum is actually running machine language programs all the time! (When it's on). It's just that you are not aware of it. Even when you're not doing anything, just watching the screen, trying to think of what to enter as the first line of your revolutionary BASIC program, the Spectrum computer is busy running under the control of a machine language program.

This program is the one that is stored in the ROM chip and is referred to as 'the operating system'. For example, the part of the program that is running when you're sitting there looking at the screen does the following things:

Scan the keyboard for entry
Note that no key has been pressed
Display the present screen (empty)

Even when you are running a BASIC program, the CPU is still under the instruction of the machine language program. This program is of the 'interpreter' type as we have alread exlained: it looks at your next BASIC instruction, converts it to machine language, executes that part of the program, and then returns to interpret the next instruction.

All this stops being true when you run your own machine language program!

Total freedom from the operating system! The use of the 'USR' function hands over total control of the CPU to whatever commands you have placed at the USR address. It will interpret whatever it finds there as valid machine language instructions.

This can be pretty terrifying as you could lose everything stored in memory should you lose control. One error, one wrong character, and you will have to turn the Spectrum off and start again from the beginning.

There are no error messages to catch what you have done wrong, no syntax checking for incorrect statements - so if you make the slightest error, the hours of work you put in to enter your program could be lost!

At the end of this book we have included a BASIC program which will allow you to enter and edit machine language programs. Once you have entered this program on your Spectrum, save it on tape as it is more than likely that you will lose control of your machine language program at least once.

On the other hand do not be afraid to experiment - you cannot damage the computer with any machine language program you enter. The worse that can happen is that you may have to turn your Spectrum off and on again.

We will now just wet your appetite with the very simplest possible machine language program. Load the BASIC "EZ Code Machine Language Editor" found at the back of this book and RUN it.

The program will ask you for a loading address. This is asking you where you will want the machine code to live. With this EZ-Code program, you cannot use an address below 31500, so let's choose 32000. Enter the number 32000 then press (ENTER).

The screen will now show:

Command or Line (###):
This means the program is waiting for you to enter a command or a new line of machine code.

Let's enter "1", then a space, then "c" and then "9". This is like entering a line of BASIC numbered line number 1, but it is a line of machine code. If everything is OK, then press (Enter). The screen should now show you all the lines you have entered:

```
1   c9
```

and at the bottom of the screen the prompt "Command or Line (###):"

At this stage you do not want to add any more lines, so let us enter a command instead.

Enter the word "dump", and then press (ENTER). What this command does is to dump the machine code in the listing into the address you have specified, namely 32000.

Congratulations: you have just entered a one instruction of machine language program! You can check this was entered correctly by now entering the command "mem", followed by (ENTER). This command allows you to examine memory, and it will ask you for a starting address. Enter 32000 then (ENTER).

You will see the contents of memory locations from 32000 through to 32087. All should show 00, except 32000 which will show C9. Press key "m" to return to the main command input stage.

What the instruction "C9" means is: RETURN!

It's a little like riding a bicycle for the first time: you really want to be let loose on your own, but as soon as you go a little way you want to "return" to the safety of earth (or operating system as the case may be).

Now we run the machine language program. To run any machine language program you have dumped to memory, enter the command "run" followed by (ENTER).

What happened? Why did the screen come up with 32000 at the bottom of the screen? This was the address used as the loading address you used at the start.

Don't forget that the function of "USR" is to execute a machine language subroutine. As part of this function, the value of USR on return from the machine language program you placed in memory will be the value of the BC register pair.

The answer lies in the way the Spectrum operating system (yes the same one) deals with the "USR" function.

When the operating system encounters the "USR" function it loads the address the user specified into the register pair BC - in this case 32000.

The value of "USR", as in

```
    Let A = USR  32000
```

naturally gave the answer 32000!

This feature of the "USR" function will prove to be a very useful one as it will enable us to monitor what is happening during the running of a machine language program.

Let us enter the following machine language program:

```
OB
C9
```

The way to enter this short two-instruction program is as follows:

Enter line 1 Ob by entering "1", then space, then "O", then "b", and then press (ENTER). Similarly enter line 2 c9. The listing should show you that you have entered the lines correctly. Enter the command "dump" and then the command "run".

This time the result will be 31999! This is because the instruction "OB" is "DEC BC" (abbreviation for decrease value of BC by 1).

Exercise:

Experiment with instruction that involve BC by looking up such instructions at the table at the back. Can you work out what the abbreviations mean?

Be careful to have the last line of all your programs as "c9". This is the RETURN instruction, and if you forget it, the program will never return.

If that should happen to you, don't worry - your computer has not been damaged. Just turn off the power and reload everything.

Exercise:

You can use the "mem" command to examine any part of memory. Try various addreses where you think you might find something interesting.

How the CPU uses its Limbs

Introduction

We have seen that your ZX Spectrum CPU has twenty four Hands and Feet. Just which operations are allowed and how easy they are for the CPU to perform is the key to machine language programming for your Spectrum.

Imagine for a moment that you are the CPU:

Possibly like most people, you are right handed and there are things you can do with your right hand that you are not quite so adapt at with your other hand. There are also certain actions which may be easy to perform one way, but more difficult another way - such as picking something off a high shelf with your left foot and passing it to your right hand is harder to do than if you used your left and right hands.

It's the same in machine language - you can perform some tasks easily one way, with more difficulty another way and it may be impossible a third way. Knowing which combination of actions are allowed is the key to success.

The equivalent hand on the CPU to your right hand is the "A" register. Remember? The ACCUMULATOR, the hand that came into existence as a result of genetic inheritence of early computers.

On the other hand (so to speak if you'll forgive the pun) you can temporarily store what you have in your right hand onto any other hand, foot and vice versa.

Computer boffins refer to this as "Register Addressing".

But this is just a big name for saying transfer information from one register to another.

```
Other examples would be LD  A, B
                        LD  H, E
and so on.
```

Please note that LD is the mnemonic (abbreviation) for "LOAD" and that when you read assembly language a comma "," is read as "with". Thus we would read

```
            "LD A, B"
 as         "LOAD A WITH B"
```

An assembly language instruction is read in the same order as a normal English sentence would be.

There are also other combinations or ways other than register addressing that information can be transferred from one register to another or from register to memory.

The ways you can use the CPU's limbs:

One of the advantages of the Z80 processor is the large number of limbs, and the possible combinations (addressing modes) that are available.

Let's look at the combinations offered by the Z80:

* Immediate addressing
* Register addressing
* Register indirect addressing
* Extended addressing
* Indexed addressing

What a list of names? Don't worry, just remain confident and we will step through them one at a time.

The list above does not cover all the possible combinations possible - only those that apply to one-handed numbers!
Let's deal with each one of these possible contortions in turn:

* Immediate Addressing

The general form for this is

```
LD  r,  n
```

(or other instruction - we use LD as an example only)
We use the abbreviation 'r' to mean any 8-bit register and 'n' any 8-bit number.

Immediate addressing is a technique that involves only a single hand. The actual data is a part of the instruction; this means the CPU can execute the instruction IMMEDIATELY it receives the instruction. It doesn't need to look in memory to find more information in order to perform this instruction.

For example, count off 215 on hand "A". I am sure you know enough about the mnemonics by now to be able to write this as:

```
LD  A,  215     or  LD  A,  OD7H
```

Once again you can do this with any of the registers, with any numbers whatsoever.

The format for the immediate addressing type of instruction is shown below:

byte 1	instruction code	(telling the computer what is this instruction)

```
        byte 2      n            (the value of the actual
                                  data for the instruction.)
```

Since there is one byte allocated for the actual data, the limitation to the size of number you can specify is within the range 0 - 255. If you don't understand this, refer back to chapter on "The Way Computers Count".

We usually use immediate addressing to initialise counters and to define constants needed in calculations.

Immediate addressing is easy to use in machine language programming. However, it is the least flexible of all transactions (addressing modes), since both the register and the data are fixed at the time of writing a program. The equivalent BASIC instruction would be

```
            LET A = 5
```

Obviously we need this kind of instruction, but we couldn't write entire programs this way!

Immediate addressing is convenient but does not solve any major problems.

But at least we're starting to get someplace: we as programmers can now specify which number gets loaded onto which registers.

* Register addressing

We dealt with this mode briefly earlier. The general format is

```
           LD  r,  r
    (or other instructions)
```

This techique only involves two Hands; in short, this is passing information from one hand to another.

The CPU will allow information passing between any two hands except the "F" hand (which we should not think of as a hand at all. It is the 'FLAG' register and does not store numbers in the normal sense).

Register address instructions only need one byte.

Instructions of this type are not only short (One byte), they are faster as well. The time needed to execute them is the time taken for 4 clock pulses, or less than 1 microsecond on the Spectrum.

There is a 'rule' in writing machine language programs that hand to hand transactions (register to register transfers) should always be used when possible to improve program efficiency in time and storage.

* Register indirect addressing

```
LD  (rr),   A   or     LD  A,  (rr)
LD  (HL),   n
```

This powerful type of instruction causes the transfer of data between the CPU and a memory location pointed to by the contents of one of the 16-bit register pairs (Feet).

Register indirect addressing is faster than ordinary indirect addressing, since the CPU need not fetch the address from memory.

However, we must load the register originally, and so register indirect addressing is only advantageous when the program uses the same or neighboring address many times.

```
For example,     LD  HL,SHAPE    ;load HL with start of
                                  shape database
        LOOP     LD  A,(HL)      ;Retrieve a data
                 INC HL          ;move pointer along
                 continue LOOP
                     until shape finished
```

* Extended Addressing

```
LD  A,  (nn)    or      LD  (nn),A
```

Now we are looking at how to store and restore information from and to your Hand and Feet from memory.

In Extended addressing, the instruction from the program supply the CPU with an address specified by two bytes.

If the transaction is to and from the accumulator, information transfer will only affect the content of memory referred to by the two-byte integer.
If transaction is to and from a register pair, both the contents of memory location referred to by the two-byte integer and the next memory location will be affected.

The format of this type of instruction is:

byte 1	op-code
byte 2	(possible additional op-code)
byte 3	low order value of the 16-bits integer value
byte 4	high order value of that integer value

Now this is the way the program can read the memory into the user registers. Again, it requires an absolute address; in other words, the resulting program using this type of addressing may not be relocatable except when the absolute address the instruction is referring to is relocatable.

```
eg. SHAPE   DB      n,n,n,...     ;shape data base
            .
            .
            LD      A,(SHAPE)     ;load first byte of shape
                                   in accumulator
```

* Indexed addressing

```
    LD  r,  (IX/IY + d)     or      LD  (IX/IY + d),    r
                (or other instructions)
```

This type of transaction involves a Foot of the CPU, the IX or IY index register.

The CPU adds the contents of the index register to the address supplied with the instruction in order to find the effective address.

This is one of the instruction type in Z80 that has 16-bit opcode. Another common 16-bit instruction type is the Block Load instructions eg. LDIR (Load increment and repeat).

One typical usage of this type of addressing technique is to perform Table operations.

The Index Registers can be used as pointer to the start of a table of data. A displacement value is supplied in the instruction to determine the address of the desired entry of the table the program want to refer to.

```
eg.     LD  IX, TABLESTART      ;initialise pointer to
                                ;start of table
        LD  A,  (IX + 3)        ;refer to the third byte
                                ;from the start of the
                                ;table
```

The format of instructions of this type is:

```
        byte 1      (op-code)
        byte 2      (op-code)
        byte 3      d                   ;displacement integer d
```

The number 'd' is an 8-bit number which has to be specified together with the instruction and can not be a variable.
ie. the range of addressing is limited from -128 to 127 from the

address pointed to by the index register.

Indexed addressing is slower because the CPU must perform an addition in order to obtain the effective address. Yet indexed addressing is much more flexible since the same instruction can handle all the elements in an array or table.

SUMMARY:

There are many ways that the CPU can fetch 8-bit information or transfer it from 8-bit registers to memory:

- Immediate addressing
  Defining in the program the number to be transferred to any register.
- Register addressing
  From any register to any other register
- Register indirect addressing
  Either using BC or DE to specify the address, and A to hold the number to be transferred.
  Or using HL to specify the address and defining the number in the program
- Extended addressing
  Specifying the address in the program and using A to hold the 8-bit number
- Indexed addressing
  Using IX or IY to specify the start of a table in memory, and any register to hold the 8-bit number. The displacement from the start of the table must be specified in the program.
  The number to be transferred to memory can also be specified in the program if desired.

These addressing modes are the only modes of transferring information to and from memory. No other combinations are allowed.

Instructions For One-Handed Loading Operations

Mnemonic	Bytes	Time Taken	Effect on flags C	Z	PV	S	N	H
LD Register, Register	1	4	-	-	-	-	-	-
LD Register, Number	2	7	-	-	-	-	-	-
LD A, (Address)	3	13	-	-	-	-	-	-
LD (Address), A	3	13	-	-	-	-	-	-
LD Register, (HL)	1	7	-	-	-	-	-	-
LD A, (BC)	1	7	-	-	-	-	-	-
LD A, (DE)	1	7	-	-	-	-	-	-
LD (HL), Register	1	7	-	-	-	-	-	-
LD (BC), A	1	7	-	-	-	-	-	-
LD (DE), A	1	7	-	-	-	-	-	-
LD Register, (IX + d)	3	19	-	-	-	-	-	-
LD Register, (IY + d)	3	19	-	-	-	-	-	-
LD (IX + d), Register	3	19	-	-	-	-	-	-
LD (IY + d), Register	3	19	-	-	-	-	-	-
LD (HL), Number	2	10	-	-	-	-	-	-
LD (IX + d),number	4	19	-	-	-	-	-	-
LD (IY + d),number	4	19	-	-	-	-	-	-

Flags notation:

# indicates flag is altered by operation
0 indicates flag is set to 0
1 indicates flag is set to 1
- indicates flag is unaffected

Counting off Numbers on One Hand

Since everything in the Spectrum CPU is designed around 8-bit hands or 8-bit memory locations, it is obviously of major importance to learn how to count off numbers on one's hands.

We discussed in the previous chapter some of the ways we can tansfer information from hand to hand. We will now deal with each one of these methods in more detail. You may recall one as being called register addressing.

As we said, that is just a big name for saying transfer information from one register to another.
Examples are:

```
      LD A,B
      LD H,E
        and so on.
```

Remember the terminology involved: "LD" means "load", "," means "with", and the mnemonic (abbreviation) instruction is read in the same order as an english sentence.

We would thus read out loud something like:

```
     LD A,B
```

as "load A with B". The next example would be read as "load H with E".

We can swap from one hand to any other hand as we mentioned earlier. Apart from one exception (the Flags register, which is not like the other registers), you can manipulate any hand to any other hand. Even the seemingly stupid instruction "LD A, A" is permitted!

A short shorthand of this is "LD r,r" where "r" represents any 8-bit register except "F".

OK: We now know we can shuffle information between hands, but that's not going to do us much good without some original information on those hands.

The second way that we can count off numbers on our hands is for us to specify how many we want the CPU to count off on which hand!

For example, count off 215 on hand "D". I am sure you know enough about the mnemonics by now to be able to write this as:

```
        LD D, D7
```

(D7 is the hexadecimal representation of 215).

You may recall this was called immediate addressing. (Pretty obvious, isn't it?).

Once again you can do this with any of the registers, with any numbers whatsoever. The limitation being of course the size of the number you can specify with 8 bits: 0 - 255.

A short shorthand of this is "LD r,n" where "r" indicates any register and "n" any number. The previous convention of one letter implies 8-bits still applies.

Now we're starting to get someplace: we can now specify which numbers get loaded onto which registers and we can spin them around from hand to hand. But we still haven't learnt how to put any of these numbers away into memory locations, and there are only so many registers!

We showed you very briefly an example of "external addressing" when we were doing the time difference exercise:

```
LD A, (Box #3)
```

The general mnemonic for this is:

```
LD A, (nn)
```

Don't forget that in our shorthand the brackets imply "the contents of".

Note two things about this:
1. You can only do it with Register A
2. You have to supply the number of the box as a two handed (16-bit) number.

The reverse instruction is also valid. This is one thing you will notice about the Z80 - there is symmetry about the instruction set:

```
LD (nn),A
```

Do notice that these instructions only apply to Register "A" -- there are of course other instructions for the other registers but none quite as clear as this one. It's the dominant hand concept again.

Let us pause here for a nanosecond and consider what these two instructions actually mean and do for us.

In the first place, the number range that can be defined by a two handed number (nn) is from 0 - 65,535. This is 64K, and means that the maximum memory that can be accessed by this instruction is only 64K! This means that all the memory - ROM, program, display, and free memory - have to fit within 64K. On a "16K Spectrum" there is actually 16K used by the ROM and 16K of RAM making a total of 32K. The "16K" refers to the RAM part only. On the "48K Spectrum", the same 16K of ROM is present plus 48K of RAM making a total of 64K. It is not possible therefore for the Z80 to access more memory than is available on a 48K Spectrum.

The instruction "LD A,(nn)" - which is read as "Load A with the contents of location nn" - is a very powerful instruction. It enables us to "read" the contents of any memory location, whether in ROM, or RAM.

You can use this instruction to explore to your heart's desire, even to a location where there is no memory - eg to try to see what is beyond the 32K memory even if you do not have additional memory. You will be surprised - it is not all zeros!

The reverse instruction "LD (nn),A" - which is read as "Load the contents of memory location nn with A" - will attempt to write to any memory location as well, but will be restricted by the physical limitations:

You can't write to a location that can't store that information, such as in non-existent memory beyond the size of your system.

One of the limitations of this instruction is that we have to know at the time of writing the program which memory location we wish to examine or write into. The abbreviation "nn" means a definite number - eg. 17100 - and not a variable.

You can't use this instruction in the machine language equivalent of a "For - Next" loop. The main use for this instruction is therefore for setting aside particular memory locations as variable storage.

```
 eg. define 32000 = speed
            32001 = height
            32002 = fuel left
```

in a lunar lander type program.

You could therefore plan a program where you got the fuel left, decreased it, and stored the new amount of fuel back into that location. You will know at the time of writing your program the address of that memory location which serves to act as a stroehouse for that information.

Let us be clear about this. Location 32002 is not a variable. It is only a memory location which you use to store information.

When writing your assembly language program you would therefore write something like

```
      LD A,(Fuel)
```

and when you or the assembler program got to specifying the actual machine code for this instruction you would replace "fuel" by the hexadecimal address of the memory location you specified.

But what if we don't know the exact address of the memory location where the information we seek is? Suppose we can only calculate where that information is going to be? Because we need 16-bits to specify the address of any memory location, we would need to store it in a 16-bit register: this means one of the register pairs BC, DE, or HL, or one of the index registers IX or IY.

One way we can do this is to have one of the register pair contain the address of the memory location. Because the register contains the information and because we don't have the address directly we call this form of addressing register indirect addressing.

The mnemonic abbreviations for these are

```
LD r,(HL)
LD A,(BC)
LD A,(DE)
```

The English reading of these instructions is

"Load the register with the contents of the memory location pointed to by HL"
"Load A with the contents of the memory location pointed to by BC"
"Load A with the contents of the memory location pointed to by DE".

Note that by using "HL" as the pointer to our memory location we can load to any register - even H or L, as strange as that may sound - but that using BC or DE we can only load into the A register.

This is because the HL register pair is the favoured register pair in the same way that the A register is the favoured single register.

Once again there is a symmetry to these instructions and we can store information into memory locations in a similar way:

```
LD (HL),r
LD (BC),A
LD (DE),A
```

This is still called "Register indirect addressing" whichever direction the information flows in.

Alternatively we could use the index registers IX and IY to point to the memory location.
The short shorthand of these instructions is:

```
LD r,(IX + d)
LD r,(IY + d)
```

"r" is again any register, and "d" is the "displacement" from the address pointed to by IX or IY. (Don't get the use of "d" confused - we don't mean register "D" but d = displacement)

The number "d" is a one handed number (8-bit number) which has to be specified at the time of programming and cannot be a variable. This is the weakness of this particular instruction and means that its use is usually limited to reading and writing tables containing data.

The symmetrical instruction is also available:

```
LD (IX + d),r
LD (IY + d),r
```

If this particular mode of addressing sounds a little complicated, don't worry: you are unlikely to need it in your first few programs.

The Z80 chip used in the Sinclair computers is nothing if not versatile, and you can combine some of the ways of loading numbers we described above.

For example, you can combine immediate addressing (ie. specifying the number you want loaded) with external addressing (ie. specifying the address to be loaded by using a register pair).

This is called - surprise, surprise - "Immediate External Addressing".

Unfortunately you can only use the HL register pair and the short shorthand is therefore:

```
LD (HL),n
```

This is useful as you can directly fill a memory location without first having to load that value in a register.

A similar combination is possible with the index registers, called "Immediate Indexed Addressing".

This is of more limited use, and the abbreviated form for these instructions are:

```
LD (IX + d),n
LD (IY + d),n
```

Using These Instructions in a Machine Language Program

Let's try to put some of these "LD" instructions into practice.

We know from the previous chapters that after returning from a 'USR' machine language program the value of the 'USR' is the contents of BC. Let's run the following program:

(Load and RUN the EZ Code Machine Language Editor first, and set the Loading address to 32000)

```
1    0e 00
2    c9
```

Now use the DUMP command to place this code into memory.

From now on, we will no longer be giving you such explicit instructions on loading and running machine language programs, as it is a cumbersome method and does not give you any additional understanding into the point of the program.

We will assume that by now you have enough familiarity with the BASIC "EZ Code Machine Language Editor" and with the tables at the back of this book to be able to enter a program. We will therefore be showing all of our programs as follows:

```
OE   00      LD C,0
C9           RET
```

This notation gives you the machine code on the left side and the Z80 assembly mnemonics in the right hand column. It also indicates very clearly which instructions require only a single byte (such as RETurn) and which instructions require 2 bytes, etc. (you will remember that some instructions on the Z80 can take up to 4 bytes!)

The other point is that we shall try to make all our programs independent of origin (where the program starts in memory) so that it does not matter what you specify as your loading address.

Nonetheless remember that these programs can be entered with the "EZ Code Machine Language Editor" program at the back of the book or any other loading program you may design yourself.

Before running this machine language program (you must "dump" the code into memory and then use the "run" command in the EZ Code program) what would you expect the result to be?

The program sets the "c" register in the register pair BC to zero, and you know that BC starts off with the address of the program, which is 32,000.

```
Will be answer be      A.  0000
                       B.  32000
                       C.  31896
```

Now run the program. Was the answer what you expected it to be?

If you are unclear about why the answer was what it was, go back and reread the chapter on "The Way Computers Count".

Now try running the following program:

```
    06   00      LD  B,0
    0E   00      LD  C,0
    C9           RET
```

This will give you the expected result of 0 as BC = 0 (both registers B and C have been set to 0).

Exercise:

You might like to try a few fancy tricks, such as loading A with a number, transferring to L, setting H to 0, and so on.

Exercise:

The attribute file starts at address 5800H. We can set HL to point to the attribute file by the following program:

```
       26 58        LD  H,58H
       2E 00        LD  L,0
```

This means that you can now change the colours in the display by using the LD (HL),n command.

The structure of the attribute file is described in the Spectrum manual. Let us set the first character to ink red, paper white, flash on. This is

```
             1 0 1 1 1 0 1 0  = BAH
```

so the next line of the program will read

```
      36 BA        LD  (HL),BAH
```

Now you must never forget to return from the machine language program, so the last line must be

```
      C9           RET
```

RUN this machine language program. Did it work?

Flags and Their Uses

Flags are those nice buntings you can wave on state occasions......... - wrong!

In machine language, the word "flag" implies "indicator". A flag is something you put up if you wish to indicate to someone else that a certain condition exists.

The obvious parallel is in boating where you run up a flag to indicate distress, country, piracy or whatever.

The reason the designers of the Z80 (and most CPU designers) use flags in their machine language is to give the programmer information about the status of the number in the CPU's dominant hand (the 'A" register) or information about the last calculation just performed.

You will remember that one of the CPU's registers is dedicated to be a flags register - the 'F' register. You may also have noticed at the start of the last chapter a table summarising the various instructions to be discussed in that chapter, and that part of that table was devoted to the effect each instruction would have on the flags. (Fortunately none of the instructions discussed in the last chapter affected any of the flags.)

The flag whose functioning is easiest to understand is the Zero Flag.

This flag will be run up the flag-pole if the contents of the 'A' register is zero.

There are many important decisions which will depend on whether 'A' is zero. Note that the zero flag is either on or off. You can't have an in-between result (shades of 'a little pregnant') so that you would only need one bit to define the zero flag.

The same is true for all the other flags as well. They are either on or off and require only one bit.

The Different Kinds Of Flags

The "F" register is a regular 8-bit register and could therefore accommodate 8 different flags. In practice however the designers could only think of 6 flags!

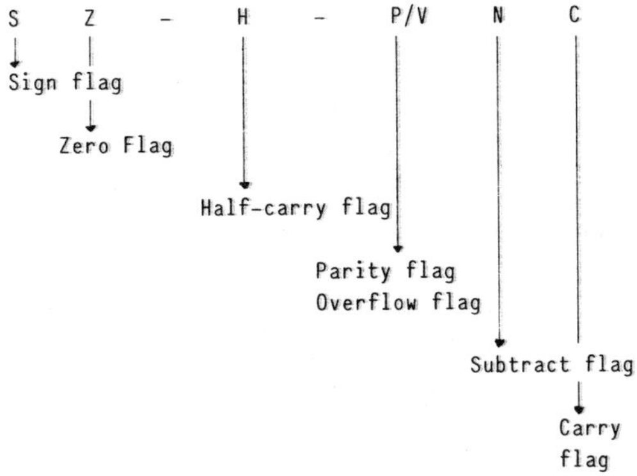

Actually the designers thought of seven flags, but decided that one register could serve as both flags: the parity/overflow flag.

Let us now look at each of these flags in detail:

Zero Flag:

This is the flag we have already discussed above. Its application is obvious, and the flag is usually set after an arithmetic operation as it serves to indicate the contents of the 'A' register.

Note carefully however that it is possible to have the 'A' register contain 0 and for the zero flag not be set. This could easily happen by using the

LD A,0

instruction. We mentioned above that none of the one-handed (8-bit) load instructions have any effect on any of the flags. The zero flag would NOT be set yet A would contain zero.

The zero flag is also set if the result of the "rotate and shift" group of instructions results in a zero.

As well, the zero flag is the only visible result of some testing instructions, such as the "bit testing" group of instructions. In those cases the zero flag is put on if the bit tested is zero.

Sign Flag:

The sign flag is very similar to the zero flag and operates on very much the same set of instructions (with the major point of departure being the "bit testing" group where the concept of a negative bit is somewhat meaningless in any case).

Carry Flag:

This is one of the more important flags available in assembly language, for without it the results of assembly language arithmetic would be totally meaningless.

The point to remember is that assembly language instructions always refer to either one-handed (8-bit) or two-handed (16-bit) numbers.

This means that the numbers we are dealing with can be either:

```
  8-bit   ==)      0 - 255
 16-bit   ==)      0 - 65535
```

or if you include carry,

```
  8-bit   ==)      0 - 256
 16-bit   ==)      0 - 65536
```

Consider the situation where we carry out the following subtraction

```
                 200
             -   201
                -----
Result =         255 !!!
```

This is a direct consequence of only having a limited number range available, and the same thing can obviously happen with 16-bit numbers.

We've already discussed that you can only count to 255 on one hand. What happens if a register is already showing 255 and you add 1? You might like to think of the register as operating the same way as the distance meter of your car. Once you have reached the maximum, it 'clocks' over and begins counting from zero again.

In the same way, if the register or car meter shows all zeros, and you turn it backwards, you will get the highest value showing, or 255 on an 8-bit register.

This is why the result of 200 - 201 gives 255. If we were car dealers we would obviously like an indication that the meter has clocked over, whether in a forward direction - in which case the car has travelled further than it seems - or a backwards direction - in which case the meter has been tampered with.

This kind of indicator exists in machine language programming and is called the carry flag. Fortunately we do not need to worry about registers being tampered with.

We have seen that the carry flag can be set by subtractions if there is an 'underflow'. The carry flag can also be set by addition operations if there should be an 'overflow'.

It is therefore convenient to think of the carry bit as the 9th bit of the 'A' register:

	Number	Carry bit	Number in bit form
	132	-	1 0 0 0 0 1 0 0
+	135	-	1 0 0 0 0 1 1 1
	----		----------------
	267	1	0 0 0 0 1 0 1 1

But as we do not have 9 bits, the 'A' register would contain the number OBH (Decimal 11) and the carry would be on (ie. = 1).

You can see that on subtraction borrowing from a 9th bit would leave a '1' there as well.

Using Flags in the Machine Language Equivalent of "If ...Then..."

In BASIC we have the ability to construct 'IF ... THEN' situations such as

```
          If A=0 then.....
   where what follows can be 'Let....'
                          or  'Goto...'
                          or  'Gosub..'
```

Exactly the same kind of decision can be programmed in machine language (except for the 'Let...'). Instead of saying "If A=0", we merely look at the zero flag: if it is on, then we know A=0.

The three flags we have been considering to date are in the main the only ones which allow us to make a choice in the next instruction to be executed.

The format of such instruction is as follows:
For example:

```
          JP    cc, End
```

where 'JP' is the mnemonic for 'jump' and 'end' is a convenient label.

The instruction is read in English as "jump on condition cc to End".

The condition "cc" could be any of:

```
Z  ( =   Zero)
NZ ( =   Not zero)
P  ( =   Positive)
M  ( =   Minus)
C  ( =   Carry set)
NC ( =   No carry)
```

The other three flags tend not to be of so much use in every day programming. They are:

Parity/Overflow Flag:

This flag acts as the parity flag for some instructions, and as the overflow flag on others, but there is rarely any confusion as the two types of operations do not commonly occur together.

The parity side of it comes into effect during logical operations and is set if there is an even number of set bits in the result. We deal with this in greater detail in the chapter on logical operations.

The overflow is a warning device that tells you that the arithmetic operation you have just performed may not fit into the 8-bits. Rather than actually telling you that the result needed a 9th bit, this tells you that the 8th bit changed as a result of the operation!

In the example above, adding 132 and 135, the 8th bit was '1' prior to the addition and '0' afterwards, so that the overflow would have been set. But the overflow would also be set by adding:

```
   64          0 1 0 0   0 0 0 0
+  65          0 1 0 0   0 0 0 1
  ---         -------------------
  129          1 0 0 0   0 0 0 1
```

Subtraction Flag:

This flag is set if the last operation was a subtraction!

Half-Carry Flag:

This flag is set in a manner similar to the carry flag but only in the case of an overflow or borrow from the 5th bit instead of from the 9th bit!

Both the subtract flag and the half-carry flag are of use only in "Binary coded decimal" arithmetic, and we deal with these flags in the chapter on "BCD Arithmetic".

SUMMARY:

Flags are used by the CPU to indicate certain conditions after instructions.

There are six such flags, each of which can be said to be ON or OFF. The six bits representing these flags are six of the eight bits in the F register. The other two bits are unused.

The conditions indicated by the various flags are

Carry
Zero
Parity or Overflow
Sign
Negate
Half Carry

Not all instructions affect each flag. Some affect all flags, some only specific flags, while others have no effect on the flags.

Counting Up and Down

In the last chapter we examined the concept of flags, and in the chapter before we found out how the CPU is able to load any desired numbers onto its fingers and toes.

Let us now examine the simplest possible way to manipulate numbers on one's fingers: we can increase the number represented on our fingers or we can decrease the number represented.

This is pretty rudimentary arithmetic, but it gets beyond loading specific numbers onto your fingers. The action of counting up is essentially: whatever number you have on your fingers, increase it by one.

This can be used in such ordinary situations as census taking or monitoring the traffic at a particular intersection.

Counting Up:

It is possible on the Z80 to increase the count on the fingers of every single hand the CPU has. This is what we mean by the general mnemonic:

```
INC r
```

"INC" is read in English as "increase" and is therefore fairly self-explanatory.

It is also possible to increase the count held on the toes of any of the feet (including the register pairs, which are not really feet, as we saw).

This increasing of the count on our toes is written as:

```
INC rr
INC IX
INC IY
```

where "rr" denotes a register pair, such as 'BC', 'DE', or 'HL'.

Note again the simple way we have of denoting which operations are using 8-bit numbers and which are 16-bit numbers:

The <u>8-bit</u> numbers are denoted by a <u>single</u> letter, while

The <u>16-bit</u> numbers are denoted by <u>two letters</u>.

But the "counting up" instruction is in fact even more powerful than this might indicate. It is possible to increase the count of any memory location if we are able to specify its address using the index registers or the 'favoured register pair', HL:

```
INC (IX + d)
INC (IY + d)
INC (HL)
```

(where 'd' is the displacement - not the register D!)

Important note:

Remember carefully our convention of reading brackets:

brackets —mean→ 'contents of'

This is very important as there is a lot of similarity between the instructions

```
INC  HL
INC (HL)
```

but a world of difference in their execution.

The first would be read as "increase HL" while the second would be read as "increase the contents of the location whose address is HL". (This second reading is often abbreviated to "increase the contents of HL").

As long as you remember the rules of the mnemonic abbreviations you will be saved from this kind of confusion. Let us examine how each operates, and let's assume that HL = 5800H.

INC HL: Look at HL. Increase the count on its fingers by one. Result:

HL = 5801H

INC (HL): Look at HL. Find the memory location referred to by this number. Increase the count in that location by one. Result:

HL = 5800H
(5800H) = (5800H) + 1

These are significantly different operations. (You might like to RUN both versions - 5800H is the start of the attribute file). Note also that while 'INC HL' is an instruction acting on a 16-bit number, 'INC (HL)' is an instruction which acts on an 8-bit number only - the number stored in location 5800H!

Decreasing the Count:

The symmetrical nature of the Z80 instruction set would almost certainly ensure that everything you can increase you can also decrease, and this is indeed the case:

```
DEC r
DEC rr
DEC IX
DEC IY
DEC (HL)
DEC (IX + d)
DEC (IY + d)
```

The mnemonic "DEC" is read in english as "decrease", and the same careful attention to the use of brackets must be applied here.

Effect on Flags:

Because the increase or decrease instructions which operate on 8-bit numbers affect every flag except the carry flag, this is a very good place to review the operation of the flags.

IMPORTANT NOTE: the increase and decrease instructions which operate on 16-byte numbers do NOT affect any of the flags. Only increase or decrease operations on 8-bit numbers affect the flags.

Sign: This flag will be set (=1) if bit 7 of the 8-bit result is 1.
This means it will be on if the thumb is up using our previous analogy. Note that this will happen whichever convention you are using for the number.

Zero: This flag will be set (=1) if the 8-bit result is zero.

Overflow: This flag will be set (=1) if the contents of bit 7 of the 8-bit number is changed by the operation.

Half-Carry: This flag will be set (=1) if there is a carry into or a borrow from bit 4 of the 8-bit number.

Negate: This flag is set if the last instruction was a subtraction. Thus it is not set (=0) for "INC" and set (=1) for "DEC".

Suggested Exercises:
====================

Use the "LD", "INC" and "DEC" group of instructions to return the numbers you want as a result of the 'USR' operation.

This will give you familiarity with these instructions.

SUMMARY:

We can increase or decrease the contents in any of the 8-bit registers or in any of the 16-bit register pairs or in either of the 16-bit indexing registers.

We can also increase or decrease the contents of memory locations whose address is specified by the HL register pair or by the indexing registers.

Increasing or decreasing 16-bit numbers will not affect any of the flags. Increasing or decreasing 8-bit numbers, either in registers or in memory, affect all the flags except the carry flag.

Instructions for One-Handed Arithmetical Operations

Mnemonic	Bytes	Time Taken	Effect on Flags C	Z	PV	S	N	H
ADD A, register	1	4	#	#	#	#	0	#
ADD A, number	2	7	#	#	#	#	0	#
ADD A, (HL)	1	7	#	#	#	#	0	#
ADD A, (IX + d)	3	19	#	#	#	#	0	#
ADD A, (IY + d)	3	19	#	#	#	#	0	#
ADC A, register	1	4	#	#	#	#	0	#
ADC A, number	2	7	#	#	#	#	0	#
ADC A, (HL)	1	7	#	#	#	#	0	#
ADC A, (IX + d)	3	19	#	#	#	#	0	#
ADC A, (IY + d)	3	19	#	#	#	#	0	#
SUB register	1	4	#	#	#	#	1	#
SUB number	2	7	#	#	#	#	1	#
SUB (HL)	1	7	#	#	#	#	1	#
SUB (IX + D)	3	19	#	#	#	#	1	#
SUB (IY + D)	3	19	#	#	#	#	1	#
SBC A, register	1	4	#	#	#	#	1	#
SBC A, number	2	7	#	#	#	#	1	#
SBC A, (HL)	1	7	#	#	#	#	1	#
SBC A, (IX + d)	3	19	#	#	#	#	1	#
SBC A, (IX + d)	3	19	#	#	#	#	1	#
CP register	1	4	#	#	#	#	1	#
CP number	2	7	#	#	#	#	1	#
CP (HL)	1	7	#	#	#	#	1	#
CP (IX + d)	3	19	#	#	#	#	1	#
CP (IY + d)	3	19	#	#	#	#	1	#

Flags Notation:

#	indicates flag is altered by operation
0	indicates flag is set to 0
1	indicates flag is set to 1
-	indicates flag is unaffected

One Handed Arithmetic

=====================

One handed arithmetic is just our reminder that all of these operations in this chapter involve only 8-bits and all of them must be carried out through our dominant hand, register A.

It seems that only our dominant hand knows how to add or subtract!

This fact is so ingrained in the Z80 machine language mnemonics that the abbreviation 'A' is even omitted in some mnemonics. For example to subtract 'B' from 'A', we would normally expect to see

```
SUB A,B
```

but in fact the mnemonic is

```
SUB B.
```

Despite this limitation on arithmetical instructions (being restricted to the A register), the Z80 language is very versatile in what we can actually add to whatever number we have on our dominant hand:

```
ADD A, r            Add any single register to A
ADD A, n            Add any 8-bit number to A
ADD A, (HL)         Add the 8-bit number in the box whose
                    address is given by HL
ADD A, (IX + d)     Add the 8-bit number in the box whose
                    address is given by IX + d
ADD A, (IY + d)     Add the 8-bit number in the box whose
                    address is given by IY + d
```

You can appreciate the extremely versatile range of possible numbers we can add to whatever number is stored in A - any number, any register and virtually any way we care to define a memory location.

The one that is missing is

```
ADD A, (nn)
```

where we define the address in the course of the program.

As a result the only way to get such an instruction would be to write:

```
LD HL,nn
ADD A, (HL)
```

Note also the favoured role of the HL register again. We cannot specify the memory location using the BC or DC register pairs.

The other limitation implicit in all this is also the inherent limitation of 8-bit numbers which can only hold values up to 255, as we have already seen.

For example,   LD   A,80H

```
ADD  A, 81H
```

will give a result of only 1 in 'A' but the carry flag will be set to indicate the result did not fit in.

If the hexadecimal arithmetic confuses you, it's a good exercise to convert the numbers to decimal and check the addition.

Hexadecimal addition and subtraction is the same as ordinary arithmetic:

```
            1 + 1 = 2
            1 + 2 = 3
```

etc. but when you get to 1+9 you get

```
            1 + 9 = A
            1 + A = B
```

etc. and when you get to 1+F you get

```
            1 + F = 10
```

This is because the 'carry' into the next column happens when you get a number bigger than 'F' instead of '9' as in decimal arithmetic.

The results of our machine language program above would therefore be as follows:

```
                 80
            +    81
               ------
               101H      as 8 + 8 = 16 → 10H
```

What can you do about this carry error?:

The designers of the Z80 have provided us with another instruction similar to ADD, but which takes into account possible overflows into the Carry.

This is a very useful instruction: "ADC", which we read as "ADD WITH CARRY".

This is exactly the same as the "ADD" instruction, with the same range of numbers, registers, etc., which can be added to Register 'A', except that the carry is added on (if it is set).

This makes it possible to add numbers greater than 255 together, by a chaining operation:

eg. to add 1000 (ie. 03E8H) to 2000 (ie. 07D0H) and store the result in BC:

```
LD  A,E8H        ;Lower part of 1st no.
ADD A,D0H        ;Lower part of 2nd no.
LD C,A           ;Store result in C
```

```
LD A,03H        ;Higher part of 1st no.
ADC A,07H       ;Higher part of 2nd no.
LD B,A          ;Store result in B
```

After the first addition (E8 + DO) we will have the carry set (because result was greater than FF) and Register A containing B8 (check this for yourselves!)

The second addition (3 + 7) will yield not OAH (= 10 decimal) as might seem on the surface but OBH (=11 decimal) because of the carry.

The final result is therefore OBB8H = 3000! This chaining could go on to take care of any size number, and the result stored in memory rather than in a register pair.

8-BIT SUBTRACTION:

This is exactly the same as 8-bit addition. Two sets of commands exist, one for ordinary subtraction, and one for subtraction with carry:

```
SUB s  -  Subtract s
SBC s  -  Subtract s with carry
```

The notation 's' is meant to denote the same range of possible operands as for the add instruction.

COMPARING TWO 8-BIT NUMBERS:

Let us step back from machine language for a moment and consider exactly what it is we mean when we compare two numbers:

We know what happens when the two numbers being compared are the same - they are 'equal'. One way to denote this in an arithmetical format would be to say that the difference between the two numbers was zero.

What if the number being compared is greater than the first number (comparison does imply relating two numbers: we compare a number with what we already have on our fingers)? Then the result after subtracting the new number would be negative.

Similarly if the new number is smaller, then the difference would be positive.

We can use these concepts to devise a system of comparisons in machine language. All we need are the flags and the subtract operation. Suppose we wish to compare a range of numbers with 5, say:

```
        LD A,5          ;Number we have
        SUB N           ;Number being compared
```

Then we will have the following results -

If N = 5	Zero flag set, carry flag not set
If N < 5	Zero flag not set, carry not set
If N > 5	Zero flag not set, carry flag set

It is therefore clear that the test for equality will be the zero flag, and the test for "greater than" will be the carry flag. (The test for "less than" is the absence of both flags).

The only inconvenience of this method is that the contents of 'A' have been altered by the operation.

Fortunately we have the "CP s" operation. This is read in English as "compare". Note that it can only compare what we already have in the 'A' register; the range of possible numbers to be compared are the same as for addition.

"Compare" is exactly the same as "subtract" except that the contents of 'A' are unchanged. The only effect is therefore on the flags.

SUMMARY:

Eight-bit arithmetic on the Z80 is limited to

- addition
- subtraction
- comparison

and can only be performed through the A register.

Given this limitation, however, a wide range of addressing modes exist.

Because of the inherent nature of 8-bit numbers, we must always be careful about overflow. The carry flag (as well as all other flags) is affected by arithmetical operations. We can use this as a warning of overflow.

Additional instructions (add with carry and subtract with carry) allow us to chain arithmetical operations to deal with overflow.

Instructions for Logical Operators

Mnemonic	Bytes	Time Taken	C	Z	PV	S	N	H
AND Register	1	4	0	#	#	#	0	1
AND Number	2	7	0	#	#	#	0	1
AND (HL)	1	7	0	#	#	#	0	1
AND (IX + d)	3	19	0	#	#	#	0	1
AND (IY + d)	3	19	0	#	#	#	0	1
OR Register	1	4	0	#	#	#	0	0
OR Number	2	7	0	#	#	#	0	0
OR (HL)	1	7	0	#	#	#	0	0
OR (IX + d)	3	19	0	#	#	#	0	0
OR (IY + d)	3	19	0	#	#	#	0	0
XOR Register	1	4	0	#	#	#	0	0
XOR Number	2	7	0	#	#	#	0	0
XOR (HL)	1	7	0	#	#	#	0	0
XOR (IX + d)	3	19	0	#	#	#	0	0
XOR (IY + d)	3	19	0	#	#	#	0	0

(Effect on Flags: C, Z, PV, S, N, H)

Flages Notation:

- \# Indicates flag is altered by operation
- 0 Indicates flag is set to 0
- 1 Indicates flag is set to 1
- \- Indicates flag is unaffected

Logical Operators

There are three operations which are as valuable in the field of machine (or assembly) language programming as the more commonly used addition, subtraction, multiplication or division are in ordinary arithmetic.

These are generally referred to as Boolean operators after the man who formulated the rules of these operations. These operations are:

AND
OR
XOR

We are already familiar with the concept of operations which apply to an entire 8-bit number, but the reason that these operations are so valuable is they operate on the individual bits of the number (or fingers of the CPU's hand).

Let us look at one of these operations, 'AND':

Bit A	Bit B	Result of Bit A 'AND' Bit B
0	0	0
1	0	0
0	1	0
1	1	1

It is obvious that the result of an 'AND' operation is to give us a '1' only if A and B both contained a '1'.

In machine language, if you AND two numbers, the result is what you would get if you 'AND'ed each of the individual bits of the two numbers.

You may be asking yourself - "What is the point of such an operation?"

The 'AND' operation is extremely useful in that it allows us to mask a byte so that it is altered to contain only certain bits:

If, for example, we wish to limit a particular variable to the range of 0 - 7 only, we quite clearly wish to indicate that we want only the bits 0 - 2 to contain information. (If bit 3 contained information, the number would be at least 8).

```
eg.      0 0 0 0   0 1 0 1        =5
         (---------)
         These bits must be '0'.
```

If we therefore take a number whose value we do not know and apply the 'AND' operation with '7', the result will be a number which lies in the range 0 - 7.

```
     eg.             0 1 1 0   1 0 0 1      = 105
                     0 0 0 0   0 1 1 1      = 7 =)Mask
                    ------------------
result of AND        0 0 0 0   0 0 0 1      = 1 =) in
                                         range 0 - 7
```

Note that the Z80 chip only allows for the 'AND' operation to take place with the 'A' register. 'A' can be 'AND'ed with an 8-bit number, any of the other 8-bit registers, with (HL), with (IX+d), or with (IY+d).

```
eg.     AND 7       Note that as only the 'A' register
        AND E       can be acted on, it need not be
        AND (HL)    mentioned in the instruction.
```

The same range of possibilities and the restriction to Register A is true for the other Boolean operations, 'OR' and 'XOR'.

The 'OR' operation is very similar in concept to the 'AND' operation:

Bit A	Bit B	Bit A 'OR' Bit B
0	0	0
0	1	1
1	0	1
1	1	1

It is obvious that the result of an 'OR' operation is to give us a '1' if either A or B contained a '1'.

Again you may be asking what is the point of such an operation.

The 'OR' operation is also extremely useful in that it allows us to set any bits in a number: if, for example, we wished to ensure that a number was odd, then quite clearly we have to set Bit 0. (The same result could be obtained by using the 'set' instruction).

```
            LD    A,Number
            OR    1                   ;make number odd
```

The above two lines would be a typical assembly listing.

The concept of 'XOR' - pronounced 'exclusive or' - is also easy to understand but its actual use in programming is more limited.

The result of 'XOR' is a '1' only if one of A or B contains a '1'.

In other words, the result is the same as for the 'OR' operation in all cases except when both A and B contain a '1'.

XOR =) OR - AND

Bit A	Bit B	Bit A 'XOR' Bit B
0	0	0
1	0	1
0	1	1
1	1	0

The last thing we must consider is the effect that these operations have on the flags.

Zero Flag	This flag will be on (=1) if the result is zero
Sign Flag	This flag will be on (=1) if bit 7 of result if set
Carry Flag	Flag will be off (=0) after 'AND' 'OR' 'XOR' ie. carry will be reset.
Parity Flag (Note that this flag also doubles as overflow flag)	This flag will be on (=1) if there is even no. of bits in the result: 0 1 1 0 1 1 1 0 =) OFF 0 1 1 0 1 0 1 0 =) ON.
Half-Carry Flag)) Subtract Flag))	Both flags turn off (=0) after 'AND' 'OR' 'XOR'. These flags are useful if 'BCD' arithmetic is being used.

Use of Boolean Operations on Flags:

There is a special case of the Boolean operators which is very handy - the case of the register A operating on itself.

```
AND A        A is unchanged, carry flag cleared
OR A         A is unchanged, carry flag cleared
XOR A        A is set to 0, carry flag cleared.
```

These instructions are often popular because they require only one byte to do what might otherwise require two, such as LD A,0.

The carry flag often needs to be cleared - eg. as a matter of routine before using any of the arithmetic operations such as

```
ADC          Add with carry
SBC          Subtract with carry.
```

and this can easily be done by the instruction AND A without affecting the contents of any of the registers.

SUMMARY:

There are three logical operators which are useful in machine language:

AND
OR
XOR

These only operate on 8-bit numbers and one of these numbers must be stored in the A register. The result of the operation is returned in the A register.

Note that the meaning of the AND operation in machine language is different to its meaning as a BASIC instruction.

The logical operators examine the individual bits of the two numbers, and are therefore useful in masking numbers or setting individual bits.

Coping with Two Handed Numbers

So far, we have been dealing only with one-handed (8-bit) numbers, but we have talked about the fact that the CPU can also handle two-handed (16-bit) numbers in some cases.

One case we have already mentioned is the index registers. These "feet" have 16 "toes" (16 bits), and can only handle 16-bit numbers.

As well, we know that using two hands together, we can sometimes hold a 16-bit number. We called these hands that go together "register pairs". They are BC, DE, and HL.

The CPU deals with 16-bit numbers in much the same way that you or I would deal with heavy objects: we need two hands, we are not very adept at manipulating such objects, and the way we handle them is slow and limited.

Let us now examine the various addressing modes (possible contortions?) available for dealing with 16-bit numbers.

Immediate Extended addressing:

```
LD rr, nn
(or other instruction)
```

This is the equivalent of 8-bit immediate addressing. It is merely immediate addressing extended so as to accomodate 16-bit data transfer.

As a general rule instructions that operate on 16-bit numbers are longer and slower than those for 8-bits. For example, while 8-bit immediate addressing instructions are 2 bytes long (one for the instruction and one for the number), the extended version - ie 16-bit - requires three bytes.

The format for Immediate Extended Addressing is as follows:

Byte 1	Instruction	
Byte 2	n1	Low order byte of the number
Byte 3	n2	High order byte of the number.

We use this type of addressing instruction to define the contents of a register pair, for example a pointer to a memory location.

Register addressing:

You may recall that register addressing is the name we give to an instruction if the value we want to manipulate is stored in one of the registers.

The same holds true for 16-bit instructions, except that there are only a few instructions of this type in the CPU's repertoire. These are mainly relating to arithmetical operations, and extremely limited in the register combinations allowed.

e.g. ADD HL, BC

We will mention here again the preference the CPU has for its HL register pair. This is where the muscle goes, and some instructions can only be carried out by this register pair. This is true of the arithmetical instructions, and we deal with this in detail in a later chapter.

Register indirect addressing:

Register indirect addressing is the name we give to instructions where the value we want is in memory, and the address of the memory location is held by a register pair.

In the Z80, this type of addressing is again mainly applied using the register pair HL

e.g. JP (HL)

Extended addressing:

Extended addressing is similar in concept to register indirect extended addressing, except that the value you want is not held in a register pair, but in a pair of memory locations.

e.g. LD HL, (nn)
where nn must be specified at the program stage.

Exercises:

Using the EZ Code Machine Language Editor, enter the following programs:

1. Immediate extended addressing:

```
    010F00     LD  BC,15        ;load BC with value 15
    C9         RET              ;return
```

When this program is run, you will see that the value of USR on return from the machine language program is 15, just as we defined it.

Note how limited this type of addressing is: you must specify the value of the number in the program.

2. Register addressing:

We will now add a line to the program above:

```
    210040     LD  HL, 4000H    ;load HL with 16384
    010F00     LD  BC, 15       ;load BC with 15
    09         ADD HL, BC       ;add the two numbers
    C9         RET              ;return
```

If you run this program, you will still get the same answer as above, namely 15! Why? Didn't we add 16384?

The answer is that we did, but it all happened in the HL register pair, so we didn't see any of it! To see what happened, we have to add a few lines, as follows:

3. Extended addressing:

```
    210040     LD  HL, 4000H
    010F00     LD  BC,15
    09         ADD HL, BC
    22647D     LD  (7D64H),HL   ;put HL in 32100 and 32101
    ED4B647D   LD  BC,(7D64H)   ;get value of BC from
                                ;32100 and 32101
    C9         RET
```

This method of transferring information from HL to BC would not actually be used in programming, as the PUSH and POP instructions are more efficient, but it does illustrate what needs to be done at times to overcome the limited addressing modes of the Z80 CPU.

You can examine memory locations 32100 and 32101 using the "mem" command to check on this program as well.

Manipulating Numbers with Two Hands

In the earlier chapters we have seen just how agile the CPU can be in manipulating numbers on one hand, and we have just discussed the way it can handle two-handed numbers.

The CPU's mathematical ability is such that he can perform very complex calculations involving large numbers with only one hand. Why then bother with two-handed numbers?

There will be times when you will find it is impossible to specify everything you want with just 8-bit numbers. If we were limited to just the range of 0 - 255 of the 8-bit numbers our computer would indeed be a very limited machine.

The most glaring example of needing 16-bit numbers is specifying the address of a memory location. We implied that such a manipulation would be possible when we discussed instructions such as LD A,(HL).

The slow way of doing things would be to load each individual register in the register pair, as we did in previous exercises.

Fortunately for us there are some (but only a few) instructions on the Z80 chip which allow us to manipulate 16-bit numbers. In this chapter we shall be dealing with loading 16-bit numbers, while the next chapter will deal with 16-bit arithmetic.

Specifying Addresses with 16-Bit Numbers:

Please note that all addresses must be specified by a 16-bit number.

You just can't specify an address with only 8-bits, even if it is only addresses from 0 to 255. The way the CPU works, it's not an address unless it is 2 bytes of 8 bits each.

We implied this when we used the short shorthand of

```
LD A, (nn)
```

So also remember that 16-bits numbers are stored in register pairs high number first (check again with our chapter on "A Look into the CPU" . . . - "HL" stands for H = "high"; L = "low").

Storing 16-Bit Numbers In Memory

There is one facet of Z80 design which is very difficult to explain or justify:

Instructions For Two-Handed Loading Operations

Mnemonic	Bytes	Time Taken	C	Z	PV	S	N	H
LD Reg pair, Number	3/4	10	-	-	-	-	-	-
LD IX, Number	4	14	-	-	-	-	-	-
LD IY, Number	4	14	-	-	-	-	-	-
LD (Address), BC or DE	4	20	-	-	-	-	-	-
LD (Address), HL	3	16	-	-	-	-	-	-
LD (Address), IX	4	20	-	-	-	-	-	-
LD (Address), IY	4	20	-	-	-	-	-	-
LD BC or DE, (Address)	4	20	-	-	-	-	-	-
LD HL, (Address)	3	16	-	-	-	-	-	-
LD IX, (Address)	4	20	-	-	-	-	-	-
LD IY, (Address)	4	20	-	-	-	-	-	-

Flags Notation:

# Indicates flag is altered by operation
0 Indicates flag is set to 0
1 Indicates flag is set to 1
- Indicates flag is unaffected

When loading 16-bit numbers into memory, the reverse convention from that of register pairs is used.

The low bit is always stored first in memory!

Let us consider a situation where we place the contents of HL into memory:

Before:		Location	Contents
		32000	00
H	L	32001	00
01	02	32002	00

Let us assume that HL contains the number 258 decimal = 0102H. The memory locations are all empty.

After:		Location	Contents
		32000	02
H	L	32001	01
01	02	32002	00

The convention with 16-bit numbers stored in memory (and in program listings) is that the low bit is always stored first.

There is no justification for that decision except to say that this was what the designers of the Z80 came up with and we now have to live with it.

Please be sure to read this carefully and make sure that you are familiar with this reversal of convention. It is likely to be the single most important source of errors in programs:

In registers: High bit stored first
In memory and programs: Low bit stored first

It is not something that can be glossed over and ignored as every time you deal with a 16-bit instruction in machine code you will need to think carefully about the order of the low and high bits.

Do not however feel put off by this - life on the Z80 would be virtually impossible without 16-bit instructions and it's a price we have to pay.

You can check this for yourselves by "running" this instruction using the "EZ Code Machine Language Editor" and then examining the contents of memory using the "mem" command.

Loading 16-Bit Numbers

The 16-bit load group at its simplest comprises of loading a 16-bit number in the register pair. The general mnemonic abbreviation is

```
LD   rr, nn
```

Once again we are using the notation of 2 letters to indicate a 16-bit number. "rr" means any register pair, "nn" any 16-bit number.

For those of you without the benefit of an assembler - that is if you have to convert the mnemonics into code by hand using the tables at the back of the book - then the discussion we had on the order of the 16-bit numbers in memory becomes crucial.

Even if you do have an assembler, you should be aware of these reversals of order to enable you to "read" the code when peeking into memory.

Let us look at a specific example:

Load HL with 258

The mnemonic for this is

```
LD HL,0102H
```

The instruction for 'LD HL,nn' is, as you will find at the end of the book,

```
21 XX XX
```

This means that the number 0102H needs to be inserted in place of the 'XX XX'. But because of the reversal rule, we do not enter this as 1002H.

The proper instruction is therefore:

```
21 02 01
```

In our examples we will show you this as

```
21 02 01          LD  HL, 0102H  ( = 258)
```

You may not have problems entering our programs, but you must be very familiar with this so that it is not a problem when you write your own programs.

Other 16-Bit Load Instructions

As well as being able to load 16-bit numbers directly into the register pairs we can also load 16-bit numbers directly into the index registers (which are both 16-toe feet, as you will remember).

```
LD  IX, nn
LD  IY, nn
```

We can also manipulate information between a register pair and two successive locations in memory. (This is the 16-bit equivalent of loading the information from a single register into a single memory location).

The general instructions are

```
LD (nn), rr
LD (nn), IX
LD (nn), IY
```

Remember that brackets are the shorthand for "contents of", so that the last instruction would be read as 'load the contents of memory location nn with the value in register IY'.

Because we are dealing with 16-bit numbers, we are actually loading the memory location specified and the following memory location into the register pair. It is not necessary to specify both addresses (because the CPU can figure out the address of the second location) but be careful not to confuse 8-bit operations with 16-bit operations.

The reciprocal nature of many of the instructions is also apparent here, and we can also load a register pair or index register with whatever is in a specific pair of memory locations:

```
LD rr, (nn)
LD IX, (nn)
LD IY, (nn)
```

Exercise:

We know from the Spectrum manual that the start of spare space can be obtained by looking at the contents of memory locations 23653 and 23654.

In BASIC we can determine this by using the line

```
PRINT PEEK 23653 + 256 * PEEK 23654
```

We will now perform the same task using machine language:
(23653 = 5C65H)

```
ED  4B  65  5C        LD  BC, (23653)
C9                    RET
```

NOTE VERY CAREFULLY THAT THE NUMBERS ARE ENTERED LOW BYTE FIRST AND YOU WOULD GET A TOTALLY ERRONEOUS ANSWER IF YOU WERE TO ENTER THEM THE OTHER WAY AROUND.

On the Spectrum, we know that once the program is finalised the position of the spare memory is fixed and we only need to determine this once in each program.

We use the BC register to get the information because, as you will recall, the value of USR is the contents of the BC register pair when the machine language program has finished.

Note that "LD BC, (NN)" is a four-byte instruction!

You can use similar programs to determine the value of any of the two byte variables listed in the Spectrum manual on pages 173 - 176.

SUMMARY:

We can load 16-bit numbers into any of the register pairs or into the index registers either by specifying the 16-bit number or the memory location where the 16-bit number is to be found.

Similarly we can transfer into memory a 16-bit number from any of the register pairs of from the index registers.

The only point to note very carefully is the peculiar order that 16-bit numbers are stored by the Z80 CPU in memory (and therefore in program instructions involving 16-bit numbers):

The low byte is always stored first !!!

Instructions for Stack Operations

Mnemonic	Bytes	Time Taken	C	Z	PV	S	N	H
PUSH Reg pair	1	11	-	-	-	-	-	-
PUSH IX or IY	2	15	-	-	-	-	-	-
POP Reg pair	1	10	-	-	-	-	-	-
POP IX or IY	2	14	-	-	-	-	-	-
LD SP, Address	3	10	-	-	-	-	-	-
LD SP, (Address)	3	20	-	-	-	-	-	-
LD SP, HL	1	6	-	-	-	-	-	-
LD SP, IX or IY	2	10	-	-	-	-	-	-

(The last six columns, C to H, are headed "Effect on flags".)

Flags Notation:

\# Indicates flag is altered by operation
0 Indicates flag is set to 0
1 Indicates flag is set to 1
\- Indicates flag is unaffected

Manipulating the Stack

You may recall the image we developed in the beginning of the book of the stack as being where the CPU was able to keep information without having to remember the address of that particular information.

One of the advantages, possibly inadvertent, of the stack operations is that we can only PUSH and POP information in two handed (16-bit) lots. This is because the stack is primarily designed to remember addresses and we need to specify addresses as 16-bit numbers.

The general instructions for pushing information to the stack are

```
PUSH rr
PUSH IX
PUSH IY
```

and the general instruction for popping information back from the stack are

```
POP rr
POP IX
POP IY
```

These are exceptionally simple instructions, and you will note the lack of need to specify an address.

For the ordinary register pairs - ie. not the index registers - these instructions are only a single byte long and therefore very economical in terms of programming space.

PUSH instructions are also not destructive: that is, the 16-bit register still contains the same information after the PUSHes.

Note that because we can PUSH any register pair and POP any register pair, the register you POP needs not be the same as the one you PUSHed!

For example

```
PUSH   BC
POP    HL
```

The effect of these two instructions is to leave the contents of the BC register unchanged but set the HL register to whatever the contents of the BC register was at the time of the PUSH instruction.

This effectively adds an instruction of the type

```
LD rr, rr'
```

to the 16-bit load group which was conspicuously missing.

As each of PUSH and POP instruction for register pairs is only one byte long, the cost in terms of memory is not expensive.

The other extra benefit is that we are able to PUSH or POP the register pair AF! This is one of the few instructions where AF is treated as a register pair, but it is obviously sensible because there are many times when we would like to preserve the contents of the flags.

What this means is that you can PUSH AF (in effect making a note of what A and F are), perform calculations which may affect the flags as an undesirable side effect, and then POP back AF, leaving the flags unchanged.

Moving the Stack Around:

As you know, the real strength of the PUSH and POP instructions is that we do not have to think about the addresses where the numbers are PUSHed to or POPed from.

You will surely agree that it does not necessarily make sense that the same area of memory should serve as a stack area whether you have 16K of memory or whether you have 48K.

The way the CPU actually keeps track of the address of the stack is by means of a "stack pointer", which can be thought of as a 16-bit register. We mentioned this briefly in our discussion of registers, but not in any of the LOAD, etc. instructions because it is not a register that can be manipulated in the same manner as the other registers.

The main thing one would want to do with the stack pointer is to define its position in memory, and that is exactly the type of instruction that is available:

```
LD SP, nn
LD SP, (nn)
LD SP, IX
LD SP, IY
```

You can examine the stack of the Spectrum by using the "mem" command of the "EZ Code Machine Language Editor" program, and looking in the last 30 - 40 bytes before RAMTOP.

****
Do not change the contents of the locations in the stack

Almost any change will cause your Spectrum to crash - the screen will go blank and you will have to turn the power on again. This is because the operating system places a lot of information it requires on the stack and changes will cause it to bomb out.

For the same reason do not try to manipulate the position of the stack pointer unless you are sure of what you are doing.

Note:

In a well organized program the number of POPs and PUSHes should end up the same no matter which path the program follows. Any miscalculation may lead to strange results.

Exercise:

We can use these instructions to examine the address at which the USR subroutine is called from by 'POP'ing the value out of the stack and into the return register BC. The following program shows how:

```
C1        POP BC     ;Get address in BC
C5        PUSH BC    ;Put it back on the stack
C9        RET
```

Instructions for Two Handed Arithmetic

Mnemonic	Bytes	Time Taken	Effect on Flags C	Z	PV	S	N	H
ADD HL, Reg pair	1	11	#	–	–	–	0	?
ADD HL, SP	2	11	#	–	–	–	0	?
ADC HL, Reg pair	2	15	#	#	#	#	0	?
ADC IX, SP	2	15	#	#	#	#	0	?
ADD IX, BC or DE	2	15	#	–	–	–	0	?
ADD IX, IX	2	15	#	–	–	–	0	?
ADD IX, SP	2	15	#	–	–	–	0	?
ADD IY, BC or DE	2	15	#	–	–	–	0	?
ADD IY, IY	2	15	#	–	–	–	0	?
ADD IY, SP	2	15	#	–	–	–	0	?
SBC HL, Reg pair	2	15	#	#	#	#	1	?
SBC HL, SP	2	15	#	#	#	#	1	?

Flags Notation:

#	Indicates flag is altered by operation
0	Indicates flag is set to 0
1	Indicates flag is set to 1
–	Indicates flag is unaffected
?	Indicates effect is not known

Two Fisted Arithmetic

One of the benefits of being able to have 16-bit capabilities on what is effectively an 8-bit processor is that we can use the 16-bits to specify addresses, or to perform calculations involving integer numbers up to 65,355 (or in the range -32,768 to +32,767 if negative numbers are to be permitted).

In this light it is easy to see why in some early microcomputers, like the original Sinclair ZX80, all arithmetic in BASIC was limited to integer numbers in the range -32,000 to +32,000.

But even though we can perform some arithmetic with two hands, our title for this chapter gives a hint of what is to come - two handed arithmetic is a little clumsy compared to one-handed arithmetic. The range of options is just not there!

Favoured Register Pair:

In the same way that the 'A' register is the favoured register in 8-bit arithmetic, so there is a favoured register pair in 16-bit arithmetic, and it is the HL register pair.

This favoritism is not quite so pronounced as in the 8-bit case, so we do not omit the name of the register pair.

Addition:

The additions are quite straightforward:

```
ADD HL,BC
ADD HL,DE
ADD HL,HL
ADD HL,SP
```

But that is it!

Note that it is not possible to add an absolute number to HL - eg. 'Add HL,nn' is not permitted. To perform that kind of calculation we need to:

```
LD  DE,nn
ADD HL,DE
```

When you consider that this now ties up four of the 8-bit registers out of a total of 7, you realise it's not something you want to do too often.

Note also that there is no addition betwen HL and the index registers. You will also remember that there is no LOAD instruction which permits you to transfer the contents of IX or IY to BC or DE, so the only way to do such an addition would be like:

```
PUSH IX
POP  DE
ADD HL,DE
```

The one point of note is the 'SP' register - the stack pointer. This is one of the very few operations where 'SP' is treated like a proper register, but obviously you can't use it as a variable! Think of what would happen to all the POPs and PUSHes if you varied the contents of 'SP' at will!

Effect on Flags

16-bit arithmetic is where the carry flag really comes into a field of its own, because as you can see from the table at the beginning of this chapter, the only other flag that is affected by the 'add' instruction is the 'subtraction' flag (and all we are saying is that the 'add' instruction is not a subtraction!)

The carry flag will be set if there is an overflow from the high bit of 'H' - any overflow from 'L' is automatically placed into 'H' by the calculation.

Add With Carry:

Because of the limited nature of 16-bits, we are able to chain additions just as in the 8-bit case. The instruction "add with carry" - mnemonic 'ADC' - operates in a similar manner to 'add' and with the same range of register pairs:

```
ADC  HL,BC
ADC  HL,DE
ADC  HL,HL
ADC  HL,SP
```

16-Bit Subtraction

16-bit subtraction is also a very straightforward operation, but there is no subtraction without carry: if you are not sure of the status of the carry flag, be sure that your program includes a line to clear the carry flag before any subtraction operation.

```
SBC   HL,BC
SBC   HL,DE
SBC   HL,HL
SBC   HL,SP
```

(That last instruction has obvious application: set HL to the end of the memory used by your program, screen display and variables, subtract SP, and the result (negative) will be the amount of free space. Can you write a simple program to do that? See the end of the chapter to confirm your solution).

Effect Of Carry Arithmetic On Flags:

You may have noticed that three other flags are affected by the 'add with carry' and 'subtract with carry' that were not affected by the simple 16-bit addition instructions.

These are the zero flag, the sign flag and overflow flag. Each of these is set according to the result of the operation.

Index Register Arithmetic:

Index registers are totally limited to addition without carry!

Furthermore the range of registers that can be added to the index registers is extremely limited:

Adding the 'BC' or 'DE' register pair
Adding the index register to itself
Adding the stack pointer.

Solution to Memory Left Exercise:

The end of the memory space the program uses is defined by the contents of the STKEND memory location. This is defined as 23653 and 23654 in the Spectrum manual.

Obviously if we load HL with the contents of that location we are halfway there:

```
        LD  HL,(STKEND)
```

then subtract the 'stack pointer' (SBC HL,SP ?)

Because of the 'carry' we need to clear the carry flag. This is most easily achieved by the 'AND A' instruction, which is covered earlier in the book (p77).

```
        AND    A
        SBC    HL,SP
```

Three-quarter marks if you knew you had to allow for the carry but didn't know how to do it. One-quarter marks if you forgot all about the carry.

Because the stack pointer is in higher memory than the top of your program (or else you are in diabolical trouble) the result will be negative.

Let us now proceed to get the number of bytes left as a positive number, using the 'BC' register ('DE' would be just as good for this). We first want to shift HL to BC, but there is no 'load' instruction to do this and we will need to use a push followed by a pop:

```
PUSH HL
POP  BC
```

HL still has the same information as before, so HL = BC.

To get HL = -BC, subtract BC from HL twice (but don't forget that the carry has just been set by the subtraction so must be cleared again):

```
AND A
SBC HL,BC
SBC HL,BC
```

HL now contains the negative value of what it contained before - ie. the positive number of bytes left.

We now need to get the number back into the BC register pair again to get a result from the 'USR' function. To get HL back into BC:

```
PUSH HL
POP BC.
```

and finally a return from the USR function:

```
RET
```

Did you get this right?
Notice how handy the stack is!

Loops and Jumps

Loops and jumps are what gives a computer program real power. Once you have the ability to make decisions and to execute different bits of programs as a result of previous calculations you are really getting places.

This freedom can also cause problems, create programs which are difficult to follow, and almost impossible to debug.

I would strongly suggest that you design your computer programs carefully before writing any machine code, and that is why we have included the chapter "Planning Your Machine Language Program". I emphasise this now because loops and jumps are what will entice you away from good program design.

Machine Language Equivalent of 'GOTO':

In BASIC, you are familiar with the instruction 'GOTO', which transfers control of your program to the instructions in the line you 'GOTO'.

Nothing could be simpler to implement in machine language: just specify the memory location where you would like the CPU to find the next instruction and you are half-way there.

The most simple instruction is "Jump To":

```
JP  XX XX
JP  (HL)
JP  (IX)
JP  (IY)
```

One of these instructions can also be made to be dependent on the status of one of the flags, such as the carry flag. This conditional jump instruction is:

```
JP  cc, nn
```

where cc is the condition to be met. If we had

```
JP  Z,0000
```

for example, this would be read "jump if zero flag is set to address '0000'. (This is the address the Spectrum jumps to when you turn the power on, and as such a 'JP' to zero might be used in a machine language program if you wanted to clear all the memory and start again with 'K').

Now note that the CPU does not allow for any mistakes. If you say 'JUMP', it will jump. Because almost any code can be construed as an instruction, the CPU does not care if you land it in the middle of data, or in the second byte of a two-byte instruction: it will read the byte at the address it finds and presumes that is the start of the next instruction.

The way the CPU works out the jump instructions is really quite simple: it has a little counter called the "program counter" which tells it where to find the next instruction to be executed. In the normal course of programming (that is, without jumps) the CPU looks at the instruction to be executed and adds however many bytes there are to the instruction to the program counter.

Thus if it meets a 2-byte instruction, it adds 2, while a 4-byte instruction will make it add 4 to the program counter.

When it comes across a "jump" instruction, it merely replaces the contents of the program counter with whatever value you have specified. That is why you cannot allow any errors to creep in.

Long Jumps and Short Jumps

We can describe the above instructions to be the machine language equivalent of a 'long jump' because the 16-bit address allows us to jump to anywhere the Z80 chip can possibly go.

The disadvantage of the long jump is that:

A. Often we don't want to jump that far but still have to use a 3-byte instruction.

B. We cannot easily relocate the program to another part of memory because we are specifying the absolute address.

It was mainly to overcome these two disadvantages that the 'short jump' was introduced. This is referred to as a "relative jump" and allows us to jump up to +127 bytes from our present position or up to -128 bytes from the present position. ie. the distance jumped can be specified in one byte!

Relative Jump Instruction:

```
        JR   d
```

where d is the relative displacement.

We can also make the relative jump dependent on some condition, such as whether the carry is set, or the zero flag is set, for example. These conditional jumps are written as

```
        JR  cc, d
```

where cc is the condition to be met.

The value of the displacement 'd' is added to the "program counter".

This means it takes the present value of the program counter and adds the relative value you have specified. The value you specify can be either positive - jumping forward - or negative - jumping backwards. If you check back to our chapter on negative numbers you will realise this means that relative jumps are limited to the range -128 to +127.

Note that, when the CPU is executing a relative jump instruction, the program counter is already pointing to the next instruction which would be executed if the condition was not met.

This is because when the CPU comes across "JR" it knows that it has a 2-byte instruction to deal with and adds 2 to the program counter - the program counter is therefore pointing to the instruction after the relative jump!

Eg. In a program such as

Location		Code
32000		ADD A,B
32001		JR Z,02H
32003		LD B,0
32005	Next	LD HL,4000H

The following is the way the CPU deals with the program if it ignores the jump instruction at 32001 (ie. zero flag not set):

```
Load byte at 32000
   Because the byte is only a 1-byte instruction so set
   program counter to 32001.
Execute instruction.
Load byte specified by Program Counter (32001)
   Byte is part of 2-byte instruction so add  2 to
   Program Counter to make it 32003
Get next byte to complete instruction
Execute instruction
Load byte specified by Program Counter (32003)
   Byte is part of 2-byte instruction so add 2 to
   Program Counter (now eaqual to 32005)
Get next byte to complete instruction
Execute Instruction
```

At location 32001 the program encounters the Relative Jump instruction. If the zero flag is not set, as in our example above, the CPU does nothing.

In general, the CPU executes jump instructions as follows:

```
If the zero flag is set, add 2 more to the Program
   Counter (this would make it = 32005)
If the zero flag is not set, do nothing
   (Program Counter remains = 32003)
```

In other words, the relative jump allows us to jump over the instruction "LD B,0" in certain cases.

This also explains why there are two times shown for the time taken for this instruction. It takes less time to do nothing than to calculate the new program counter.

The CPU will therefore execute either the instruction at 32003 or the instruction at 32005 depending on the zero flag.

It is also possible to make the relative jump negative as we have already mentioned.

Exercise:

Because the relative jump is a 2-byte instruction, and the program counter is pointing to the next instruction after the relative jump, what would be the effect of an instruction which read:

```
        JR  -2
```

Machine Language "For ..... Next" Loops:

You are, I am sure, familiar with the BASIC form of the "For . . . Next" loops:

```
       FOR I = 1 to 6
       LET C = C+1
       NEXT I
```

The machine language equivalent is similar but takes a different form. Let us consider how we could implement the machine language loop using the arithmetic functions and the relative jump:

```
        LD B,1          ;Set counter to 1
        LD A,7          ;Max. of counter + 1
LOOP    INC C           ;C = C + 1
        INC B           ;Increment counter
        CP B            ; Is B = A?
        JR  NZ,LOOP     ; If not loop again
```

This will work, but note the following:

We are tying up 2 register pairs, one to increase, and one to hold the maximum; and the instruction which increments the counter does not set any flags on completion.

A much better way would be if we counted down!

We know that we have to do the loop 6 times, so why not set 'B' to 6 and count down?
This will give us:

```
        LD B,6          ;set counter
LOOP    INC C           ; C = C + 1
        DEC B           ;Decrease counter
        JR NZ,LOOP      ;Loop is not finished
```

You can see that this is a much more efficient way of doing things.

The Z80 chip has a special instruction which combines the last two lines above.

This instruction is written as:

```
            DJNZ  d
```

and is read as "decrease (B) and jump if not zero". (The d is the relative displacement). This instruction is a 2-byte instruction and therefore saves one byte on the above coding.

Because of the existence of this special instruction, the 'B' register is usually used as a counting register.

The limitation of the 'DJNZ' instruction is that one can only count up to 256. DJNZ instructions can however be nested, if required:

```
        LD B,10H            ; B=16
BIGLOOP PUSH BC             ;Save value of 'B'
        LD B,0              ;Set B=256
LITLOOP .....
                            ;Whatever calculation
        ......
        DJNZ LITLOOP        ;Done 256 times?
        POP BC              ;Get back value of B
        DJNZ                ;Do bigloop 16 times
```

Exercise:

Try and write down on a piece of paper what would appear in each register after each instruction in the above program.

Waiting Loops:

There are times in machine language programs when things happen so fast it is necessary to just wait a little while.
Examples that spring to mind are sending information to a cassette (the pips have to be spaced sufficiently far apart to be able to read them later) or sending information to a typewriter (imagine printing thousands of characters a second).

It is therefore useful to set up waiting loops using the DJNZ instruction:

```
          LD B, Count
  WAIT    DJNZ  WAIT
```

The instruction 'DJNZ WAIT' will cause the CPU to jump back to the DJNZ instruction as many times as required to set 'B' back to zero before proceeding again.

This should give you the answer to our exercise of what happens when you write

```
   WAIT         JR  WAIT
```

You might be waiting quite awhile for the CPU to exit this loop!

Instructions for Call and Return Group

Mnemonic	Bytes	Time Taken	C	Z	PV	S	N	H
			Effect on Flags					
Call address	3	17	-	-	-	-	-	-
Call cc,address	3	10/17	-	-	-	-	-	-
RET	1	10	-	-	-	-	-	-
RET cc	1	5/11	-	-	-	-	-	-

Note: cc is condition to be met for instruction to be executed. The following are the conditions which can be used:

Flag	Abbreviation	Meaning
Carry	C	Carry Set (=1)
	NC	Carry Clear (=0)
Zero	Z	Zero Set (=1)
	NZ	Zero Clear (=0)
Parity	PE	Parity Even (=1)
	PO	Parity Odd (=0)
Sign	M	Sign Minus (=1)
	P	Sign Pos. (=0)

Flags Effected:

Note that none of the flags are effected by the call or return instructions.

Timing:

Where two times are shown, the shorter time indicated is for the case of the condition not being met.

Use of Subroutines

The use of subroutines is as easy in machine language programming as it is in ordinary BASIC programs, if not easier.

In fact, remember that using the 'USR' function in your BASIC program is really calling a subroutine: you will recall we need to have a 'RETurn' instruction to finish!

Therefore it is very easy for you to test certain subroutines independently of your main machine language program.

The major difference that you will face in implementing subroutines in your machine language program is that it is necessary for you to know the address where the subroutine starts.

This can cause a problem if you store the machine language routines in a variable array, because the address of this variable is not necessarily fixed. It also means that machine language programs that use subroutines cannot easily be relocated to new positions in memory.

Subroutines can also be called conditionally. This is the machine language equivalent of the basic statement:

```
IF (condition) then GOSUB (line)
```

Care should be taken when in a subroutine so as to not affect any flags or registers which are needed for the next comparisons. This is so you don't branch off again on a following CALL statement, "after returning to where you left off."

The difference is that the only conditions allowed are the status of four of the flags:

- Carry flag
- Zero flag
- Parity flag (also overflow flag)
- Sign flag

Remember that all these flags are set according to the last instruction which affected that particular flag.

It is therefore good practice to have 'CALL' or 'RETURN' instruction immediately after the instruction which sets the flag.

eg.

```
LD      A, (Number)
CP      1
CALL    Z,One
CP      2
CALL    Z,Two
```

```
            CP      3
            CALL    Z,Three
```

The above routine allows you jump to various routines depending on the value stored in the location 'number', but note that it assumes that the subroutines do not change the value in Register A !!! (Why?).

A shorter routine is possible if you know that there are only the above three possibilities for the value stored in 'number':

```
        LD          A,(Number)
        CP          2
        CALL        Z,Two        ; A = 2
        CALL        C,One        ; A ( 2 = ) A = 1
        CALL        Three        ; A ) 2 = ) A = 3
```

This is because the instruction 'CP 2' sets both the zero and carry flags and the call instructions do not affect any flags.

Similarly the use of the conditional return from a subroutine is very useful. (But not considered to be good programming practice).

Instructions for Block Compare and Move Group

Mnemonic	Bytes	Time Taken	Effect on Flags C	Z	PV	S	N	H
LDI	2	16	-	-	#	-	0	0
LDD	2	16	-	-	#	-	0	0
LDIR	2	21/16	-	-	0	-	0	0
LDDR	2	21/16	-	-	0	-	0	0
CPI	2	16	-	#	#	#	1	#
CPD	2	16	-	#	#	#	1	#
CPIR	2	21/16	-	#	#	#	1	#
CPDR	2	21/16	-	#	#	#	1	#

Flags Notation:

# Indicates flag is altered by operation
0 Indicates flag is set to 0
1 Indicates flag is set to 1
- Indicates flag is unaffected

Timing:

For repeat instructions, the times shown are for each cycle. The shorter time indicated is for the case of the instruction terminating - eg. for CPIR, either BC = 0 or A = (HL).

Block Operations

You should by now be very familiar with the language your computer understands - it's very much like learning a foreign language: when you can think in that language you know you have mastered it.

This chapter covers the last set of very useful instructions - the next few chapters deal with instructions that are nice to have around and in some circumstances come into their own, but in general terms you should be able to write machine language programs with what you already know.

Be sure however to read the chapter on planning your machine language program!

The instructions covered in this chapter are by their very nature able to leap tall buildings in a single bound, faster than a speeding bullet - in other words, instructions which can operate on a block of memory rather than just single 8-bit bytes.

Let's start with the simplest of these:

CPI

With your knowledge of the Z80 language, you should be able to immediately recognise this as a member of the "compare" family, and it is in fact an extended compare.

It is read in English as "compare and increase". (You will remember that one can only compare anything with the contents of Register 'A', and this does not need to be mentioned in the instruction.)

"CPI" compares 'A' with (HL) and increases HL automatically. This means that after the CPI operation, HL is already pointing to the next location ready for a repeat.

With such an instruction we might be able to write a routine to search all of memory for a particular match, as follows:

```
Search          CPI
                JR     NZ, Search
```

In this way, unless a match is found (zero flag will be set as in all compare instructions) the program will keep on looking.

Unfortunately this is not such a good idea because unless a match is found the program will never end! Fortunately the designers of the Z80 language thought of this and the CPI instruction also automatically decreases BC!

We can therefore select at will the length of the block we wish to search through and thus specify an end to the search.

Let's assume that the length of the block we are searching through is less than 255 bytes long, so that the BC count would only be stored in the C register, we could write:

```
Search      CPI
            JR  Z, Found
            INC C
            DEC C
            JR  NZ, Search
Notfound    .......
            ...
Found       .......
```

Obviously a different routine would be implemented if the length of the block was more than 255 bytes. Note the use of the INC and DEC instructions to test whether C = 0. These two instructions only require one byte each, and as they both affect the zero flag the net effect is to set the flag only if C was originally zero. The other benefit is that this coding does not alter any of the other registers.

Now we could also wish to search a block of memory starting from the top rather than from the bottom, and we therefore have the instruction:

CPD

which is read in English as "compare and decrease". The decrease refers to HL of course, and the effect on BC is still the same!

Even more powerful than these two instructions are the real supermen:

CPIR
CPDR

These are read as "compare, increase and repeat".
and "compare, decrease and repeat".

These 2-byte instructions are unbelievably powerful: they allow the CPU to automatically continue searching through the block of memory until either a match is found or the end of block is reached. (Naturally we have to specify A, HL and BC before starting, but even so this is unbelievably economical coding).

Because the instruction will stop for one of two possibilities (ie. match found in middle of block or no match at all) we have to ensure we use some code at the end to differentiate between the two possibilities.

You should be aware however that no matter the speed of machine language, CPIR and other similar instructions can be very time consuming instructions.

CPIR, for example, requires 21 cycles for each byte to be searched. Admittedly there are 3,500,000 cycles in each second, but even so this means that searching through 3,500 bytes requires 1/50th of a second.

This may not seem like a very long time to you but when you realise that the screen is displayed every 1/50th of a second or so you realise that it can be significant.

The remaining block operations are along the lines of "Move it, Mate":

These are:

```
          LDI        LDIR
          LDD        LDDR
```

Obviously part of the "load" family these are read as:

Load and increase
Load, increase and repeat
Load and decrease
Load, decrease, and repeat

Taking the simplest one first, 'LDI' is really a combination of the following set of actions:

Load (DE) with (HL)
Increment DE, HL
Decrement BC

Note that this is the only instruction that will load from one memory location to another without having to be loaded into a register first.

The use of the 'DE' register as the destination address is very clever - this way you never forget which register holds the de-stination address!

The symmetrical instruction 'LDD' is exactly the same except that HL and DE are decreased as loading proceeds. The difference between 'LDI' and 'LDD' is more important when the two blocks (the one where the information is and the one where the information is going) overlap.

Suppose we are using this instruction in a word processing application, and we want to delete a word from a sentence:

```
     The big brown dog jumped over the fox.
     1 3 5 7 9 1 3 5 7 9 1 3 5 7 9 1 3 5 7 9
```

If we want to delete the word 'brown' all we need to do is to move the rest of the sentence to the left by 6 characters.

```
       DE = destination    = character 9
       HL = source         = character 15
       BC = count          = 24 characters.
```

Let us start with LDI: after one instruction we have

```
original = The big brown dog jumped over the fox.
move one char:     d (---d
new      = The big drown dog jumped over the fox.
```

and HL = 10, DE = 16, BC = 23.

After 2 more instructions:

```
     The big dogwn dog jumped over the fox.
```

And after all the instructions have been completed:

```
   The big dog jumped over the fox.e fox.
```

(If we had wanted the portion after the full stop to be blanked out this could have been achieved by adding blanks at the end of the original sentence and increasing BC to say 30.)

If we now want to reverse the process and return the word 'brown' to the sentence, we can't simply use 'LDI' again because we will overwrite the information we want to shift:

```
eg.      HL = Source         = Character 9
         DE = Destination    = Character 15
         BC = Count          = 24 Characters
```

After one instruction we would have:

```
original = The big dog jumped over the fox.e fox.
move char          d---) d
new      = The big dog judped over the fox.e fox.
```

After 6 instructions we would have:

```
     The big dog judog juver the fox.e fox.
```

So far so good. But another three gives:

```
     The big dog judog jud og the fox.e fox.
```

The problem is that we have overwritten the information we want to transfer. You can verify this by trying to move one character at a time yourslef by hand.

It is therefore better to use the 'LDI' instruction, with the DE register pointing to the end of the sentence.x This will ensure the information woll not be overwritten in the move.

The instructions 'LDIR' and 'LDDR' are even more powerful, able to shift thousands of bytes around very quickly.

Exercise:

Write a short routine to transfer 32 bytes from the ROM part of memory to the screen.

Note how the 32 first bytes in the screen are arranged.

Now try 256 bytes, then 2048 bytes.

Instructions that are less frequently used

Register Exchanges

We briefly discussed in the first few chapters the idea of the CPU having gloves it could put on or take off, and thus store some information in a place that is more accessible than memory locations.

You must remember that you cannot manipulate these alternate registers and the analogy with gloves is a very valuable one. While they will retain their shape, there is no way they can do any arithmetic or counting by themselves.

The first instruction is:

```
          EX   AF,AF'
```

This does exactly what its name suggests: "Exchange the register pairs AF and AF'". In the gloves analogy we would say "Swap gloves on the pair of hands AF". In other words, put on the spare set of AF gloves - you will remember the spare set is always denoted as AF'.

The next general swap gloves instruction is:

```
        EXX
```

This instruction swaps the gloves on all other 8-bit registers as follows:

```
      B    C                B'  C'
      D    E    ( = )       D'  E'
      H    L                H'  L'
```

This is therefore a very powerful instruction but its very power makes it limited in use. This is because it acts on all the registers at once and it is not possible to hold any value back.

(Except in register 'A' which is not affected by "EXX").

The only way around this problem is to write a short routine along the lines of:

```
               PUSH      HL
               EXX
               POP       HL
```

This means that you have saved the values of BC, DE and HL in the alternate set of registers but still have HL's value to work with.

The last instruction in this group does not really fall within the swap gloves type:

```
               EX    DE,HL
```

In this instruction DE gets the contents of HL and HL the contents of DE.

This instruction is indeed very useful, because as we saw HL is a favoured register pair in many applications and there are times when the value we want to manipulate is in DE.

Bit, Set and Reset

So far all the instructions we have been dealing with have involved the manipulation of 8-bit or 16-bit numbers.

The "Bit, Set and Reset" group allows us to manipulate the single fingers on the CPU's hand (single bits of the registers) and/or contents of memory locations. Because of the very tedious nature of fiddling with single bits this is not a very commonly used group of instructions.

Furthermore, it tends to take even longer to set a single bit in a register or memory location than it does to change or examine the entire 8 bits of that memory location or register.

Nonetheless there are times when you need to know whether a bit in the middle is set or not, or even to set a bit. Note however that many of the bit setting or resetting can be carried out using the logical operators.

The "Bit, Set and Reset" group of instructions allows us to turn any bit "on" or "off" at will, or even just look at a specified bit to see what its status is.

Let us look at the first set of instructions:

```
SET n, r
SET n, (HL)
SET n, (IX + d)
SET n, (IY + d)
```

The "SET" instruction turns "on" (ie. = 1) the bit numbered 'n' (using the notation 0 - 7) in register 'r' or in the specified memory location.

No changes are made to any of the flags.

The "RESET" group of instructions operate on exactly the same range of registers or memory locations, but instead of turning the bits "on", it turns the bits "off" (ie. = 0).

The "BIT" instructions should really be read as "BIT?" in English as the function of this instruction is to test the contents of the indicated bit.

No changes are made to the registers or memory locations but the zero flag is altered according to the status of the bit tested.

```
If Bit = 0    then   zero flag is set on ( = 1)
If Bit = 1    then   zero flag is set off ( = 0)
```

This may seem confusing at first glance but think of it this way: if the bit is zero, then the zero flag is raised; if the bit is on, then naturally the zero flag would not be raised.

Rotates and Shifts

You can move them to the left, you can move them to the right, you can shift those registers any way you like.

The trick is to differentiate between the various shifts and rotations in order to know which one to use when, and to remember that the 'carry' bit can often be considered to be a 9th bit of the registers. (ie. the carry is bit number 8 if the bits are numbered 0 - 7).

Some rotate instructions go right through the carry (as the 9th bit) so that the entire rotation goes through a cycle of 9 bits.

For example, let us look at 'RLA' (the meaning of each instruction will be made clear later in this chapter):

Other rotations involve only an 8-bit cycle, although the carry flag is changed according to the bit which has to go the 'long way round'. An example of this is the 'RLCA' instruction:

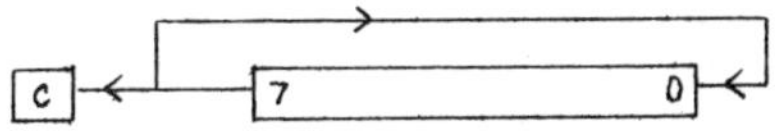

This means that in a left rotation as above the contents of bit 0 are transferred to bit 1, bit 1 to 2, etc., but the contents of bit 7 are transferred to both the carry bit and to bit 0. Compare this with the 'RLA' instruction above where bit 7 gets transferred to the carry bit and the carry bit gets transferred to bit 0.

Left Rotations:

There are basically two types of left rotations:

* ROTATE LEFT REGISTERS - this is a 9-bit cycle rotation as illustrated above for 'RLA'

RLA - "Rotate Left Accumulator"
RL r - "Rotate Left Register r"

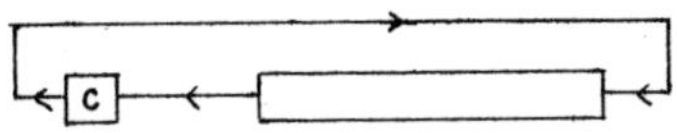

* ROTATE LEFT CIRCULAR - the 'circular' means that the cycle is only 8-bits as with the RLCA instruction illustrated above.

RLCA	-	Rotate left circular 'A"
RLC r	-	Rotate left circular 'r'
RLC (HL)	-	Rotate left circular (HL)
RLC (IX + d)	-	Rotate left circular (IX + d)
RLC (IY + d)	-	Rotate left circular (IY + d)

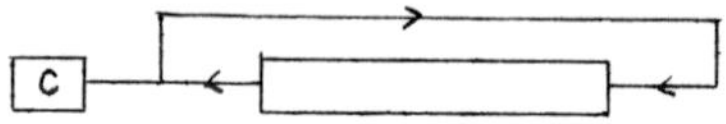

As well as these two left rotate instructions there is a shift left instruction available, but this can only operate on register 'A':

SLA - Shift Left Accumulator

This is different in that the contents of the carry bit are lost and bit zero is filled with 0. This is effectively multiplying 'A" by 2 as long as nothing is transferred to the accumulator. (Think about 'SLA' if A = 80H).

RIGHT ROTATIONS:

Once again we have the two basic modes of rotations but this time to the right. Exactly the same range of possible memory locations and rotations can be spinned to the right as to the left.

RRA	-	Rotate Right Accumulator
RR r	-	Rotate Right Register

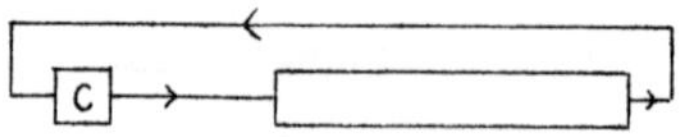

RRCA - Rotate Right Circular 'A'
RRC r - Rotate Right Circular 'r'
RRC (HL) - Rotate Right Circular (HL)
RRC (IX+d)- Rotate Right Circular (IX+d)
RRC (IY+d)- Rotate Right Circular (IY+d)

A similar shift right is available as for shift left:

SRL r - Shift Right Logical Register 'r'

In this case this is pure division by 2 as long as we are using unsigned numbers (ie. the number range we wish to represent is 0 - 255).

Because in some applications we use the convention to indicate negative numbers by setting bit 7 to 1 (ie. giving us a range of -128 to +127) there is an addition shift right instruction called

SRA r - Shift Right Arithmetic 'r'

As you can see this is also a division by 2 but it preserves the sign bit.

In and Out

In and out are just about a simple a concept as you could get in machine language programming.

There are times when the CPU needs to get information from the outside world ("No CPU is an island?"), such as from the keyboard or from the cassette player.

As far as the CPU is concerned that's totally foreign territory and as all good CPUs it will never leave home. The most it is prepared to do is to open a door to allow deliveries. The CPU doesn't know and doesn't care to know how a cassette player works.

All the relevant information is which door the cassette man is going to be delivering his goodies to - there is a choice of up to 256 doors for the Z80 chip but the actual number available to a particular CPU is a result of decisions made by the hardware manufacturers. As far as the Sinclair is concerned there is only the keyboard, the printer and the cassette player.

The other thing the CPU doesn't want to know about is how the data is being transmitted. As far as it's concerned, if it's coming in or going out, it's an 8-bit byte.

The keyboard and the cassette player are both on the other side of door FEH (254 in decimal), so that to get data in from the keyboard you use the instruction

```
IN A,(FE)
```

Now you may be asking yourselves how the 40 keys of the keyboard are arranged so as to be represented by 8-bit bytes.

The answer is not what you would expect - the keyboard only returns information from 5 keys at a time. It is the value of 'A' as the door is opened which determines which set of 5 keys are going to be examined!

The keyboard is divided into 4 rows, each comprising two blocks of 5 keys:

```
3 = )    1  2  3  4  5     6  7  8  9   0   (=4
2 = )    Q  W  E  R  T     Q  U  I  O   P   (=5
1 = )    A  S  D  F  G     H  J  K  L  N/L  (=6
0 = )  SFT  Z  X  C  V     B  N  M  .  SPC  (=7
```

You can see that there are 8 blocks of letters and we should therefore be able to correlate this with the 8 bits of 'A'.

This is in fact the case:

All of the bits of 'A' are set to 'ON' except for one bit which specifies the block to be read.

You can think of it as something like a secret handshake - as the CPU goes to the door to get the information the handshake determines which piece of information it gets.

Thus to read the keys in the block "1 2 3 4 5", it is bit 3 of 'A' which should be off:

A = 1 1 1 1 0 1 1 1 = F7

The contents of the keyboard are returned in 'A' with the information coming into the lower bits of 'A":

ie. Key '1' -) Bit 0 of 'A"
Key '2' -) Bit 1 of 'A'

If block 4 was chosen instead (ie. A = EFH) then the information would come in as:

Key '0' -) Bit 0 of 'A'
Key '9' -) Bit 1 of 'A'

You can think of the information coming into 'A' from the outside edges first, so that both '0' and '1' would both go to bit '0' of register 'A'.

For some games applications you may wish to allow all of the top row to be read, and it is possible to read it all in one instruction (rather than the two instructions which would be required if we read one block at a time).

This is done by fooling the doorman into giving you two lots of information at once:

eg. A = 1 1 1 0 0 1 1 1 = E7

Note that both bits '3' and '4' are 'OFF'

This handshake tells the doorman that the CPU wants the information from block 3 and block 4, and that is what it will get. Of course the two lots of information get jumbled and it is not possible for you to tell whether key '0' or key '1' was pressed, for example - both would set bit 0 of 'A'.

ie. '1' or '0' -) Bit 0 of A
'2' or '9' -) Bit 1 of A
etc.

This is useful in movement games because it enables keys '5' and '8' to be used as the left and right direction arrows even though they belong to different blocks in the keyboard.

Note that if you use the instruction

```
            IN  r, (C)
```

where register C specifies which door you want, then it is the contents of register B which define which keyboard block is being selected.

The other doors which may be of interest to you are obviously the cassette input/output doors.

This is still door FE, as mentioned above. The major problem involved is the timing of the data going out and going in; this kind of problem requires a lot of experience with machine language programming and calculations of the time required for each instruction path.

The OUT instruction is also used to generate sound on the Spectrum and to set the border colour.

Page 160 of the Spectrum manual discusses the BASIC OUT instruction, and machine code programming of the OUT command is exactly the same. In other words, bits 0, 1 and 2 define the border colour, bit 3 sends a pulse out to the MIC and EAR sockets, while bit 4 sends a pulse to the internal loudspeaker.

To change the border colour, load A with the appropriate colour value and then execute the OUT (FE),A instruction. Note that this is only a TEMPORARY change in border colour. To change the border colour permanently, you must perform the above OUT instruction and also change the value of the memory location 23624, which is the operating system's variable BORDCR (see page 174 of Spectrum manual).

The reason for this is that the hardware in the Spectrum (the ULA chip in the Spectrum) controls the border colour, and that it obtains its information by looking at the contents of that memory location. You can stop the hardware from messing about with the border colour only if you disable all interrupts (DI instruction). Note that some of the subroutines in the ROM re-enable interrupts (EI instruction).

Creating your own sound:

You can create your own sound on the Spectrum, but there are some limitations due to the hardware construction for users with only 16K of RAM.

Because the screen is constantly being updated, the hardware regularly interrupts the Z80 from performing its tasks in order to show what is on the display file. This is done by bringing the WAIT line low.

The effect of this is that any program that requires exact or regular timing is impossible as it is not possible to predict the timing effects of these WAIT interruptions. The design of the Spectrum is such that the Z80 is only interrupted if the Z80 is trying to process information contained in the first 16K of RAM. No such interruptions occur if the program and data the Z80 is accessing is in the ROM or in the upper 32K of memory.

To summarise this in layman's terms: you can produce sounds and noises using the OUT command if you have a 16K machine, but not pure notes. (It is possible to get around this by calling the ROM's BEEP routine - see the chapter on the Spectrum's features).

To create sound, you need to send a pulse to turn on the loudspeaker (and/or MIC socket if it is to be amplified). Then a little while later, you need to send another pulse to turn it off. Then a little while later, on again, ...

In this way sound is created. The total length of time between turning the loudspeaker on and the next time you turn it on again determines the frequency of the sound. The length of time you leave the pulse ON, as opposed to the total time between pulses can give you a minimal degree of control over volume.

Note that you must use a value of A for on and off such that the border colour remains unchanged. Otherwise, you will get a banding pattern similar to the LOADing pattern.

Exercise:

Write a routine which simulates an ambulance siren (frequency increasing, then frequency decreasing). Note that you must sound each frequency for a short period before moving on to the next frequency.

BCD Representation

BCD stands for binary-coded decimal. This is a way of representing information in decimal format.

In order to encode each of the digits from 0 to 9, only four bits are necessary and six of the possible codes will not be used in this representation.

Since four bits are needed to encode a decimal digit, two digits may be encoded in every byte. This is called BCD representation.

```
eg. 00000000     is BCD representation for decimal 00.
    10011001     is BCD representation for decimal 99. What is the
BCD representation for "58"? "10"?
Is "10100000" a valid BCD representation?
```

BCD ARITHMETIC

This strange convention in representing numbers can lead to potential problems in addition and subtraction.

```
    Try adding the following
            BCD       08        0000 1000
        +   BCD       03        0000 0011
        -----------------------------
            BCD       11        0000 1011
```

You will notice that the result of the second operation is wrong and is an invalid BCD number. To compensate, a special instruction, "DAA", called "decimal adjust arithmetic" must be used to adjust the result of the addition. (ie. Add 6 if the result is greater than 9).

The next problem is illustrated by the same example. The carry will be generated from the lower BCD digit (the right-most one) into the left-most one. This internal carry must be taken into account and added to the second BCD digit.

The "half carry flag ", H is used to detect this carry.

```
LD  A,  12H      ;load literal BCD "12"
ADD A,  24H      ;add literal BCD "24"
DAA              ;decimal adjust result
LD  (addr), A    ;store result
```

You will be unlikely to use BCD representation in your programming. But it is good to know that the Z80 chip still supports this representation and the DAA instruction will make the life of a small group of BCD users simpler.

Interrupts

An interrupt is a signal sent to the microprocessor, which may occur at any time and will generally suspend the execution of the current program (without the program knowing it).

Three interruption machanisms are provided on the Z80: the bus request(BUSRQ), the non-maskable interrupt(NMI) and the usual interrupt(INT).

From programming point of view, we will only look into the usual maskable interrupt (INT).

The DI (disable interrupt) instruction is used to reset (mask), while the EI (enable interrupt) instruction is used to set (unmask).

Generally, an ordinary interrupt will result in the current program counter pushed onto the stack follows by a branch of execution to the zero page of the ROM by the RST instruction. A RETI (return from interrupt) instruction is required to return from the interrupt.

In normal operation, the Spectrum has interrupts enabled (EI), and in fact the programme is interrupted 50 times per second. This interrupt allows the keyboard to be scanned by the ROM's routine.

You may wish to disable interrupts in your programs as this will speed execution. You can still read the keyboard as long as you use your own routine to do so.

Be sure to enable interrupts when you finish from your program, as otherwise the system will not be able to read the keyboard!

Restarts

This is rather a "leftover" from the 8080 implemented for compatibility. That is why you will be unlikely to use RST instructions in your program.

The RST performs the same actions as a call, but allows a jump to only one of eight addresses in the first 256 memory locations: 00H, 08H, 10H, 18H, 20H, 28H, 30H or 38H.

The advantage of the RST instruction is that frequently called subroutines can be called using only one byte. The RST instruction also takes less time than a CALL instruction.

The disadvantage of RST instruction is that it can only be used to call one of the above eight possible locations.

As all those locations are within the ROM, you cannot gain this advantage in your own programs. It is possible however to make use of the ROM's subroutines if you know what they do, and thus use the RST instructions.

You will be able to know more about the RST instructions from our book "UNDERSTANDING YOUR SPECTRUM" by Dr Ian Logan.

Programming Your Spectrum

Planning Your Program

Machine language programming is extremely flexible in that it allows you to do anything at all.

Since all the higher level languages ultimately have to come down to machine language, it follows that anything you can program in Fortran or Cobol or any other language can be done in machine language.

With the additional benefit that the machine language program will be the faster one.

This total flexibility can however also be a trap to the unwary programmer. With so much freedom, it is possible to do anything. Unlike the SPECTRUM's BASIC operating system, for example, there are no checks on whether the statement is a legal one.

Since all numbers you can enter will be an instruction of one kind or another, the Z80 chip will process everything.

But even beyond the problems of checking whether the syntax is legal, machine language programming has no constraints on your logic - you can perform functions, jumps, etc. which would be totally illegal in any higher level language.

It is therefore of the utmost importance to discipline yourself in the design of machine language programming. I cannot recommend too highly the concept of the 'top-down' approach in programming in general, but especially in machine language programming.

The 'top-down' approach forces you to break down the problem into smaller units, and enables you to check the logic of your design without doing any coding for a long time.

Suppose you wanted to write a lunar lander program:
The very first approach might be something along the lines

```
INSTR          Display instructions
               Jump back to INSTR till ENTER pressed
DRAW           Draw landscape, start Lander at top
LAND           Move Lander
                   If fuel finished go to CRASH
                   Jump back to LAND if not ground
GROUND         Print Congratulations
                   Jump back to INSTR for next GO
CRASH          Print commiserations on bad landing
                   Jump back to INSTR for next GO
```

Notice how this 'program' is written totally in English. At this stage, no decision has been made whether the program is to be written in BASIC or machine language. Nor is it necessary to make that decision - the concept of the Lunar Lander program is not dependent on the coding.

Now comes the part of logic testing.
You play the part of the computer and see if all the possibilities you wish to see included in the program are covered.

Are there any jumps to things you meant to write in but forgot? Is everything there? Are some routines redundant? Should some of the things be put into subroutines?

Let us look at the 'program' again - oh, oh: we forgot to allow any way to finish the program!

The above logic might be fine for some applications, such as an arcade machine, but in your program you may decide you would like to be able to turn the program off.

We now change the last part of the program as follows:

```
GROUND        Print Congratulations
                  Jump to Finish
CRASH         Print commiserations on bad landing
FINISH        Ask player if finished
              If not, jump to INSTR
              If yes, STOP
```

Note that we have used labels to describe certain lines in the program. These are very valuable, the more so if you choose short labels which are descriptive in their meaning.

Once this level is finished, you move one level down to do the same thing to one of the lines or modules above.
This is why this approach is called the top down approach.

For example we can expand the 'finish' module above:

```
FINISH            Clear screen
                  Print "Would you like to stop now?"
                  Scan keyboard for input
                  If input = yes then stop
                  Jump to INSTR
```

The other benefit of the top down approach is that you can test and run a particular module on its own, so that it is ready for the final program.

Let us go down one level further again, and look at the
Clear screen

line in more detail.

By this stage we do have to decide on what language we will write the program in, and let us choose machine language on the Sinclair.

If you were writing in BASIC, all you would have to say is:

```
900 CLS
```

but in machine language that simple sentence, 'Clear screen' can be deceptive.)

We might therefore do something like:

```
CLEAR           Find screen beginning
                Fill next 6144 positions with blanks
```

We still haven't done any coding, but obviously the approach is based on machine language. Let's look more closely at exactly what this clear screen routine is meant to do and what it will actually do.

You may recall from the Spectrum manual that the screen is made up of 6144 locations, and that there are a further 768 locations which describe the attributes of the screen - paper colour, ink colour, and so on.

The short program description above will indeed clear the screen portion, but does not have any effect on the attribute file. If not all the screen has the same paper colour, or if some character positions have flashing or bright set 'on', then the clear screen routine above will clearly be inadequate.

We need to work on the attribute file as well. (Note how much more complex certain tasks can be in machine language than in BASIC.)

We therefore need to expand the program to read

```
          Find screen beginning
          Load next 6144 bytes with blanks
          Find attribute file beginning
          Load next 768 bytes with paper/ink desired
```

The next level down is the one where you must finally do the coding, so let us look at filling the screen with blanks:

```
CLEAR       LD   HL,SCREEN        ;Screen start
            LD   BC,6144          ;Bytes to clear
            LD   D,0              ;D=blank
LOOP        LD   (HL),D           ;Fill blank
            INC HL                ;Next position
            DEC BC                ;Reduce count
            LD  A,B
            OR C                  ;Test if BC = 0
            JR NZ,LOOP            ;Again if not end
```

Now you can deal with programs of such length quite easily and in this way build up very complex programs indeed.
By the way, you no doubt understand now why machine language programs tend to be so long and why people invented the higher language programs!

Exercises:

There are more ways than one to write any particular routines, so let us look at the simple clear screen routine written above.

This could be handled by several different approaches.

Exercise 1:

Can you think of a way that would enable the loop to blank 6144 positions without using the BC register, but using the B register only so that we may make use of the 'DJNZ' instruction?

Exercise 2:

Can you think of a way that would enable the 6144 positions to be blanked using the more powerful 'LDIR' instruction?

Think carefully of what 'LDIR' does: it is not always necessary to have 6144 blank positions elsewhere!

Answers:

More than one possible answer can be "right" - the only test is does it work? In other words does it do what YOU want?

Using DJNZ:

```
CLEAR       LD  HL,SCREEN
            LD  A,0
            LD  B,24          ;Set B=24
BIGLOOP     PUSH BC           ;save value
            LD  B,A           ;Set B=256
LITLOOP     LD  (HL),A        ;
            INC HL            ;Fill in 256 blanks
            DJNZ LITLOOP
            POP  BC           ;Get back value of B
            DJNZ BIGLOOP      ;Do it until end
```

We have been able to use 24 times 256 (=6144) to clear the screen.

Points of note are:

We can set B = 0 to go through the DJNZ loop 256 times. (Why?)

This procedure would not normally be used in a program unless we were also using register C for other purposes.

Using LDIR:

```
CLEAR       LD HL,SCREEN        ;Source
            PUSH HL
            POP DE
            INC DE              ;DEST = HL + 1
            LD BC,6144          ;How Many
            LD (HL),0           ;1st POS = 0
            LDIR                ;Move it
```

Note that we have found DE = HL +1 by getting DE = HL and increasing DE. This can be achieved more easily by loading the value of SCREEN +1 into DE directly but this requires 1 more byte!

The reason this LDIR works is because we are using the fact that the data is overwriting the block to be written as we proceed. This is using in a positive manner the problem we discussed in the Block Move Chapter.

If you add up the memory required, the first method requires 14 bytes, the second 16 bytes, and the last 13 bytes.

Features of the Spectrum

It is time then to have a look into features of your ZX Spectrum that are useful when you develope machine language programs for it.

Input - keyboard

As far as input to the Spectrum is concerned, we will ignore cassette input and concentrate on the keyboard.

The keyboard is the only input which provides real-time communication. It can dynamically affect the processing of any program, either the operating system in ROM or the user's program in RAM.

Logically we can see the keyboard as a two dimensional matrix with eight rows and five columns as in appendix A.

Each of the forty intersections represents a key of the keyboard. In their normal state (when they are not pressed), they are always in a high mood ie. the intersection is set as 1.

When a particular key is pressed and "pressurized" the intersection corresponding to that key will be reset to a low mood ie. 0.

Knowing the relationship between the keyboard and this inner matrix representation, we can derive a logical way of testing key pressing which can be used in machine language programming.

In BASIC, when we scan the keyboard we need to provide an address for that particular half row of keyboard where the desired key resides before using the IN function as described in chapter 23 (p 160) of the Spectrum manual.

Similarly, in a machine language program, we need to load into the accumulator a value corresponding to the address of the half row of keys we want to test. The required value for each half row is listed in the leftmost column of the table in appendix A.

eg. For the "H - ENTER" half-row we load A with value BFH

```
LD  A, BFH
```

The value in A will then be used to fetch the byte which contains the state of that particular half-row of keys and return to A when the INPUT instruction is issued.
eg. The port used is the FEH port

```
IN  A, (FEH)
```

Since there are five keys per half row, we are only interested in the five low order bits of the returned byte in A.

If no key is pressed in that half-row, the value of the low order five bits will be (2**4 + 2**3 + 2**2 + 2**1 + 2**0 ie. 16 + 8 + 4 + 2 + 1 = 31).

register A = xxx11111 when no key is pressed.

If we want to test whether the rightmost bit is pressed, we check to see whether that bit is low.

There are two ways to test that:

i. Use Bit test instructions, eg BIT 0, A
   If the bit is low (not set) then the Zero flag will be set.

ii. Use Logical AND instructions AND 1
   If the bit is low (not set) then the result will be zero and the Zero flag will be set.

The first method is easier because the particular bit we want to test is specified directly in the Bit-test instruction. But it has a shortfall in that if we want to test two keys of that half-row we will need to use two Bit-test instructions and possibly two relative jumps.

eg. To test bit 0 and bit 1 using the first method

```
        BIT 0,  A       ;test bit 0 of A set or not
        JR  Z,  NPRESS  ;jump if not pressed
        BIT 1,  A       ;test bit 1 of A set or not
        JR  Z,  NPRESS  ;jump if not pressed
            .
            .
        do whatever if both are pressed
            .
NPRESS  .
        .
```

The second method of testing using logical AND requires a little more logic. To test bit 0 we use "AND 1"; to test bit 1 we use "AND 2"; to test bit 2 we use "AND 4" and so on.

To test two keys, we use "AND x" where x is the sum of the value we will use when testing each one key individually.

eg. To test both bit 0 and bit 1 of A are set:

```
        AND     3           ;test both bit 0 and bit 1
                            ;is set
        CP      3           ;test if both set
```

```
        JR      NZ,NBOTH    ;jump if not both pressed
        .
        .
```

To test if either bit 0 or bit 1 of A are set

```
        AND     3           ;test either bit 0 and bit
                            ;1 is set
        JR      Z,NOTONE    ;jump if not one is pressed
        .
        .
```

Exercise:

To summarise what we have learnt relating to the keyboard, can you code a machine language subroutine trapping the (ENTER) key pressed for your Spectrum.

You will need to
a. check the row address that needs to be loaded into A.
b. send it to the input port FEH.
c. test the bit that is set by the (ENTER) key.

Output - Video Screen display

The Video screen display is the main source of output for the computer to communicate to the user.

The following machine language program will demonstrate the way the screen memory of the Spectrum is organised:

```
210040    LD  HL,4000H            ;load HL with start of
                                  ;display file
36FF      LD  (HL), FFH           ;fill that screen location
110140    LD  DE,4001H            ;load DE with next byte
                                  ;in display
010100    LD  BC,1                ;BC contains number of
                                  ;bytes to be transferred
EDBO      LDIR                    ;move a block length BC
                                  ;from (HL) to (DE)
C9        RET                     ;end of program
```

Load the above program into your Spectrum and run the machine code program. The way it is written above, one byte only will be transferred from (HL) to (DE).

Now change the fourth line to read LD BC, 31 (011F00). You may be surprised at which are the first 32 bytes of the screen display. Note how a very thin line has been drawn across the top of the screen. The first 32 bytes of the screen memory relate to the first byte of each of the first 32 characters.

Now change that line to read LD BC,255 (01FF00). Again you may be surprised. The next byte after the 32nd one is not on the second row of dots on the screen! It is the first byte of the 32nd character! And so on up to the 256th character.

Are you prepared to predict where the next byte would go? Change that line to LD BC, 2047 (Ø1FFØ7) and run the program. You will find that the top third of the screen only has been filled.

You can experiment with this, using different values for BC up to LD BC, 6143 (Ø1FF17). In this way you can watch the way Spectrum organises the screen.

The screen memory is actually divided into three lots.

i. Memory 4000H - 47FFH (===) first eight lines.
ii. Memory 4800H - 4FFFH (===) second eight lines.
iii. Memory 5000H - 57FFH (===) third eight lines.

Not only that, but you will recall that each character of the Spectrum is composed of eight 8-bit bytes which makes up 64 dots.

eg. For the character " ! ", its character represntation is

0	00000000	0H
16	00010000	10H
16	00010000	10H
16	00010000	10H
16	00010000	10H
0	00000000	0H
16	00010000	10H
0	00000000	0H

The organisation of the Spectrum screen display memory is such that the first 256 bytes from 4000H to 40FFH correspond to the first byte of each of the 256 8-byte character of the first eight lines.

Then the next 256 bytes from memory location 4100H to 41FFH correspond to the second byte of each of the 256 8-byte character of the first eight lines and so on.

Thus, the memory location of the eight bytes corresponding to the first character of the screen is:

1st byte	4000H
2nd byte	4100H
3rd byte	4200H
4th byte	4300H
5th byte	4400H
6th byte	4500H
7th byte	4600H
8th byte	4700H

Strange, isn't it? But we have to accept the Spectrum the way it is built.

Can you write down the eight bytes that correspond to the 31st character of the third line of the screen? You can refer to Appendix B, the screen memory map.
(405EH, 415EH, 425EH,...,475EH).

To follow on the concept we have developed about the screen display, the memory locations that correspond to the first character of the second eight lines lot is:
4800H, 4900H, 4A00H, 4B00H, 4C00H, 4D00H, 4E00H, 4F00H.

Similarly, the first character of the third eight lines lot has its eight-bytes in memory locations:
5000H, 5100H, 5200H, 5300H, 5400H, 5500H, 5600H, 5700H.

There are some advantages, however, in using machine language. The apparent complexities are worth overcoming. As a trivial example, in BASIC, if you try to PRINT into the input section of the screen (the bottom two lines), the BASIC system will object most violently. But in machine language you have full access to the whole screen.

If you observe the screen display organisation more closely, you will see that the High Order Byte of First Byte (HOBFB) of each character determines which lot of the three memory portions the character is in.

For example,if 40H =(HOBFB (41H	char is in first eight lines lot
if 48H =(HOBFB (49H	char is in second eight lines lot
if 50H =(HOBFB (51H	char is in third eight lines lot

Not only that, the low order three bits of the HOB (High Order Byte) determines which byte of the eight bytes of the character it belongs.

Things starting to blurr now? Turn to appendix B and try to observe the relationship between memory locations and the display screen (if any?!!).

Try the following example,:
Suppose we are given an address as 4A36H. The High Order Byte of the address is 4AH so:

i. we know that it is within the screen display memory since its value is in between 40H and 58H.

ii. its binary representation is 01001010

iii. from the lower three bits we know that it belongs to the third byte of a character position on the screen.

iv. if we made the lower three bits zero, then the value of the HOB would be 48H. Thus we know this belongs to the second eight lines lot, ie the middle portion of the screen display.

The conclusion we can reach is that the byte given refers to the third byte of a character in the middle portion of the display memory.

Which character of the middle portion does the byte belongs to? To answer this question, we'll need to know the value of the Low Order Byte of the address.

We know the LOB of the address is 36H. So the address refers to character 36H (48+6), the 54th position away from the first character of the middle portion.

Since each line has 32 characters, the position referred to is in the second line of the middle screen display portion and is the (54-32+1)th character of that line.

The conclusion we can make is that the byte given is the third byte of the 23rd character of the 10th line from the start of the screen.

Exercise:

Which byte of which character does the address 564FH refer to?

Exercise:

Can you write a short routine to write an exclamation mark to the screen? The bytes that make up this character are given above.

Output - Video display attribute

The display attribute memory is easier to understand than the display memory because it has a one-to-one relationship with the screen display characters.

The attribute file is located in memory from 5800H to 5AFFH. It is 768 bytes, which correspond to 24 lines of 32 character each. In other words, there is one attribute byte for each character position.

Thus, 5800H corresponds to the attribute of the first character of the first line, 5801H the second character, 5802H the third,...581FH the thirty second character of the first line.

Similarly, 5820H holds the attribute of the first character of the second line, 5840H of the third line, ... and 5AE0H the attribute of the first character of the last line of the screen.

We know that for each character position on the screen, there is a corresponding attribute byte in the attribute memory, made up as follows:

```
        attribute byte      b b bbb bbb

    bit 0 - 2          represents the ink colour of the
                       character 0 to 7.
    bit 3 - 5          represents the paper colour of the
                       character 0 to 7.
    bit 6              Bright if 1, normal if 0.
    bit 7              Flash if 1, not flash if 0.
```

Exercise:

What is the address of the attribute byte that corresponds to the first byte of the middle screen section? What is the address for the first byte of the third section? Answers are given on the next page, but try to work it out for yourself.

Exercise:

Can you write a subroutine that converts a given address on the screen to its corresponding attribute address.
eg. 4529H

You must in effect determine which character of this screen this belongs to, and then add this to 5800H.

The following program shows a short method of achieving this:

```
LD   HL, 4529H          ;load the given address to HL
LD   A,  H              ;load the high order byte to A
AND  18H                ;trap bits 3 and 4 to
                        ;determine which portion of the
                        ;screen the address belongs
SRA  A                  ;shift right accumulator
SRA  A                  ;three times - ie divide by 8
SRA  A                  ;result can either be 0,1 or 2
                        ;depending whether H was
                        ;   48H, 50H or 50H
ADD  A,58H              ;transform to attribute memory
LD   H,A                ;HL contain attribute address
                        ;ie H = 58H, 59H or 60H
                        ;L remains the same!!!
```

You may need to think about this for a while!

The way the program works is related to the answer of the first exercise:

```
1st char. of 1st screen section = 4000H   Attribute address = 5800H
1st char. of 2nd screen section = 4800H   Attribute address = 5900H
1st char. of 3rd screen section = 5000H   Attribute address = 5A00H


2nd char. of 1st screen section = 4801H   Attribute address = 59Ø1H
             etc. ...
                                etc. ...
```

This should make things a little clearer!

Output - Sound

Another real time communication that your Spectrum microcomputer offers is sound. It would be a waste if we didn't make full use of this facility.

In machine language on the Spectrum, there are two major ways of generating sound.

i. Sending signals to the cassette output port 254 for certain duration of time using the OUT instruction 254.

```
eg.     OUT (254),  A
```

ii. Set HL, DE to certain values and call the ROM sound routine used to generate sound.
    The input parameters are:

```
    DE  -   duration in sec * frequency
    HL  -   (437,500 / frequency) - 30.125
Then
    CALL    03B5H.
```

The first way of sound generation has the advantage of being free from any ROM calls. It is shorter in terms of time to execute. But ... there is always a BUT!

Since the ULA is constantly accessing the first 16K memory of the RAM to perform the video display, your program, if it resides within the first 16K, will frequently be temporarily interrupted.

If the program is generating sound, the sound will be in bursts of unpredictable duration. One solution is to move the part of the program that generates sound to the higher memory region if you have a 48K machine.

If you haven't got a 48K machine, then you can still generate sound using this method, but it will not be 'clean sound'. You have to use the second method of sound generation (of calling the ROM routine) to get that result.

Note that as we send values to output port 254, it will also affect the border colour, and turn the MIC on, as well as the loudspeaker depending on what value is sent. Refer to chapter 23 (p 160) of your Spectrum user manual.

On the other hand, the ROM routine for generating sound in effect allows you to use the BEEP command from your machine language program. You can think of the DE register pair as holding a value for the duration of the sound, and HL a value for the frequency. Experiment with different values for HL and DE until you get the sound you want.

The limitation of this method of course is that you are restricted to whatever sounds you can create with the BEEP command.

Monitor Programs

EZ-Code Machine Language Editor

This is a machine code monitor program that allows you to:

i. INPUT your machine language program module in
either a fully assembled format
or a semi-assembled format with all relative jump and absolute jumps expressed in the form of line number.

ii. LIST the source input program module.

iii. DUMP the input program module into the specified memory address.

iv. EXAMINE a range of memory locations.

v. SAVE EITHER the "source module"
OR the dumped program in fully machine code format.

vi. LOAD a saved "source program" from the cassette.

vii. RUN the dumped machine program module.

PREREQUISITE for the EZ-code

Before using this monitor program to input any machine language programs, you must assemble your assembly language program. You do not need to calculate relative or absolute jumps!

Your program module must not be greater than 800 bytes or more than 200 instructions.

You cannot load the final program below memory 31499 (in order not to wipe off the EZ-code program.)

CONCEPT behind the EZ-code

The concept behind this program is to enable you to enter machine code instruction in a numbered line format, much like the listing of a BASIC program.

Each line of the "source program" (the name of the lines of machine code) has a line number and up to 4 bytes of machine code.

A major benefit is therefore the ability to "edit" any line. The "source program" can also be SAVED separately to tape, allowing work in progress to be saved.

A major innovation in this program is the ability to insert relative jumps or absolute jumps without having to calculate the numbers involved in any jump can be made by referring to the line number you wish to jump to!

This means that changes can be made without problems even within the scope of a relative jump.

The machine code of the "source program" is transferred to memory by the "dump" command. The resulting machine code can also be SAVED to memory.

EZ-code Instruction Summary

Note that the first question the program will ask you is

"Loading address".

This is the address where you wish the machine code program to go. This cannot be below 31500.

**** Entering LINEs ****

i. To ENTER lines of "source program":

(line-no)(blank)(maximum of 4 bytes in Hexadecimal)
(ENTER)

eg. 1 210040 will insert the machine code instruction
LD HL,4000H into line number 1.

ii. To EDIT a line:

(line-no)(blank)(retype new bytes)(ENTER)

eg. 1 210140 will change line number 1 to the instruction
LD HL,4001H.

iii.To DELETE an instruction line:

(line-no)(ENTER)

eg. 1 (ENTER) will delete line number 1.

iv. To specify RELATIVE or ABSOLUTE jump

```
(line-no)(blank)(jump instruction)("lower case "L"")
    (line-no)(ENTER)
```

```
eg. 1 c312  represents the instruction JP to line 2.
    2 1811  represents the instruction JR to line 1.
```

**** COMMANDs ****

i. dump(ENTER)
  * dump the source listing into the memory starting from the specified LOADING address.
  * this must be done before running the machine code program.

abbreviation: du

ii. exit(ENTER)
  * exit from the EZ-code and re-enter BASIC system.

abbreviation: ex

iii.list(ENTER)
  * list the first twenty-two instruction lines of the source listing.
  * press any key except "m" and "BREAK" to continue listing

abbreviation: li

list#(ENTER)
  * list twenty-two lines of the source listing starting from line number #, a number between 1 and 200 inclusively.

abbreviation: NO ABBREV

iv. load(ENTER)
  * load a source listing module from the cassette replacing the existing module.

abbreviation: lo

v. mem(ENTER)
prompt: Starting address:
  * enter memory address you want to start displaying from.
  * can be from 0 to 32767 for 16K Spectrum or 0 to 65535 for 48K Spectrum.
  * press "m" to exit memory examine mode.

abbreviation: me

vi. new(ENTER)
 * clear the current module and re-run the EZ-code.
 * this is useful when you want to start coding in another program module.

abbreviation: ne

vii.run(ENTER)
 * run the dumped program module from LOADING address you specified when you start running the EZ-code program or when you LOAD a new source listing.

abbreviation: ru

viii.save(ENTER)
 * save either the source listing or dumped machine code onto cassette.

```
prompt: Enter name:
            enter the name you want to use.
        Source or Machine code: (s or m)
            enter s for source listing saving
            enter m for machine code saving
        Start tape, then press any key.
            make sure that the cassette lead is properly
            winded.
            press any key when the cassette is ready.
```

abbreviation: sa

NOTES
-----

1. If you don't want the result of BC register returned after running, change line 3090 to :
   `3090 IF k$="ru" THEN LET L=USR R`

2. To restart the EZ-code :
   Either use RUN and resulting with all vaiables reinitialised
   Or use GOTO 2020 which returns the prompt "Command or Line(###): ".

3. All numeric entry except machine instruction code has to be in decimal format.

4. To enable you to insert additional lines in the current listing, it is good to space out the listing.
   ie.instead of entering instruction lines as 1, 2, 3 enter as 1, 5, 10 etc.
   This will makes the input of the module more flexible.

EXERCISE on EZ-code

Enter the following codes.

```
        210040        LD  HL,4000H          ;fill screen
        110140        LD  DE,4001H
        01FF17        LD  BC,6143
        3EFF          LD  A,  OFFH
        77            LD  (HL), A
        EDBO          LDIR
        3E7F   LOOP:LD  A,  7FH          ;trap BREAK key
        DBFE          IN  A,(OFEH)
        E601          AND 1
        20F8          JR  NZ, LOOP
        C9            RET
```

To enter the above code using EZ-code:

```
(RUN)
Loading address: 31500(ENTER)
Command or Line(###): 1 210040(ENTER)
Command or Line(###): 5 110140(ENTER)
Command or Line(###): 10 01ff17(ENTER)
Command or Line(###): 15 3eff(ENTER)
Command or LIne(###): 20 77(ENTER)
Command or Line(###): 25 edb0(ENTER)
Command or Line(###): 30 3e7f(ENTER)
Command or Line(###): 35 dbfe(ENTER)
Command or Line(###): 40 e601(ENTER)
Command or Line(###): 45 20l30(ENTER)
(This is 20 then lower case "L", then 30. In other words
        JR  NZ, line 30 )
Command or Line(###): 50 c9(ENTER)
Command or Line(###): list(ENTER)
Command or Line(###): dump(ENTER)
Command or Line(###): mem(ENTER)
Starting address: 31500(ENTER)
                    m     (this is the key to exit the memory
                           display mode)
Command or Line(###): run(ENTER)
                      (BREAK)
```

Note how there must be a space after the line numbers.

```
EZCODE
Copyright (c) 1982 by William Tang and A.M.Sullivan

 100 REM machine
 110 REM machine▲code▲monitor
 120 GO TO 9000
 130 DEF FN d(s$) = (s$ > "9")*( CODE s$-55)
       +(s$ <= "9")*( CODE s$-48)-(s$ > "`")*32
 140 DEF FN o(O$) = ((O$ = "ca")+(O$ = "da")
       +(O$ = "ea")+(O$ = "fa")+(O$ = "c2")
       +(O$ = "d2")+(O$ = "e2")+(O$ = "f2")
       +(O$ = "c3"))-((O$ = "38")+(O$ = "30")
       +(O$ = "28")+(O$ = "20")+(O$ = "18")
       +(O$ = "10"))
1000 REM
1010 REM  INV LINE▲PRINTING▲routine TRU
1020 CLS : PRINT AT ze, 25; INVERSE on; FLASH on; "LISTING TRU
1030 LET F = ze : PRINT AT ze, ze;
1040 FOR J = pl1 TO pl2
1050 IF C$(J, on) = "▲▲" THEN GO TO 1110
1060 PRINT TAB tr- LEN STR$ J; J; TAB fr; "▲";
1070 IF C$(J, tw, on TO on) = "1"
       THEN PRINT C$(J, on)+"▲"+C$(J, tw)+C$(J, tr)
     : GO TO 1090
1080 PRINT C$(J, on); "▲"; C$(J, tw); "▲"
       ; C$(J, tr); "▲"; C$(J, fr)
1090 LET F = F+on
1100 IF F = 22 THEN GO TO 1120
1110 NEXT J
1120 PRINT AT ze, 25; "▲▲▲▲▲▲▲"
1130 RETURN
2000 REM
2010 REM  INV main▲routine TRU
2020 INPUT "Command▲or▲Line(###) :▲"; A$
2030 IF A$( TO fr) = "▲▲▲▲" THEN GO TO mr
2040 IF A$(on) > "9" THEN GO TO 3000
2050 LET k$ = "" : FOR K = on TO fr
2060 IF A$(K TO K) = "▲" THEN GO TO 2090
2070 LET k$ = k$+A$(K TO K)
2080 NEXT K
2090 IF K = 5 OR VAL k$ = ze OR VAL k$ > ln
       THEN GO TO mr
2100 LET J = VAL k$ : LET n = J
     : REM line▲number▲must▲be▲3▲bytes
2110 LET A$ = A$(K+on TO )
2120 LET k$ = ""
2130 FOR K = on TO LEN A$
2140 IF A$(K TO K) <> "▲"
       THEN LET k$ = k$+A$(K TO K)
2150 NEXT K
2160 LET A$ = k$
2162 IF A$(on) = "1" THEN GO TO mr
```

```
2170 CLS : FOR I = on TO 7 STEP tw
2180 LET K = INT (I/tw+on)
2190 LET C$(J, K) = A$(I TO I+on)
2200 NEXT I
2210 IF C$(n, on) = "▲▲" THEN GO TO 2250
2220 IF n < TP THEN LET TP = n
2230 IF n > BP THEN LET BP = n
2240 GO TO 2320
2250 IF n <> BP THEN GO TO 2280
2260 IF BP = on OR C$(BP, on) <> "▲▲"
      THEN GO TO 2320
2270 LET BP = BP-on : GO TO 2260
2280 IF n <> TP THEN GO TO 2320
2290 IF C$(TP, on) <> "▲▲" THEN GO TO 2320
2300 IF TP <> BP AND TP <> ln THEN LET TP = TP+on
     : GO TO 2290
2310 LET TP = on
2320 LET pp = n
2330 IF n < TP THEN LET pp = TP : GO TO 2380
2340 LET numlp = ze
2350 IF pp = TP OR numlp = 11 THEN GO TO 2380
2360 IF C$(pp, on) <> "▲▲"
      THEN LET numlp = numlp+on
2370 LET pp = pp-on : GO TO 2350
2380 LET pl1 = pp : LET pl2 = BP
2390 GO SUB 1000
     : REM print▲a▲block▲of▲lines
2400 GO TO mr
3000 REM
3010 REM  INV Commands************** TRU
3020 LET k$ = A$( TO tw)
3030 IF k$ = "du" THEN GO TO 5000
3040 IF k$ = "ex" THEN STOP
3050 IF k$ = "li" THEN GO TO 4000
3060 IF k$ = "lo" THEN GO TO 7000
3070 IF k$ = "me" THEN GO TO 6000
3080 IF k$ = "ne" THEN RUN
3090 IF k$ = "ru" THEN PRINT USR R
3100 IF k$ = "sa" THEN GO TO 8000
3110 GO TO mr
4000 REM
4010 REM  INV List▲routine********** TRU
4020 LET pl1 = TP : LET pl2 = BP
4030 LET n1 = CODE A$(6 TO 6)
4040 IF LEN A$ > fr AND n1 > 47 AND n1 < 58
      THEN LET pl1 = VAL A$(5 TO 8)
4050 GO SUB 1000
4060 GO TO mr
5000 REM
5010 REM  INV DUMP▲routine********** TRU
5020 CLS : PRINT AT ze, 25; INK on; INVERSE on
      ; FLASH on; "DUMPING" : LET G = R
```

```
5030 PRINT AT on, ze;
5040 FOR J = TP TO BP
5050 IF C$(J, on) = "▲▲" THEN GO TO 5470
5060 IF C$(J, tw, on TO on) <> "1" THEN GO TO 5380
5070 POKE G, ze ÷ POKE G+on, ze ÷ POKE G+tw, ze
     ÷ POKE G+tr, ze
5080 LET jl = VAL (C$(J, tw, tw TO tw)+C$(J, tr))
5090 PRINT TAB tr- LEN STR$ J; INVERSE on; J
       ; TAB fr; INVERSE ze; "▲"
       ; C$(J, on)+"▲"+C$(J, tw)+C$(J, tr)
       ; " =  > ";
5100 IF jl < ze OR jl > ln THEN GO TO 5460
5110 LET CJ = FN O(C$(J, on))
5120 PRINT TAB 17- LEN STR$ jl; INVERSE on; jl
       ; TAB 18; INVERSE ze; "▲"; C$(jl, on)
       ; "▲"; C$(jl, tw); "▲"; C$(jl, tr); "▲"
       ; C$(jl, fr);
5130 IF ABS CJ <> on THEN GO TO 5460
5140 LET dd = (jl > J)-(jl < J)
5150 LET ja = G ÷ LET dp = ze
5160 IF jl = J THEN GO TO 5270
5170 LET cl = J+dd
5180 LET n1 = ze ÷ IF C$(cl, on) = "▲▲"
       THEN GO TO 5220
5190 IF C$(cl, tw, on TO on) <> "1"
       THEN LET n1 = on+(C$(cl, tw) <> "▲▲")
             +(C$(cl, tr) <> "▲▲")
             +(C$(cl, fr) <> "▲▲")
     ÷ GO TO 5220
5200 LET TJ = FN o(C$(cl, on))
5210 LET n1 = (TJ = on)*tr+(TJ = -on)*tw
5220 IF cl = jl AND dd > ze THEN GO TO 5270
5230 LET dp = dp+n1
5240 IF cl = jl THEN GO TO 5270
5250 LET cl = cl+dd
5260 GO TO 5180
5270 IF CJ = on THEN LET ja = ja+dd*dp+(dd > ze)*tr
     ÷ GO TO 5310
5280 IF dd > ze THEN LET dp = dp+2
5290 IF dp > 126 AND dd < ze THEN GO TO 5460
5300 IF dp > 129 AND dd > ze THEN GO TO 5460
5310 LET V = 16* FN d(C$(J, on, on TO on))
     + FN d(C$(J, on, tw TO tw))
5320 POKE G, V ÷ LET G = G+on
5330 IF CJ = on THEN POKE G, ja- INT (ja/qk)*qk
     ÷ LET G = G+on ÷ POKE G, INT (ja/qk)
     ÷ LET G = G+on ÷ GO TO 5360
5340 IF dd < ze THEN LET dp = -dp
5350 LET dp = dp-tw ÷ POKE G, dp ÷ LET G = G+on
5360 PRINT "ok"
5370 GO TO 5470
5380 FOR I = on TO 7 STEP tw
```

```
5390 LET K = INT (I/tw+on)
5400 LET V = 16* FN d(C$(J, K, on TO on))
     + FN d(C$(J, K, tw TO tw))
5410 IF V < ze THEN GO TO 5440
5420 POKE G, V
5430 LET G = G+on
5440 NEXT I
5450 GO TO 5470
5460 PRINT "**"
5470 NEXT J
5480 PRINT AT ze, 25; "▲▲▲▲▲▲▲▲"
     : GO TO mr
6000 REM
6010 REM  INV Memory▲display********* IRU
6020 INPUT "Starting▲address :▲"; dm
6030 CLS : PRINT AT ze, ze;
6040 LET G = dm : LET F = ze
6050 LET F = F+on
     : PRINT TAB 5- LEN STR$ G; G ; TAB 6;
6060 FOR I = on TO fr
6070 LET V = PEEK G
6080 LET H = INT (V/16)
6090 LET L = V-16*H
6100 PRINT D$(H+on); D$(L+on); "▲";
6110 LET G = G+on
6120 NEXT I
6130 PRINT "▲"
6140 IF F <> 22 THEN GO TO 6050
6150 LET k$ = INKEY$ : IF k$ = "" THEN GO TO 6150
6160 IF k$ <> "m" AND k$ <> "M" THEN LET F = ze
     : POKE 23692, qk-on : GO TO 6050
6200 POKE 23692, on : PAUSE 20 : GO TO mr
7000 REM
7010 REM  INV LOAD****************** IRU
7020 CLS
7030 INPUT
     "Load▲array :Press▲any▲key▲when▲▲▲ready.▲"
     ; k$
7040 PRINT AT ze, 25; INVERSE on; FLASH on; "LOADING"
7050 LOAD "source" DATA C$()
7060 FOR I = on TO ln
7070 LET TP = I
7080 IF C$(I, on) <> "▲▲" THEN GO TO 7100
7090 NEXT I
7100 FOR I = ln TO on STEP -1
7110 LET BP = I
7120 IF C$(I, on) <> "▲▲" THEN GO TO 7140
7130 NEXT I
7140 PRINT AT ze, 25; "▲▲▲▲▲▲▲"
7150 GO TO 9150
8000 REM
8010 REM  INV SAVE****************** IRU
```

```
8020 INPUT "Enter▲name :▲"; n$
8030 IF n$ = "" THEN GO TO 8020
8040 INPUT
        "Source▲or▲Machine▲code :▲(s▲or▲m)"
        ; k$
8050 IF k$ <> "s" AND k$ <> "m" THEN GO TO 8040
8060 IF k$ = "s" THEN SAVE n$ DATA C$() : GO TO mr
8070 INPUT "Starting▲address :▲"; ss
8080 INPUT "Finishing▲address :▲"; sf
8090 LET sb = sf-ss+on
8100 SAVE n$ CODE ss, sb
8110 GO TO mr
9000 REM
9010 REM initialisation
9020 LET ze = PI - PI : LET on = PI / PI
     : LET tw = on+on : LET tr = on+tw
     : LET fr = tw+tw : LET qk = 256
     : LET mr = 2020 : LET ln = 200
9025 BORDER 7 : PAPER 7 : INK on : INVERSE ze
     : OVER ze : FLASH ze : BRIGHT ze
     : BEEP .25, 24 : BEEP .25, 12
9030 DIM A$(15) : DIM O$(tw)
9040 LET TP = ln : LET BP = on
     : REM line▲number▲buffer
9050 DIM C$(ln, fr, tw) : REM holds▲code
9060 PRINT AT ze, 20; INVERSE on; FLASH on
        ; "INITIALISING"
9070 FOR I = on TO ln
9080 FOR J = on TO fr
9090 LET C$(I, J) = "▲"
9100 NEXT J
9110 BEEP .01, 20
9120 NEXT I
9130 PRINT AT ze, 20; "▲▲▲▲▲▲▲▲▲▲▲▲"
9140 LET D$ = "0123456789ABCDEF"
9150 CLS : PRINT "Lowest▲address :▲"; 31500
9160 INPUT "Loading▲address :▲"; R : PAUSE 20
9170▲ IF R < 31500 THEN GO TO 9160
9180 CLS : GO TO mr
```

Hexload Machine Code Monitor

This BASIC program can be a monitor program on its own as it can be used to WRITE hexcode onto the memory, LIST memory, MOVE memory content around, SAVE the memory onto cassette and LOAD from the cassette to memory.

On the other hand we can use Hexload as a semi-linking loader for code created by the EZ-CODE program. This is because EZ-code can only be used to input small modules of less than 800 bytes and less than 200 instructions.

So for large programs, we use EZ-code to develop the modules and save each module as machine code on cassette.
Then we use HexLoad, which is a much smaller BASIC program, to load these modules and link them together by moving the modules into their appropriate memory locations.

We will actually apply this technique as we develop the FREEWAY FROG program.

Concept behind Hexload

The concept behind Hexload is extremely simple.
The monitor program actually set the RAMTOP of BASIC system to 26999.

That means you can input your machine code program anywhere betweem memory locations 27000 to 32578 for 16K Spectrum and 27000 to 65346 for 48K Spectrum.

Hexload is a straight forward machine code monitor program.
It offers basic monitoring functions like:

```
WRITE   onto memory in Hex format
SAVE    from memory to cassette
LOAD    from cassette to memory
LIST    memory contents from a starting address
MOVE    memory contents from one locations to another.
```

Hexload Instructions Summary

1. WRITE
   Write code in HEX format onto the memory.

Procedure:

a. Input start of memory where you want to write to in decimal format in response to the prompt.

The address is limited to 27000 - 32578 for 16K
27000 - 65346 for 48K

eg. Write to address: 27000(ENTER)

b. Enter codes in hex format.
c. Press "m" to return to main menu.

2. SAVE

Save memory to cassette.

Procedure:

a. Input memory from which saving starts, can be any address 0 - 32767 for 16K
0 - 65535 for 48K
b. Input number of bytes to be saved.
c. Input name of the module to be saved.
d. Press any key when the cassette is ready.
e. Option of verifying the module saved on to the cassette.
It is good to verify so as to ensure that there is no corruption of the module during the saving procedure.

3. LOAD

Load machine code module from cassette.

Procedure:

a. Input memory address to which the module is start loading. The address is limited to same range as in write command.
b. Enter the name used when the module is saved.
If you are not sure of the name, just press (ENTER).

4. LIST

Display memory contents starting from an address.

Procedure:

a. Input address start listing from.
Can be any address as in SAVE command above.
b. Type any key to continue the display.
c. Type "m" to return to main menu.

5. MOVE

Move memory contents from start address to finish address into new memory address.

Procedure:

a. Input move from memory, any address as in the range of SAVE command.
b. Input move until memory, any address as in the range of SAVE command.
c. Input move to memory, address range as in WRITE command.
d. You can even copy the ROM into RAM by using this command.

eg. Move from memory: 0(ENTER)
    Move until memory: 1000(ENTER)
    Move to memory: 32000(ENTER)

this will move ROM 0 to 1000 to RAM address 32000.

NOTES: Any of the input in above commands which breaches the address range will result in the input being reprompted.

EXERCISE:

Try using this monitor to input the module we have developed with EZ-code.

HEXLOAD
Copyright (c) 1982 by William Tang and David Webb

```
 100 REM
 110 REM monitor▴program
 120 CLEAR 26999 : LET ze = PI - PI
     : LET on = PI / PI : LET tw = on+on
     : LET qk = 256 : LET lm = 27000
     : LET mr = 140 : LET wl = 340
 130 GO SUB 2000
 140 CLS
     : PRINT "Start▴of▴machine▴code▴area = "
       ; lm
 150 PRINT "menu" : PRINT
     : PRINT
       "▴▴▴▴Write▴machine▴code.........1"
 160 PRINT
     : PRINT
       "▴▴▴▴Save▴▴machine▴code.........2"
 170 PRINT
     : PRINT
       "▴▴▴▴Load▴▴machine▴code.........3"
 180 PRINT
     : PRINT
       "▴▴▴▴List▴▴machine▴code.........4"
 190 PRINT
     : PRINT
       "▴▴▴▴Move▴▴machine▴code.........5"
 200 PRINT
     : PRINT
       "Please▴press▴appropriate▴key."
 210 LET g$ = INKEY$
 220 IF g$ = "m" OR g$ = "M" THEN STOP
 230 IF g$ = "" OR g$ < "1" OR g$ > "5"
       THEN GO TO 210
 240 CLS
     : PRINT "Start▴of▴machine▴code▴area = "
       ; lm
 250 GO TO 300* VAL g$
 300 REM  INV Write****************** TRU
 310 INPUT "Write▴to▴address :"; d
 320 IF d > mm OR d < lm THEN GO TO 310
 330 PRINT : PRINT "Write▴Address :▴"; d
     : PRINT "To▴return▴to▴menu▴enter▴""m"""
 340 LET a$ = ""
 350 IF a$ = "" THEN INPUT "Enter▴hex.▴code :"
       ; a$
 360 IF a$(on) = "m" OR a$(on) = "M"
       THEN GO TO mr
 370 IF LEN a$/tw <> INT ( LEN a$/tw)
       THEN PRINT "Incorrect▴entry▴";
     : GO TO wl
```

```
380 LET c = ze
390 FOR f = 16 TO on  STEP -15
400 LET a = CODE a$((f = 16)+tw*(f = on))
410 IF a < 48 OR a > 102 OR (a > 57 AND a < 65)
      OR (a > 70 AND a < 97)
      THEN PRINT "Incorrect▲entry▲";
   : GO TO wl
420 LET c = c+f*((a < 58)*(a-48)
      +(a > 64 AND a < 71)*(a-55)+(a > 96)*(a-87))
430 NEXT f : POKE d, c : LET d = d+on
440 PRINT a$( TO tw); "▲▲";
450 LET a$ = a$(3 TO )
460 IF d = UDG
      THEN PRINT
      "Warning :you▲are▲now▲in▲the▲user
      graphics▲area!"
   : GO TO wl
470 IF d = UDG-20
      THEN PRINT
      "Warning :you▲are▲now▲in▲routines
      memory▲area!"
   : GO TO wl
480 GO TO wl+on
600 REM  INV Save******************** TRU
610 INPUT "Save▲M.C.▲from▲address :"; a
620 INPUT "Number▲of▲bytes▲to▲be▲saved :"; n
630 INPUT "Name▲of▲the▲routine :"; a$
640 SAVE a$ CODE a, n
650 PRINT "Do▲you▲wish▲to▲verify?"
660 INPUT v$
670 IF v$ <> "y" THEN GO TO mr
680 PRINT "Rewind▲tape▲and▲press▲""PLAY""."
690 VERIFY a$ CODE a, n
700 PRINT "O.K." : PAUSE 50
710 GO TO mr
900 REM  INV Load******************** TRU
910 INPUT
      "Load▲M.C.▲to▲address▲starting▲▲▲ :▲"
      ; a
920 IF a > mm OR a < lm THEN GO TO 910
930 INPUT "Program▲name :"; a$
940 PRINT "Press▲""PLAY""▲on▲tape."
950 LOAD a$ CODE a : GO TO mr
1200 REM  INV List******************** TRU
1210 LET a$ = "0123456789ABCDEF"
1220 INPUT "List▲Address :"; d
1230 PRINT "Press▲""M""▲to▲return▲to▲Menu."
1240 LET a = INT ( PEEK d/16)
     : LET b = PEEK d-16* INT ( PEEK d/16)
1250 PRINT d; TAB 7; a$(a+on); a$(b+on)
1260 LET d = d+on
1270 IF INKEY$ = "m" OR INKEY$ = "M" THEN GO TO mr
1280 GO TO 1240
1500 REM  INV Move******************** TRU
```

```
1510 INPUT "Move from memory : "; fm
1520 INPUT "Move until memory : "; um
1530 INPUT "Move to memory : "; tm
1540 IF tm > fm THEN GO TO 1610
1550 LET mp = tm
1560 FOR I = fm TO um
1570 POKE mp, PEEK I
1580 LET mp = mp+on
1590 NEXT I
1600 GO TO mr
1610 LET mp = um+tm-fm
1620 FOR I = um TO fm STEP -on
1630 POKE mp, PEEK I
1640 LET mp = mp-on
1650 NEXT I
1660 GO TO mr
2000 LET RT = PEEK 23732+qk* PEEK 23733
2010 IF RT = 65535 THEN LET mm = 65347
     : LET UDG = 65367
2020 IF RT = 32767 THEN LET mm = 32579
     : LET UDG = 32599
2030 LET n1 = INT (UDG/qk)
2040 POKE 23675, UDG-n1*qk : POKE 23676, n1
2050 RETURN
```

The Freeway Frog Program

Program Design

This program is about frogs hopping their way home by crossing from one side of a highway to the other.

There are trucks and cars and motor bicycles on the highway with police cars frequently patrolling the highway.

Scores are given by the number of moves hopped from one side to the other side.

You must understand the game very clearly because you are the programmer.
This is merely the problem definition stage.
Unless we can clearly define and understand the problem it will be very hard for us to know where we are heading in the later stage of the design and development of the whole project.

FREEWAY FROG program structure

Now we can apply what we have learnt about TOP DOWN MODULAR program design. We proceed from very high level and divide the whole program up into well-defined logical modules.

They are as follows:

1. INITIALISATION
   perform all initial tasks.

2. TRAFFIC FLOW
   control of traffic on the highway.
   This can again be logically subdivided into
   i. regular traffic flow eg. trucks, cars and motorcycles.
   ii. irregular flow traffic eg. police car.

3. FROG
   control the movement of the FROG, crash testing as well as home testing.

4. GENERAL PROGRAM CONTROL
   this part of the program takes care of the score calculation and display, testing for termination of the game.

5. TERMINATION
perform the house keeping job before returning from the program.

Developing the FREEWAY FROG program

In developing the FREEWAY FROG program we have divided it into six stages. The division into these six stages follows very closely to the logical breaks shown above.

With each stage of development, we will have testing to ensure each stage is working before proceeding to the next stage.

The six stages will be:

1. Data Base design
involving the design of objects shape, the creation of database for each object and variables that the program will work on.

2. Initialisation
involves the setting up of the screen, and the initialisation of various variables.

3. Traffic flow
here we develop only the regular traffic flow and test it separately from the irregular police car appearance which involves different logic.

4. Police car
we develop and test the police car movement.

5. Frog
this will involve testing of frog movement, moving the frog by blanking the old frog and drawing the new frog, test for crashing, calculating scores ...etc.

6. Program control
handles updating of highscore, restart of game, abortion of game, return from the program.

Before we proceed to develop the stages of FREEWAY FROG, we will introduce here a BASIC program which will adds up thecontents of a block of memory and generate the sum as a "checksum".

You may find this checksum useful to check for data entry errors.

```
9000    REM
9010    REM checksum
```

```
9020    INPUT "From address: ";f
9030    INPUT "To address   : ";t
9040    LET s=0
9050    FOR I=f TO t
9060    LET s=s+PEEK I
9070    NEXT I
9080    PRINT "Checksum: ";s
9090    GO TO 9020
```

Enter the start of the memory block, then the end of the memory block which you want to do the checksum in decimal value. The BASIC program will generate the checksum value.

Stage 1 - Data Base

**** Design of object shape ****

As this is a two way traffic game, we need to design two truck shapes: a left truck shape and a right truck shape etc...

For the FROG, there will be four possible directions and so there will be four shapes, one for each direction.

Let us adopt the following convention for position of an object and for drawing each object:

If the shape is composed of four characters

```
C   D
A   B
```

the position pointer will be pointing to character A.

Character A is drawn first, then character B ...until the whole row is finished.
Then we'll draw the next row up. That is, repositioning to one line above to character C.

Thus, we will organise the shape database as

```
Shape   ABCD
```

Don't forget that each character shape is defined as eight bytes.

If we adopt the principle of drawing each character from top byte to the bottom byte, then we will need to organise the shape database also from top to bottom. Thus, the shape database will look like this:

```
Shape   a1, a2, a3, a4, a5, a6, a7, a8
        b1, b2, b3, b4, b5, b6, b7, b8
        c1, c2, c3, c4, c5, c6, c7, c8
        d1, d2, d3, d4, d5, d6, d7, d8
```

Let's adopt another principle that when we draw a shape, we will draw the whole shape into its screen memory location first, then we change the attribute file.

We will therefore store the attribute data that relates to that shape after its screen memory data.

Unlike the shape, for each character there is only one corresponding attribute data byte.

So, to cater for the attributes data we have four attribute data bytes after the above thirty two shape data bytes. (for a four character shape).

**** Input of object shape ****

label	line#	from(H)	to(H)	from(D)	to(D)	chechsum
FRGSHP	120	69AFH	6A36H	27055	27190	18085
LBIKE	340	6A37H	6A76H	27191	27254	3647
LBATT	430	6A77H	6A7EH	27255	27262	28
RBIKE	460	6A7FH	6ABEH	27263	27326	3355
RBATT	560	6ABFH	6AC6H	27327	27334	28
LCAR	600	6AC7H	6B26H	27335	27430	5073
LCATT	730	6B27H	6B32H	27431	27442	36
RCAR	770	6B33H	6B92H	27443	27538	4902
RCATT	900	6B93H	6B9EH	27539	27550	12
LTRUCK	940	6B9FH	6C76H	27551	27766	22023
LTATT	1230	6C77H	6C91H	27767	27793	87
RTRUCK	1280	6C92H	6D69H	27794	28009	21834
RTATT	1570	6D6AH	6D84H	28010	28036	87
BLANK	1620	6D85H	6D88H	28037	28040	0

Module from 27055 to 28040, 986 bytes, checksum is 79197.

Suggested name "shapdb",(shape database).

All the above objects except the Frog can be grouped into SHAPE data bytes followed by attribute data bytes.

The reason why the Frog shape database is not of that format is because we have decided that the frog has only one colour at any one time, either GREEN when it is alive, or RED when it is dying, or YELLOW when it reaches home.

In this game, we use BLACK (0) as the paper colour except for the highway boundary and the top information line where we use WHITE (7) as paper colour.

For objects that move only on the highway, paper attribute will be 0 and the ink colour will be that given in its database.

Before we input the shape data base into memory and store it onto cassette, it is assumed that you understand character representation in memory.

We will now explain the assembler listing using the example of shape FROG1, starting at line 160.

In line 160, you will see

```
69B7    6F   160 FROG1    DB  111,15,31,159,220,216,120,48
        0F 1F 9F DC D8 78 30
```

69B7 is the memory address in hexadecimal format

6F is the start of the eight bytes of the current DB instruction in Hexadecimal value.
The hexadecimal value of the next seven bytes are in the next line between line 160 and line 170.
ie OFH, 1FH, 9FH, DCH, D8H, 78H,30H.

160 is the line number of the assembler listing.

FROG1 is the label. This is for our benefit only.

DB is a mnemonic. It means that what follows is a sequence of bytes. (Similar to DATA in BASIC).

111,15,31,159,220,216,120,48
are the bytes to be loaded into the memory.

Now let's build the FROG1 shape.

00	00000000	00000000	00
01	00000001	10000000	80
23	00100011	11000100	C4
25	00100101	10100100	A4
6F	01101111	11110110	F6
4F	01001111	11110010	F2
DF	11011111	11111011	FB
FF	11111111	11111111	FF
6F	01101111	11110110	F6
OF	00001111	11110000	FO
1F	00011111	11111000	F8
9F	10011111	11111001	F9
DC	11011100	00111011	3B
D8	11011000	00011011	1B
78	01111000	00011110	1E
30	00110000	00001100	OC

Remember:
i. we draw the bottom row first from left to right.
ii. Then we draw the next row up.
iii.For each character, we draw the eight bytes from top to bottom.
iv. Then at the very last, we fill in the attributes.

FRGSHP in line 120 defines one of four pointers pointing to the four shapes of the frog. In the program, we will therefore be able to find the correct shape given the direction of the frog.

DEFW is a mnemonic that means we want to define a 2-byte "nn". The least significant byte is first while the most significant byte is next.

**** Input of shape database ****

Use the Hexload program to input lines 120 to 1590 in the assembler listing. Enter only the hex bytes as shown in column 2.

Remember to save and verify the code before you proceed to the next part of this stage!

**** Design of the objects database ****

We have decided that there will be a regular flow of six vehicles in the two lane of the highway.
These are randomly distributed between the two lanes.

Object database will store information about the current status of the traffic:

For example, for each object we need to know:

Existence, Movement cycle count, Direction of movement, whether it's partly on the screen or not, Position pointer,
Shape database pointer, Attribute database pointer,
Number of Rows the shape occupies,
Number of column the shape occupies.

The database carries this information about each object in each game cylce.

The first six group of databases from program line 1710 to 2040 represent the six vehicles that are going to be on the highway. When any vehicle moves off the highway, another vehicle will be generated randomly.

One simple way is to prepare the initial information for each possible vehicle and store this in memory.
When a new vehicle is generated, we just go to the corresponding memory locations and restore the database.

We will apply the same principle to the Police car and the Frog.

Therefore, when we build up the object database, we need not build up the temporary database, as this will be initialised by the program.

* temporary database memory map

Format: for the six existing vehicles, the frog and the police car:

Existence	DEFB	1 byte
Cycle count	DEFB	1 byte
Direction	DEFB	1 byte
Real/abstract	DEFB	1 byte
Position	DEFW	2 bytes
Shape pointer	DEFW	2 bytes
Attribute	DEFW	2 bytes
Row	DEFB	1 byte
Column	DEFB	1 byte
	TOTAL	12 bytes

label	line#	from(H)	to(H)	from(D)	to(D)
OB1EXT	1710	6E25H	6E30H	28197	28208
OB2EXT	1800	6E31H	6E3CH	28109	28220
OB3EXT	1850	6E3DH	6E48H	28221	28232
OB4EXT	1900	6E49H	6E54H	28233	28244
OB5EXT	1950	6E55H	6E60H	28245	28256
OB6EXT	2000	6E61H	6E6CH	28257	28268
PCAREXT	2070	6E6DH	6E78H	28269	28280
FRGEXT	2180	6E79H	6E80H	28281	28288

As mentioned above, these are only temporary working storage. The information that they contain changes as the game proceeds.

There are two other major temporary working storage area.
They are used to store what is underneath the frog and the police car respectively.

label	line#	from(H)	to(H)	from(D)	to(D)
FRGSTR	1650	6D89H	6DACH	28041	28076
PCSTR	1660	6DADH	6F24H	28077	28196

We do not need to define any of these locations - only allow for them. We only need to build up the following database.

The object database is organised in the following way:

FRGDB	frog database
DBINDEX	other object database index
RBDB	right bycycle database
LBDB	left bycycle database
RCDB	right car database
LCDB	left car database
RTDB	right truck database
LTDB	left truck database

LPCDB	left police car database
LPCATT	left police attribute database
RPCDB	right police car database
RPCATT	right police car database

label	line#	from(H)	to(H)	from(D)	to(D)	checksum
FRGDB	2260	6E81H	6E88H	28289	28296	561
DBINDEX	2320	6E89H	6E94H	28297	28308	1734
RBDB	2400	6E95H	6EAOH	28309	28320	640
LBDB	2470	6EA1H	6EACH	28321	28332	692
RCDB	2540	6EADH	6EB8H	28333	28344	523
LCDB	2610	6EB9H	6EC4H	28345	28356	760
RTDB	2680	6EC5H	6EDOH	28357	28368	584
LTDB	2750	6ED1H	6EDCH	28369	28380	809
LPCDB	2820	6EDDH	6EE8H	28381	28392	955
LPCATT	2890	6EE9H	6EF4H	28393	28404	30
RPCDB	2930	6EF5H	6FOOH	28405	28416	379
RPCATT	3000	6FO1H	6FOCH	28417	28428	30

Module from 28289 to 28428, 140 bytes, checksum 7697.

Suggested name is "objdb". (object database).

We know that all objects except the FROG have a twelve bytes database.

The meaning and contents of each byte is:

* Existence (1 byte)
  - set to zero when the object is nonexistant.
  - set to value n where (n - 1) is the number of cycles that the object will wait before it is allowed to move.

n value for	left and right cycle	is	2
	left and right car	is	3
	left and right truck	is	6
	police car	is	1
	frog	is	8

  in other words, the police car moves every cycle, the motorcycle move every alternate cycle etc.

* Cycle count (1 byte)
  - initially set as 1 so that it is ready to move straight away and decrement by one every cycle.
  - when it reaches zero, the object will be allowed to move and the count will be reinitialised to the value held in the existence byte.

* Direction (1 byte)
  - all left to right traffic (ie. top lane traffic) will have direction value zero.

- all right to left traffic (ie. bottom lane traffic) will have direction value one.

* Abstract/Real flag (1 byte)
- this defines whether objects is partly off the screen
- all left to right traffic will start off with value zero (abstract).
- left to right traffic will change this to one when their position points to the real screen 4820H.
- all right to left traffic will have flag start off with value one (real); the object has a position pointing to the screen. ie 48DFH.
- as the right to left traffic moves off the screen, ie.when the position pointer moves from 48C0H to 48BFH, this will be changed from real to abstract.

* Position pointer (2 bytes)
- 2 bytes pointer storing the current position of the object.

* Shape pointer (2 bytes)
- 2 bytes pointer pointing to the shape database of the object.

* Attribute pointer (2 bytes)
- 2 bytes pointer pointing to the attribute database of the object.

* Row (1 byte)
- store how many rows the object shape occupies.

* Column (1 byte)
- store how many columns the object shape takes.
- this value includes two columns of blanks, one at each end of the object.
  The purpose of these two extra columns of blanks is to avoid the traffic getting too close to each other.

Now you can key in the object initialise database from listing 2270 to 3010.

You can use EZ-code or Hexload to enter this module.
If you use EZ-code, remember to save the source listing as well as the dumped listing.

**** General database ****

We have covered so far the database from 69AFH to 6F0CH (27055 to 28428).

Now we are going to build up the rest of the database and we classify this as "general database".

This is organised as below:

line	500 to 630	SOUND	
	660 to 690	SCORE MESSAGE	
	720 to 1210	GENERAL	

label	line#	from(H)	to(H)	from(D)	to(D)	checksum
PCTON1	500	6F0DH	6F10H	28429	28432	282
PCTON2	510	6F11H	6F14H	28433	28436	166
HOMTON	540	6F15H	6F3CH	28437	28476	2565
SCRMS1	660	6F3DH	6F42H	28477	28482	540
SCORE	670	6F43H	6F48H	28483	28488	288
SCRMS2	680	6F49H	6F53H	28489	28499	732
HISCR	690	6F54H	6F58H	28500	28504	240

Module from 28429 to 28504, 76 bytes, checksum 4813.

Suggested name "gendb". (general database).

You only need to input from line 500 to line 690.

From line 720 to line 1210, memory 6F59H to 6F82H (28505 to 28546), these are all variables used by the program.

Line 1100 to 1150 are instructions with mnemonic EQU. This assigns a value to the corresponding label and is used by the assembler program. You do not have to enter anything.

Conclusion

Now we have covered the whole database area from memory 69AFH TO 6F82H (27055 to 28546).

Examine all modules that you have built, their names, their memory range before you proceed the next stage of the building up of the FREEWAY FROG program.

You should have now developed three modules:

name	from mem	to mem	length	checksum
shpdb	27055	28040	986	79197
objdb	28289	28428	140	7697
gendb	28429	28504	76	4818

Note that the database occupies nearly 1400 bytes!!

Stage 2 - Initialisation

**** Screen Setup ****

In this module, we set up the highway, the score display, the frog as well as initialise all control variables.

We will do it in three parts.
First, clear the screen and put in the highway.
Secondly, put in all the frogs.
Thirdly, display the score.

This module includes the following routines:

routine	line#	from(H)	to(H)	from(D)	to(D)	checksum
INIT	1240	6F83H	700AH	28547	28682	11996
CLRSCR	7060	72D7H	7316H	29399	29462	5236
DRWHWY	1820	700BH	7040H	28683	28736	4802
HIGHWY	1980	7038H	7040H	28728	28736	696
FILHWY	2070	7041H	7054H	28737	28756	2609
LINEUP	2290	7055H	7079H	28757	28793	4325
DISASC	7630	7328H	7349H	29480	29513	3580
SCRIMG	14500	776FH	7786H	30575	30598	1855
FINAL	15390	77FEH	781DH	30718	30749	2466

Module spread from 28547 to 30749, 2201 bytes.

Suggested name "init". (intialisation).

Enter first CLRSCR, DRWHWY, FILHWY, FINAL into their corresponding memory locations.

Then enter INIT routine. Enter three bytes of zero for the following lines instead of the CALLs because the routine which are called haven't been developed yet.

line#	address(H)	address(D)
1430	6FAFH	28591
1470	6FBAH	28602
1490	6FC0H	28608
1530	6FCBH	28619
1570	6FD6H	28630
1590	6FDCH	28636
1630	6FE7H	28647

Then enter the following codes into memory starting from 32000. Save the module from 28547 to 30598, 2052 bytes before running the code in memory 32000.

```
F3              DI                    ;Disable interrupt
D9              EXX                   ;Preserve HL'
E5              PUSH     HL
D9              EXX
CD836F          CALL     INIT
3E7F     KEY    LD       A,7FH        ;TRAP SPACE KEY
DBFE            IN       A,(FEH)
E601            AND      1
20F8            JR       NZ,KEY       ;loop if not press
CDFE77          CALL     FINAL        ;finalisation
D9              EXX                   ;restore HL'
E1              POP      HL
D9              EXX
FB              EI                    ;enable interrupt
C9              RET
```

You should see the screen blacken and four white linesappear on the screen.

The following is a brief description of what each routine does.

```
INIT
    set border colour to black
    initialise frog-crash flag, frog existence, gameflag
              number of frog
    set random ROM pointer
    set frog station (also initial position of frog) to
              50ACH
    call clear-screen
    call draw highway
    call line-up frogs (five of them)
    load score message
    print score
    load high score message
    print high score
    initialise all objects as nonexistent
    initialise chase flag, siren sound flag and score


DRWHWY
    fill top highway line (32 characters of 40A0H)
    fill middle highway line (32 characters of 4860H)
    fill bottom highway line (32 characters of 5020H)
*remember that highway is white paper black ink
    unfill top two-character bytes of top highway
                                (therefore, they are white)
    unfill bottom two-character bytes of bottom highway
                                (they are also white now)
    redraw middle two-bytes of the middle highway
```

```
FILHWY
    initialise fill character ()FFH)
    set loop count to 32      (one line 32 characters)
    draw one character (8 bytes)
    move pointer to next character each time

FINAL
    set white border
    blank screen
    set screen attribute file to white paper and black ink
```

If everything is fine, save the module first from memory location 28500 to 30800, 2300 bytes.

Now enter LINEUP, DRWFRG routines. Check the checksum and save the whole module again under the same name, same addresses.
Then change memory from 6FAFH (28591) to 6FB1H (28593) to that it corresponds to line 1430 of the assembly listing.
ie. CD 55 70.

Run 32000 and you will see five frogs line up at the left bottom of the screen.

The following are descriptions of what these two routines do:

```
LINEUP
    set frog direction to 1 (facing right)
    set frog shape to FROG2
    set attribute number to 2 (green)
    if no frog left
        then return
    else
        for number of frog
            push BC, DE, HL onto stack
            draw the frog by calling DRWFRG routine
            pop  HL, DE, BC from stack
            update draw position


DRWFRG
    draw shape using convention discussed earlier
    calculate attribute pointer
    fill attribute of frog
```

Now input DISASC, SCRIMG routines. Check the checksum and save the module again as above.

Now change the memories referred to by the following lines in the assembly listing to the correct codes shown on the listing.

line#   1470, 1490, 1530, 1570, 1590, 1630.

Run 32000 and you should see the whole screen set up with highway drawn, frog and score displayed.

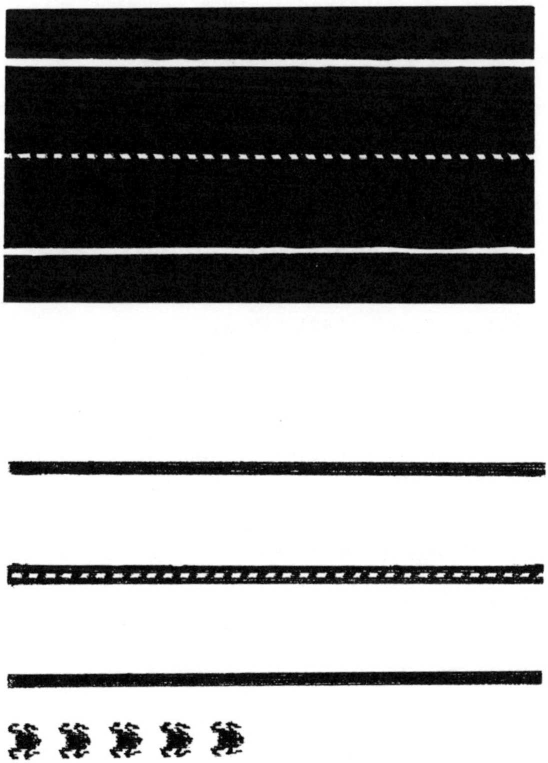

Stage 3 - Regular Traffic

In this stage, we develop the regular flow of traffic. ie. all traffic except police car:

```
    Traffic control ( including regeneration of traffic)
        regenerate traffic
    Moving traffic
        moving control
            drawing traffic
                determine drawn shape
```

Below is a table of all routines in this module.

name	line#	from(H)	to(H)	from(D)	to(D)	checksum
TFCTRL	3090	70BDH	70D8H	28861	28888	2587
REGEN	3320	70D9H	710EH	28889	28942	5673
MOVTRF	3700	710FH	71AEH	28943	29102	14831
MVCTRL	4720	71AFH	7208H	29103	29192	9222
DRAW	5560	7209H	7295H	29193	29333	13923
RSHAPE	6630	7296H	72D6H	29334	29398	6803
RANDNO	15050	77CCH	77DDH	30668	30685	2194

Module from 28861 to 30685, 1824 bytes.

Suggested name "regtrf". (regular traffic).

Again, it is useless to generate a total checksum of the whole module because the memory range covers some undeveloped memory area. But it is important that you check the checksum of each routine after entering it.

We develop this module in two parts.

Firstly, the draw routine for traffic.
Secondly, the traffic control and draw control.

Input DRAW, RSHAPE routines into their memory region, checksum and save them.

Then entering the following testing program starting from memory 32000.

```
F3                  DI
D9                  EXX
E5                  PUSH    HL
D9                  EXX
CD836F              CALL    INIT
3E03                LD      A, 3          ;row count
32606F              LD      (ROW), A      ;store in ROW
3E09                LD      A, 9          ;column count
325F6F              LD      (COLUMN), A   ;store in COLUMN
11926C              LD      DE, RTRUCK    ;right truck shape
216A6D              LD      HL, RTATT     ;right truck attri
226A6F              LD      (ATTPTR), HL;store in ATTPTR
3E01                LD      A, 1          ;set to real pos
212248              LD      HL, 4822H     ;top lane
CD0972              CALL    DRAW          ;draw shape
3E7F      KEY       LD      A, 7FH        ;key trap
DBFE                IN      A,(OFEH)
E601                AND     1
20F8                JR      NZ, KEY
CDFE77              CALL    FINAL
D9                  EXX
E1                  POP     HL
D9                  EXX
FB                  EI
C9                  RET
```

Load the database modules in the order they are created.
Load the init module.
Load the routines you developed in this stage.
Save memory 27000, 4000 bytes into "frog" module. This will includes all routines you have developed so far.
Enter and save the above test routine in memory 32000.

Run 32000 and you should see the screen set up and a right truck on the top lane as well.

You can change the parameters in the program above between CALL INIT and CALL DRAW to test all other object shapes.

Below is a brief description of the two routines.

DRAW

Similar logic to DRWFRG

RSHAPE

trap lower 5 bits of low order byte of position parameter
subtract from 1FH and add 1

```
    trap lower 5 bits again
    determine SKIP and FILL depending on real or abstract
    calculate attribute position and store in ATTPOS
```

Enter TFCTRL, REGEN and MVCTRL routines in their memory region and save the whole module.

Edit the testing routine as follows:

```
                DI
                EXX
                PUSH    HL
                EXX
                CALL    INIT
CDBD70  MOVE    CALL    TFCTRL
CD0F71          CALL    MOVTRF
3E7F            LD      A, 7FH
DBFE            IN      A,(0FEH)
E601            AND     1
20F2            JR      NZ, MOVE
                CALL    FINAL
                EXX
                POP     HL
                EXX
                EI
                RET
```

By now you should realise that we save the whole stage module while we are developing that stage.
Once a module is fully developed and tested, it will be merged together with previous modules and saved into the "frog" module.

We test the modules by a small testing program starting from memory 32000.

After you have done all the housekeeping work for your modules, test run the new "frog" module.

If everything is correct, you should see the whole screen as before plus all traffic moving at a very fast speed in the two lanes. This is because there is no delay between each program cycle.

A short description of the routines.

```
TFCTRL
    load generation flag
    if not regeneration
        decrement flag count
        return
    else
        regenerate the first nonexistence object by calling
```

```
        the REGEN routine
    return


REGEN
    save existence database pointer
    generate random number 0 to 5
    test the first two character of the screen position
        where the object is created
    if the sum of the attributes of those two position is
        not equal to zero
            then return (traffic jam)
    else
        determine the initialise database
        load into temporary working database
        set regeneration cycle count to 2
        return


MOVTRF
    for all existing objects
        decrement cycle count
        if count reaches zero
            reload count from existence
            move one character left or right
            store new position in NEWPOS
            test attribute correspondence of the front of
                objects
            if any nonzero ink
                if not green
                    set jam flag
                else
                    set crash flag
            if jam flag set
                load cycle count with 2(move one cycle
                                        later)
                return
            else
                store new position
                call MVCTRL (move control)


MVCTRL
    if edge reached
        change real/abstract flag
    if left moving
        if on edge (position low order byte = 1FH)
            if abstract flag
                set non exist, return
            else
                goto L1
        else
```

```
            goto L1
    else
        get end of object
        if reach end of screen (low order byte is OCOH)
            set non exist, return
L1: refill cycle count
    retrieve shape pointer
    store attribute pointer in ATTPTR
    retrieve ROW and COLUMN of shape
    DRAW from new position.


RANDNO
    push HL,BC onto stack
    retrieve what random pointer pointing to in ROM
    update pointer (move down ROM)
```

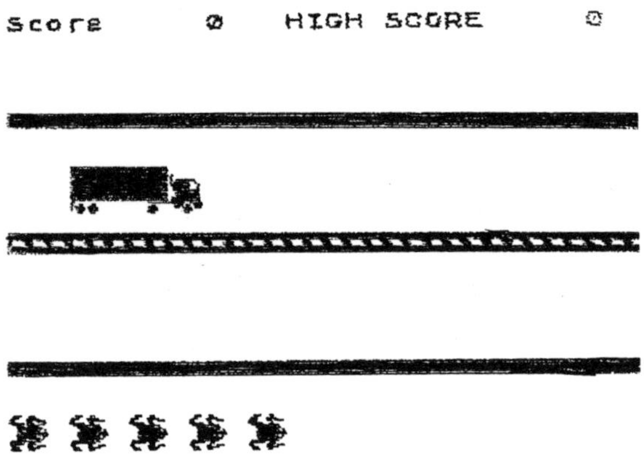

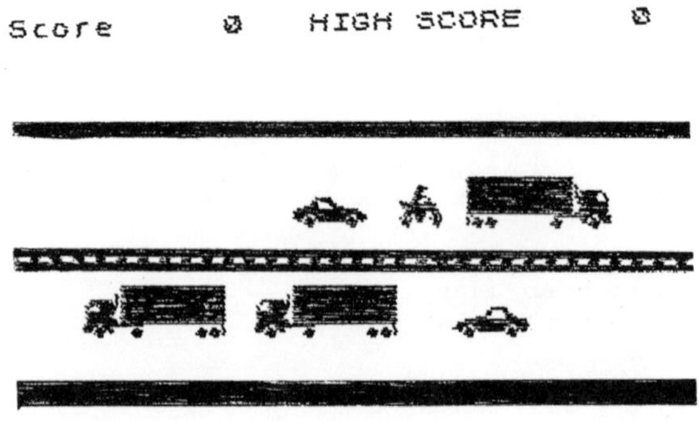

Stage 4 - Police Car

In this stage, we will introduce the POLICE car into the program.

The POLICE car will be generated randomly and enter with SIREN sounding. It moves every cycle and there is no traffic jam in its course. It will overtake any regular traffic before it.

That is why the program needs to save what is underneath the police car and put it back when the police car moves on.

Below are all routines in this module.

name	line#	from(H)	to(H)	from(D)	to(D)	checksum
RESPC	9560	7450H	74C1H	29776	29889	11011
POLICE	7930	734AH	73DEH	29514	29662	15769
STRPC	8830	73DFH	744FH	29663	29775	10615

There are routines which are called in this module which has been developed in previous modules.

Module from 29514 to 29889, 376 bytes.

Suggested name "police".

Enter POLICE and STRPC routines. Checksum and save them in the "police" module.

Then edit the testing program to the following:

```
                  DI
                  EXX
                  PUSH    HL
                  EXX
                  CALL    INIT
         MOVE     CALL    TFCTRL
                  CALL    MOVTRF
CD4A73   MOVE1    CALL    POLICE
                  LD      A,7FH
                  IN      A,(OFEH)
                  AND     1
20F5              JR      NZ,MOVE1
                  CALL    FINAL
                  EXX
                  POP     HL
                  EXX
                  EI
                  RET
```

Load the "frog" module, then the "police" module.

Run the testing program. You should see the POLICE car moving very fast on the highway.

If you want to put in other traffic as well, change the relative jump to   JR NZ, MOVE.
Remember to recalculate the displacement offset. (EFH).

As it moves, you would see the POLICE car wipe off the traffic shape as it overtakes them. It may be so fast that you wouldn't notice.
But you can tell when some traffic starts to run into the vehicle in front of them.

Let's look at these routines:

```
POLICE
    if police car non-exist
        get a random number
        if not a mutiple of 31
            return
        else
            set chase flag
            determine top or bottom lane randomly
            load corresponding initial database.
    get direction
    store position pointer
    retrieve position
    move and store NEWPOS
    set ROW, COLUMN, REAL/ABSTRACT flag, POS before
        call RSHAPE
    get resulted ATTPOS and test head of shape for green
    if green attribute
        set crash flag
        blank front of police car
    call STRPC (for storing of what's underneath policecar)
    update position database
    call MVCTRL (for moving on and off the screen)
    turn off chase flag if non-exist
```

```
STRPC
    set HL points to NEWPOS
    set DE points to PCSTR (police car store)
    store position and 5 byte of information starting from
        ROW variable
    store according to SKIP/FILL format
        all screen memory first
        then attribute file
```

Enter the RESPC routine and merge with the previous two routines. Save the whole module as "police".

You need to edit the testing program again to test the storing and restoring.

Although we included the STRPC routine we are not sure that it saved the correct data underneath the police car. Only the RESPC can help us to know that, because it puts what was stored back onto the screen.

change the tesing program to the following:

```
                    .
                    .
                    .
        MOVE    CALL    TFCTRL
CD5074          CALL    RESPC   (----------
                CALL    MOVTRF
                CALL    POLICE
                LD      A,7FH
                IN      A,(OFEH)
                AND     1
20EC            JR      NZ,MOVE
                    .
                    .
                    .
```

Adjust the relative jump before you test run the module with "frog".

You should see the POLICE car overtaking vehicles without wiping them off.

The RESPC's logic is as below:

```
RESPC
    return if police car nonexist
    restore the position and 5 bytes into variables
        starting from ROW
    restore screen memory then attribute according to
        SKIP/FILL format
    return
```

Finally, enter SIREN routine, checksum and merge it with the rest of the "police" module.

Load "frog" module then reload the new "police" module.

Edit the testing program in memory 32000's as following:

```
                      .
                      .
                      .
                CALL    INIT
        MOVE    CALL    TFCTRL
                CALL    RESPC
                CALL    MOVTRF
                CALL    POLICE
CD8777          CALL    SIREN   (---------
                LD      A,7FH
                IN      A,(OFEH)
                AND     1
                JR      NZ,MOVE
                      .
                      .
```

Run the testing program and you will find the whole traffic flow will slow down. This is because of a constant delay either because of the sound output or a downcount delay loop.

```
SIREN
    trap (ENTER) key pressed
    if pressed
        change siren to no siren or vice versa
    if no sound
        go to DELAY
    else
        if no police car
            go to delay
        else
            determine the correct tone database
            load onto DE, HL
            call 03B5H
            return
DELAY:  down count 6144
```

Merge this module with "frog" in the memory and reload in "frog".

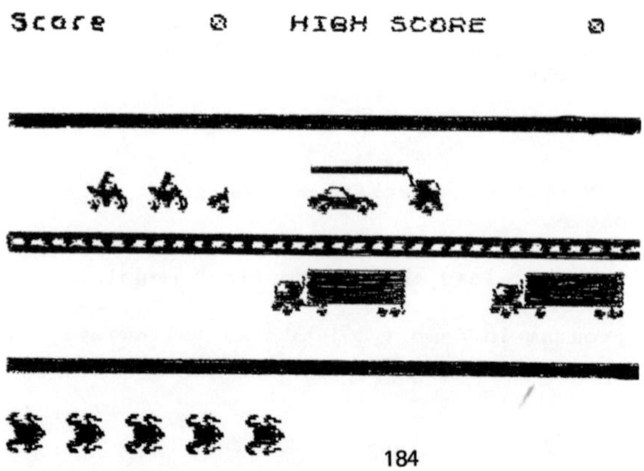

Stage 5 - The Frog

In this stage we develop the frog routines.

We need to regenerate the frog when a frog dies.

We also need to handle the frog movement, save what is underneath it and restore what was stored back when the frog moves.

We also need to handle the frog crashing or home run and calculate score.

We build up this module in three parts as below.
    Regenerate and move frog
    store and restore what is underneath
    handle crashing, homerun and score

All routines within this module is as follows:

name	line#	from(H)	to(H)	from(D)	to(D)	checksum
FROG	10280	74C2H	74E2H	29890	29922	3818
REGFRG	10520	74E3H	750FH	29923	29967	4079
MOVFRG	10770	7510H	75D5H	29968	30165	19943
RESFRG	11870	75D6H	7627H	30166	30247	8492
STRFRG	12440	7628H	7690H	30248	30352	10136
CRASH	13160	7691H	76A6H	30353	30374	2767
FRGDIE	13280	76A7H	7707H	30375	30471	9965
FRGTON	13890	7708H	771CH	30472	30492	2435
CALSCR	14040	771DH	776EH	30493	30574	8106

Module from 29890 to 30574, 685 bytes.

Suggested name "frgrtn" (frog routine).

Enter FROG, REGFRG, MOVFRG, RESFRG, STRFRG and CRASH routines.

Edit the testing program as following:

```
                .
                .
                .
                CALL    INIT
        MOVE    CALL    TFCTRL
                CALL    RESPC
                CALL    MOVTRF
                CALL    POLICE
                CALL    FROG      (-----------
                CALL    SIREN
```

```
        LD      A,7FH
        IN      A,(OFEH)
        AND     1
        JR      NZ,MOVE
        .
        .
```

Since we haven't entered the FRGDIE routine yet, replace the coding in line 13190 of the assembly listing by

```
        00, 00, 00
```

Run the testing program and you should be able to move the frog. The controls are "1"=up, "a"=down, "i"=left, "p"=right.

When the frog crashed, it will simply disappear because the FRGDIE routine which handles the dying procedure of the frog hasn't been put in yet.

The description of these few routines are as following:

FROG
the control routine for the whole FROG module.

```
    if frog crashed
        goto CRH
    else
        set score-flag to no score (0)
        call REGFRG
        decrement cycle count
        if count non zero
            return
        else
            reset cycle count
            call MOVFRG
            if not crash
                return
CRH:call CRASH routine
    return
```

REGFRG

```
    if frog does not exist
        load frog initial database to working database
        update frog station to three position left
        initialise OLDFRG and NEWFRG to FRGPOS
        initialise frog storage area to 0
    return
```

MOVFRG

```
    initialise registers
                C - absolute movement
                B - frog direction
```

```
            DE- frog shape
    test frog movement
            1 - up, a - down, i - left, p - right
    store shape, direction
    if absolute move is zero
        return
    else
        restore old frog position
        calculate new frog position and store
    test up screen position, right screen, bottom screen,
        frog station
    if valid
        store position into NEWFRG
        set score flag.
    restore OLDFRG
    if OLDFRG equal NEWFRG
        return
    else
        call RESFRG
        set OLDFRG equal NEWFRG
        move stored direction, shape pointer to frog
            database
        call STRFRG
        return


RESFRG
    restore underneath frog based on OLDFRG position
    memory first then attributes


STRFRG
    store underneath frog based on NEWFRG position
    draw frog while drawing as well


CRASH
    reset crash flag
    set frog nonexist
    call FRGDIE routine (dying procedures)
    call RESFRG routine (place back what was underneath)
    decrement number of frog
```

After you have saved up all the modules, enter the CALSCR, FRGDIE and FRGTON routine.

To test the crash handling routine, replace 13190 of the listing by the following instruction:

```
7698    CDA776      CALL    FRGDIE      (30360)
```

Edit the testing program to the following:

```
            .
            .
        CALL    FROG
        CALL    CALSCR  (--------
        CALL    SIREN
            .
            .
            .
```

Merge the routine in the "frgrtn" module and run memory 32000 together with the "frog" module.

When the frog crashes, it will flash red and vanish.

```
FRGDIE
    test frog reaches home or die
    set die tone, red colour attribute
    if reaches home
        add one to third digit of score
            (bonus 100 points)
        call DISSCR (display score)
        set home tone, yellow colour attribute
    draw frog based on OLDFRG, FROGSH, and attribute just
        set by call DRWFRG
    flash frog with the attribute five times


FRGTON
    call TONE1 (tone code from SIREN routine)
    move up or down the tone database depends upon attibute
        used to flash the frog ( if yellow then down db )
                               ( if red    then up   db )


CALSCR
    if frog non-exist
        return
    else
        if score flag not set
            return
        else
            if go up
                add one to tenth digit of score
                    (10 points)
            else
                if not within the highway
                    return
                else
                    add one to tenth digit
```

readjust all score digits
build up score printing image
display score printing image

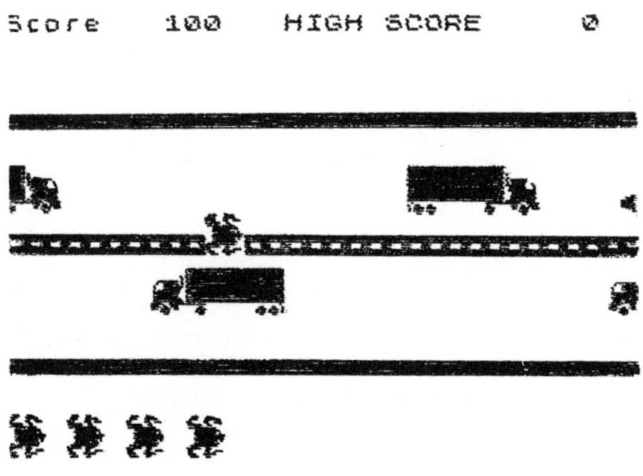

Stage 6 - Control

In this stage we develop the control routine for the whole program.

The main control is that when the game is finished, high score is updated and the game is restarted automically.

In any cycle, the user can abort the game by pressing the space key.

You will find that line 180 to 440 of the listing looks very similar to the testing program we have been developing.

Routines left for program are as follows:

name	line#	from(H)	to(H)	from(D)	to(D)	checksum
START	180	6978H	69AEH	27000	27054	8427
OVER	15200	77DEH	77FDH	30686	30717	2491

Now enter these routines into the memory. Save them together with the "frog" module and save the whole module as "frog".

Run 27000 instead of 32000 and you will have the whole program working.

```
OVER
    compare all digits of HISCR and SCORE+1
    for the first nonequal digit
        if HISCR digit is lower
            update HISCR to SCORE+1
        else
            return
    return
```

Congratulations and I hope you enjoyed the development of the FREEWAY FROG program.

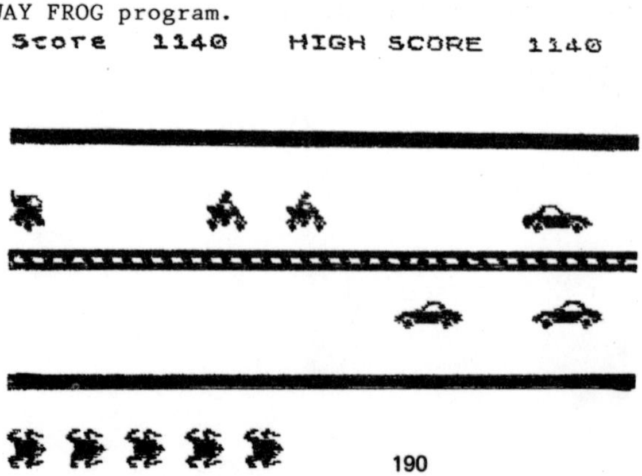

```
                00100 ;**********  FREEWAY FROG  **********
                00110 ;
                00120 ;
                00130 ;
                00140 ;
                00150 ;
6978            00160         ORG     27000
                00170 ;
6978 F3         00180 START   DI              ;DISABLE BASIC SYSTEM AFFECTING
6979 D9         00190         EXX             ;THE KEYBOARD SCANNING
697A E5         00200         PUSH    HL      ;PRESERVE THE HL' REGISTER PAIR
697B D9         00210         EXX             ;POP BACK BEFORE RETURN
697C CD836F     00220 AGAIN   CALL    INIT    ;INITIALISATION
697F CDBD70     00230 MOVE    CALL    TFCTRL  ;TRAFFIC CONTROL ROUTINE
6982 CD5074     00240         CALL    RESPC   ;RESTORE UNDERNEATH
6985 CD0F71     00250         CALL    MOVTRF  ;MOVE TRAFFIC
6988 CD4A73     00260         CALL    POLICE  ;POLICE CAR ROUTINE
698B CDC274     00270         CALL    FROG    ;FROG MODULE
698E CD1D77     00280         CALL    CALSCR  ;CALCULATE AND DISPLAY SCORE
6991 CD8777     00290         CALL    SIREN   ;SIREN OR DELAY
6994 3A776F     00300         LD      A,(GAMFLG)      ;FINISH WHEN NO FROG
6997 A7         00310         AND     A
6998 2005       00320         JR      NZ,CONTIN
699A CDDE77     00330         CALL    OVER    ;HIGHSCORE MANAGEMENT
699D 18DD       00340         JR      AGAIN   ;NEW GAME AGAIN
699F 3E7F       00350 CONTIN  LD      A,7FH   ;TRAP SPACE KEY PRESSED
69A1 DBFE       00360         IN      A,(0FEH)        ;SCAN KEYBOARD
69A3 E601       00370         AND     1
69A5 20D8       00380         JR      NZ,MOVE
69A7 CDFE77     00390         CALL    FINAL   ;RESET SCREEN AND BORDER COLOUR
69AA D9         00400         EXX
69AB E1         00410         POP     HL      ;RETRIEVE HL'
69AC D9         00420         EXX
69AD FB         00430         EI              ;ENABLE INTERRUPTS
69AE C9         00440         RET             ;RETURN TO BASIC SYSTEM
                00450 ;
                00460 ;
69AF            00470
                00100 ;**********  FROGDB/ASM  **********
                00110 ;
69AF B769       00120 FRGSHP  DEFW    FROG1           ;UP FROG
69B1 D769       00130         DEFW    FROG2           ;RIGHT FROG
69B3 F769       00140         DEFW    FROG3           ;DOWN FROG
69B5 176A       00150         DEFW    FROG4           ;LEFT FROG
69B7 6F         00160 FROG1   DB      111,15,31,159,220,216,120,48
     0F 1F 9F DC D8 78 30
69BF F6         00170         DB      246,240,248,249,59,27,30,12
     F0 F8 F9 3B 1B 1E 0C
69C7 00         00180         DB      0,1,35,37,111,79,223,255
     01 23 25 6F 4F DF FF
69CF 00         00190         DB      0,128,196,164,246,242,251,255
     80 C4 A4 F6 F2 FB FF
69D7 1F         00200 FROG2   DB      31,31,31,127,252,193,113,56
     1F 1F 7F FC C1 71 38
69DF FE         00210         DB      254,244,248,240,192,156,240,192
     F4 F8 F0 C0 9C F0 C0
69E7 38         00220         DB      56,113,193,252,127,31,31,31
```

```
       71 C1 FC 7F 1F 1F 1F
69EF C0          00230          DB        192,240,156,192,240,248,244,254
       F0 9C C0 F0 F8 F4 FE
69F7 FF          00240 FROG3    DB        255,223,79,111,37,35,1,0
       DF 4F 6F 25 23 01 00
69FF FF          00250          DB        255,251,242,246,164,196,128,0
       FB F2 F6 A4 C4 80 00
6A07 30          00260          DB        48,120,216,220,159,31,15,111
       78 D8 DC 9F 1F 0F 6F
6A0F 0C          00270          DB        12,30,27,59,249,248,240,246
       1E 1B 3B F9 F8 F0 F6
6A17 7F          00280 FROG4    DB        127,47,31,15,3,57,15,3
       2F 1F 0F 03 39 0F 03
6A1F F0          00290          DB        240,240,248,254,63,131,142,28
       F0 F8 FE 3F 83 8E 1C
6A27 03          00300          DB        3,15,57,3,15,31,47,127
       0F 39 03 0F 1F 2F 7F
6A2F 1C          00310          DB        28,142,131,63,254,248,240,240
       8E 83 3F FE F8 F0 F0
                 00320 ;
                 00330 ;
6A37 00          00340 LBIKE    DB        0,0,0,0,0,0,0,0
       00 00 00 00 00 00 00
6A3F 1F          00350          DB        31,63,115,81,169,112,112,32
       3F 73 51 A9 70 70 20
6A47 FE          00360          DB        254,252,252,234,213,206,14,4
       FC FC EA D5 CE 0E 04
6A4F 00          00370          DB        0,0,0,0,0,0,0,0
       00 00 00 00 00 00 00
6A57 00          00380          DB        0,0,0,0,0,0,0,0
       00 00 00 00 00 00 00
6A5F 01          00390          DB        1,3,1,0,3,4,14,31
       03 01 00 03 04 0E 1F
6A67 80          00400          DB        128,192,192,224,224,112,119,255
       C0 C0 E0 E0 70 77 FF
6A6F 00          00410          DB        0,0,0,0,0,0,0,0
       00 00 00 00 00 00 00
                 00420 ;
6A77 00          00430 LBATT    DB        0,7,7,0
       07 07 00
6A7B 00          00440          DB        0,7,7,0
       07 07 00
                 00450 ;
6A7F 00          00460 RBIKE    DB        0,0,0,0,0,0,0,0
       00 00 00 00 00 00 00
6A87 7F          00470          DB        127,63,63,87,171,115,112,32
       3F 3F 57 AB 73 70 20
6A8F F8          00480          DB        248,252,206,138,149,14,14,4
       FC CE 8A 95 0E 0E 04
6A97 00          00490          DB        0,0,0,0,0,0,0,0
       00 00 00 00 00 00 00
6A9F 00          00500          DB        0,0,0,0,0,0,0,0
       00 00 00 00 00 00 00
6AA7 01          00510          DB        1,3,3,7,7,14,238,255
       03 03 07 07 0E EE FF
6AAF 80          00520          DB        128,192,128,0,192,32,112,248
```

```
     C0 80 00 C0 20 70 F8
6AB7 00          00530         DB      0,0,0,0,0,0,0,0
     00 00 00 00 00 00 00
                 00540 ;
                 00550 ;
6ABF 00          00560 RBATT   DB      0,7,7,0
     07 07 00
6AC3 00          00570         DB      0,7,7,0
     07 07 00
                 00580 ;
                 00590 ;
6AC7 00          00600 LCAR    DB      0,0,0,0,0,0,0,0
     00 00 00 00 00 00 00
6ACF 00          00610         DB      0,0,3,7,15,2,0,0
     00 03 07 0F 02 00 00
6AD7 07          00620         DB      7,255,255,159,111,247,240,96
     FF FF 9F 6F F7 F0 60
6ADF 80          00630         DB      128,255,255,255,255,254,0,0
     FF FF FF FF FE 00 00
6AE7 F0          00640         DB      240,254,255,159,111,246,240,96
     FE FF 9F 6F F6 F0 60
6AEF 00          00650         DB      0,0,0,0,0,0,0,0
     00 00 00 00 00 00 00
6AF7 00          00660         DB      0,0,0,0,0,0,0,0
     00 00 00 00 00 00 00
6AFF 00          00670         DB      0,0,0,0,0,0,0,0
     00 00 00 00 00 00 00
6B07 00          00680         DB      0,0,0,0,0,0,0,0
     00 00 00 00 00 00 00
6B0F 00          00690         DB      0,0,0,0,0,63,97,193
     00 00 00 00 3F 61 C1
6B17 00          00700         DB      0,0,0,0,0,0,128,192
     00 00 00 00 00 80 C0
6B1F 00          00710         DB      0,0,0,0,0,0,0,0
     00 00 00 00 00 00 00
                 00720 ;
6B27 00          00730 LCATT   DB      0,6,6,6,6,0
     06 06 06 06 00
6B2D 00          00740         DB      0,0,0,6,6,0
     00 00 06 06 00
                 00750 ;
                 00760 ;
6B33 00          00770 RCAR    DB      0,0,0,0,0,0,0,0
     00 00 00 00 00 00 00
6B3B 0F          00780         DB      15,127,255,249,246,111,15,6
     7F FF F9 F6 6F 0F 06
6B43 01          00790         DB      1,255,255,255,255,127,0,0
     FF FF FF FF 7F 00 00
6B4B E0          00800         DB      224,255,255,249,246,239,15,6
     FF FF F9 F6 EF 0F 06
6B53 00          00810         DB      0,0,192,224,240,64,0,0
     00 C0 E0 F0 40 00 00
6B5B 00          00820         DB      0,0,0,0,0,0,0,0
     00 00 00 00 00 00 00
6B63 00          00830         DB      0,0,0,0,0,0,0,0
     00 00 00 00 00 00 00
```

```
6B6B 00          00840          DB         0,0,0,0,0,0,1,3
     00 00 00 00 00 01 03
6B73 00          00850          DB         0,0,0,0,0,252,134,131
     00 00 00 00 FC 86 83
6B7B 00          00860          DB         0,0,0,0,0,0,0,0
     00 00 00 00 00 00 00
6B83 00          00870          DB         0,0,0,0,0,0,0,0
     00 00 00 00 00 00 00
6B8B 00          00880          DB         0,0,0,0,0,0,0,0
     00 00 00 00 00 00 00
                 00890 ;
6B93 00          00900 RCATT    DB         0,2,2,2,2,0
     02 02 02 02 00
6B99 00          00910          DB         0,2,2,0,0,0
     02 02 00 00 00
                 00920 ;
                 00930 ;
6B9F 00          00940 LTRUCK   DB         0,0,0,0,0,0,0,0
     00 00 00 00 00 00 00
6BA7 1F          00950          DB         31,31,31,62,61,59,3,1
     1F 1F 3E 3D 3B 03 01
6BAF F8          00960          DB         248,252,254,127,184,216,192,128
     FC FE 7F B8 D8 C0 80
6BB7 FF          00970          DB         255,255,255,255,6,15,15,6
     FF FF FF 06 0F 0F 06
6BBF FF          00980          DB         255,255,255,0,0,0,0,0
     FF FF 00 00 00 00 00
6BC7 FF          00990          DB         255,255,255,0,0,0,0,0
     FF FF 00 00 00 00 00
6BCF FF          01000          DB         255,255,255,0,6,15,15,6
     FF FF 00 06 0F 0F 06
6BD7 FE          01010          DB         254,254,254,4,50,122,122,48
     FE FE 04 32 7A 7A 30
6BDF 00          01020          DB         0,0,0,0,0,0,0,0
     00 00 00 00 00 00 00
6BE7 00          01030          DB         0,0,0,0,0,0,0,0
     00 00 00 00 00 00 00
6BEF 00          01040          DB         0,0,7,9,17,17,31,31
     00 07 09 11 11 1F 1F
6BF7 02          01050          DB         2,2,250,250,254,252,252,248
     02 FA FA FE FC FC F8
6BFF FF          01060          DB         255,255,255,255,255,255,255,255
     FF FF FF FF FF FF FF
6C07 FF          01070          DB         255,255,255,255,255,255,255,255
     FF FF FF FF FF FF FF
6C0F FF          01080          DB         255,255,255,255,255,255,255,255
     FF FF FF FF FF FF FF
6C17 FF          01090          DB         255,255,255,255,255,255,255,255
     FF FF FF FF FF FF FF
6C1F FE          01100          DB         254,254,254,254,254,254,254,254
     FE FE FE FE FE FE FE
6C27 00          01110          DB         0,0,0,0,0,0,0,0
     00 00 00 00 00 00 00
6C2F 00          01120          DB         0,0,0,0,0,0,0,0
     00 00 00 00 00 00 00
6C37 00          01130          DB         0,0,0,0,0,0,0,0
```

```
      00 00 00 00 00 00 00
6C3F  00          01140            DB        0,0,0,0,0,0,0,0
      00 00 00 00 00 00 00
6C47  00          01150            DB        0,0,0,0,0,255,255,255
      00 00 00 00 FF FF FF
6C4F  00          01160            DB        0,0,0,0,0,255,255,255
      00 00 00 00 FF FF FF
6C57  00          01170            DB        0,0,0,0,0,255,255,255
      00 00 00 00 FF FF FF
6C5F  00          01180            DB        0,0,0,0,0,255,255,255
      00 00 00 00 FF FF FF
6C67  00          01190            DB        0,0,0,0,0,254,254,254
      00 00 00 00 FE FE FE
6C6F  00          01200            DB        0,0,0,0,0,0,0,0
      00 00 00 00 00 00 00
                  01210 ;
                  01220 ;
6C77  00          01230 LTATT      DB        0,3,3,5,5,5,5,5,0
      03 03 05 05 05 05 05 00
6C80  00          01240            DB        0,3,3,5,5,5,5,5,0
      03 03 05 05 05 05 05 00
6C89  00          01250            DB        0,0,0,5,5,5,5,5,0
      00 00 05 05 05 05 05 00
                  01260 ;
                  01270 ;
6C92  00          01280 RTRUCK     DB        0,0,0,0,0,0,0,0
      00 00 00 00 00 00 00
6C9A  7F          01290            DB        127,127,127,32,76,94,94,12
      7F 7F 20 4C 5E 5E 0C
6CA2  FF          01300            DB        255,255,255,0,96,240,240,96
      FF FF 00 60 F0 F0 60
6CAA  FF          01310            DB        255,255,255,0,0,0,0,0
      FF FF 00 00 00 00 00
6CB2  FF          01320            DB        255,255,255,0,0,0,0,0
      FF FF 00 00 00 00 00
6CBA  FF          01330            DB        255,255,255,255,96,240,240,96
      FF FF FF 60 F0 F0 60
6CC2  1F          01340            DB        31,63,127,254,29,27,3,1
      3F 7F FE 1D 1B 03 01
6CCA  F8          01350            DB        248,248,248,124,188,220,192,128
      F8 F8 7C BC DC C0 80
6CD2  00          01360            DB        0,0,0,0,0,0,0,0
      00 00 00 00 00 00 00
6CDA  00          01370            DB        0,0,0,0,0,0,0,0
      00 00 00 00 00 00 00
6CE2  7F          01380            DB        127,127,127,127,127,127,127,127
      7F 7F 7F 7F 7F 7F 7F
6CEA  FF          01390            DB        255,255,255,255,255,255,255,255
      FF FF FF FF FF FF FF
6CF2  FF          01400            DB        255,255,255,255,255,255,255,255
      FF FF FF FF FF FF FF
6CFA  FF          01410            DB        255,255,255,255,255,255,255,255
      FF FF FF FF FF FF FF
6D02  FF          01420            DB        255,255,255,255,255,255,255,255
      FF FF FF FF FF FF FF
6D0A  40          01430            DB        64,64,95,95,127,63,63,31
```

```
     40 5F 5F 7F 3F 3F 1F
6D12 00         01440          DB       0,0,224,144,136,136,248,248
     00 E0 90 88 88 F8 F8
6D1A 00         01450          DB       0,0,0,0,0,0,0,0
     00 00 00 00 00 00 00
6D22 00         01460          DB       0,0,0,0,0,0,0,0
     00 00 00 00 00 00 00
6D2A 00         01470          DB       0,0,0,0,0,127,127,127
     00 00 00 00 7F 7F 7F
6D32 00         01480          DB       0,0,0,0,0,255,255,255
     00 00 00 00 FF FF FF
6D3A 00         01490          DB       0,0,0,0,0,255,255,255
     00 00 00 00 FF FF FF
6D42 00         01500          DB       0,0,0,0,0,255,255,255
     00 00 00 00 FF FF FF
6D4A 00         01510          DB       0,0,0,0,0,255,255,255
     00 00 00 00 FF FF FF
6D52 00         01520          DB       0,0,0,0,0,0,0,0
     00 00 00 00 00 00 00
6D5A 00         01530          DB       0,0,0,0,0,0,0,0
     00 00 00 00 00 00 00
6D62 00         01540          DB       0,0,0,0,0,0,0,0
     00 00 00 00 00 00 00
                01550 ;
                01560 ;
6D6A 00         01570 RTATT    DB       0,5,5,5,5,5,3,3,0
     05 05 05 05 05 03 03 00
6D73 00         01580          DB       0,5,5,5,5,5,3,3,0
     05 05 05 05 05 03 03 00
6D7C 00         01590          DB       0,5,5,5,5,5,0,0,0
     05 05 05 05 05 00 00 00
                01600 ;
                01610 ;
6D85 00         01620 BLANK    DB       0,0,0,0
     00 00 00
                01630 ;
                01640 ;
0024            01650 FRGSTR   DS       36                 ;4*8+4
0078            01660 PCSTR    DS       120                ;12*8+12+7
                01670 ;
                01680 ;
                01690 ;********  DATA BASE  ********
                01700 ;
6E25 00         01710 OB1EXT   DEFB     0                  ;OBJECT 1 EXISTENCE
6E26 00         01720          DEFB     0                  ;CYCLE COUNT
6E27 00         01730          DEFB     0                  ;DIRECTION, 0=>RIGHT
6E28 00         01740          DEFB     0                  ;OBJECT 1 POS REAL/ABS
6E29 0000       01750          DEFW     0                  ;POSITION COUNTER
6E2B 0000       01760          DEFW     0                  ;SHAPE POINTER
6E2D 0000       01770          DEFW     0                  ;ATTRIBUTE POINTER
6E2F 00         01780          DEFB     0                  ;ROW COUNTER
6E30 00         01790          DEFB     0                  ;COLUMN POINTER
6E31 00         01800 OB2EXT   DB       0,0,0,0
     00 00 00
6E35 0000       01810          DEFW     0                  ;OB2 POS REAL/ABS FLAG
6E37 0000       01820          DEFW     0
```

```
6E39 0000       01830            DEFW    0
6E3B 00         01840            DB      0,0
     00
6E3D 00         01850 OB3EXT     DB      0,0,0,0
     00 00 00
6E41 0000       01860            DEFW    0
6E43 0000       01870            DEFW    0
6E45 0000       01880            DEFW    0
6E47 00         01890            DB      0,0
     00
6E49 00         01900 OB4EXT     DB      0,0,0,0
     00 00 00
6E4D 0000       01910            DEFW    0
6E4F 0000       01920            DEFW    0
6E51 0000       01930            DEFW    0
6E53 00         01940            DB      0,0
     00
6E55 00         01950 OB5EXT     DB      0,0,0,0
     00 00 00
6E59 0000       01960            DEFW    0
6E5B 0000       01970            DEFW    0
6E5D 0000       01980            DEFW    0
6E5F 00         01990            DB      0,0
     00
6E61 00         02000 OB6EXT     DB      0,0,0,0
     00 00 00
6E65 0000       02010            DEFW    0
6E67 0000       02020            DEFW    0
6E69 0000       02030            DEFW    0
6E6B 00         02040            DB      0,0
     00
                02050 ;
                02060 ;
6E6D 00         02070 PCAREXT DEFB   0                ;POLICE CAR DATABASE
6E6E 00         02080 PCARCYC DEFB   0
6E6F 00         02090 PCARDIR DEFB   0
6E70 00         02100 PCARRAP DEFB   0
6E71 0000       02110 PCARPOS DEFW   0
6E73 0000       02120 PCARSHP DEFW   0
6E75 0000       02130 PCARATT DEFW   0
6E77 02         02140 PCARROW DEFB   2
6E78 06         02150 PCARCOL DEFB   6
                02160 ;
                02170 ;
6E79 00         02180 FRGEXT  DEFB   0                ;FROG DATABASE
6E7A 00         02190 FRGCYC  DEFB   0
6E7B 00         02200 FRGDIR  DEFB   0                ;0:UP 1:RHT 2:DWN 3:LFT
6E7C 0000       02210 FRGPOS  DEFW   0
6E7E 0000       02220 FROGSH  DEFW   0
6E80 00         02230 FRGATR  DEFB   0
                02240 ;
                02250 ;
6E81 08         02260 FRGDB   DB     8,8,1
     08 01
6E84 AC50       02270 FRGSTN  DEFW   50ACH            ;INITIAL POSITION OF FROG
6E86 B769       02280         DEFW   FROG1
```

```
6E88 04         02290              DB       4             ;ATTR. TOTAL 8 CHARS
                02300 ;
                02310 ;
6E89 956E       02320 DBINDEX DEFW     RBDB          ;RIGHT BYTE DB
6E8B A16E       02330         DEFW     LBDB          ;LEFT BIKE DB
6E8D AD6E       02340         DEFW     RCDB          ;RIGHT CAR DB
6E8F B96E       02350         DEFW     LCDB          ;LEFT CAR DB
6E91 C56E       02360         DEFW     RTDB          ;RIGHT TRUCK DB
6E93 D16E       02370         DEFW     LTDB          ;LEFT TRUCK DB
                02380 ;
                02390 ;
6E95 02         02400 RBDB    DB       2,1,0,0       ;EXT CNT DIR RAF
     01 00 00
6E99 1D48       02410         DEFW     481DH         ;POS
6E9B 7F6A       02420         DEFW     RBIKE         ;RIGHT BIKE
6E9D BF6A       02430         DEFW     RBATT         ;ATTRIBUTE
6E9F 02         02440         DB       2,4           ;ROW COL
     04
                02450 ;
                02460 ;
6EA1 02         02470 LBDB    DB       2,1,1,1
     01 01 01
6EA5 DF48       02480         DEFW     48DFH
6EA7 376A       02490         DEFW     LBIKE
6EA9 776A       02500         DEFW     LBATT
6EAB 02         02510         DB       2,4
     04
                02520 ;
                02530 ;
6EAD 03         02540 RCDB    DB       3,1,0,0
     01 00 00
6EB1 1B48       02550         DEFW     481BH
6EB3 336B       02560         DEFW     RCAR
6EB5 936B       02570         DEFW     RCATT
6EB7 02         02580         DB       2,6
     06
                02590 ;
                02600 ;
6EB9 03         02610 LCDB    DB       3,1,1,1
     01 01 01
6EBD DF48       02620         DEFW     48DFH
6EBF C76A       02630         DEFW     LCAR
6EC1 276B       02640         DEFW     LCATT
6EC3 02         02650         DB       2,6
     06
                02660 ;
                02670 ;
6EC5 06         02680 RTDB    DB       6,1,0,0
     01 00 00
6EC9 1848       02690         DEFW     4818H
6ECB 926C       02700         DEFW     RTRUCK
6ECD 6A6D       02710         DEFW     RTATT
6ECF 03         02720         DB       3,9
     09
                02730 ;
                02740 ;
```

```
6ED1 06          02750 LTDB     DB      6,1,1,1
     01 01 01
6ED5 DF48        02760          DEFW    48DFH
6ED7 9F6B        02770          DEFW    LTRUCK
6ED9 776C        02780          DEFW    LTATT
6EDB 03          02790          DB      3,9
     09
                 02800 ;
                 02810 ;
6EDD 01          02820 LPCDB    DB      1,1,1,1
     01 01 01
6EE1 DF48        02830          DEFW    48DFH
6EE3 C76A        02840          DEFW    LCAR
6EE5 E96E        02850          DEFW    LPCATT
6EE7 02          02860          DB      2,6
     06
                 02870 ;
                 02880 ;
6EE9 00          02890 LPCATT   DB      0,5,5,5,5,0
     05 05 05 05 00
6EEF 00          02900          DB      0,0,0,5,5,0
     00 00 05 05 00
                 02910 ;
                 02920 ;
6EF5 01          02930 RPCDB    DB      1,1,0,0
     01 00 00
6EF9 1B48        02940          DEFW    481BH
6EFB 336B        02950          DEFW    RCAR
6EFD 016F        02960          DEFW    RPCATT
6EFF 02          02970          DB      2,6
     06
                 02980 ;
                 02990 ;
6F01 00          03000 RPCATT   DB      0,5,5,5,5,0
     05 05 05 05 00
6F07 00          03010          DB      0,5,5,0,0,0
     05 05 00 00 00
                 03020 ;
                 03030 ;
                 00480 ;
                 00490 ;
6F0D 29          00500 PCTON1   DB      41,0,0F0H,1     ;FIRST POLICE CAR TONE
     00 F0 01
6F11 17          00510 PCTON2   DB      23,0,8CH,3      ;SECOND POLICE CAR TONE
     00 8C 03
                 00520 ;
                 00530 ;
6F15 46          00540 HOMTON   DB      46H,0,0C7H,4    ;FROG REACH HOME TONE
     00 C7 04
6F19 5D          00550          DB      5DH,0,8CH,3
     00 8C 03
6F1D 7C          00560          DB      7CH,0,0A1H,2
     00 A1 02
6F21 AA          00570          DB      0AAH,0,0F1H,1
     00 F1 01
6F25 DE          00580          DB      0DEH,0,6DH,1
```

```
      00 6D 01
6F29 28         00590          DB      28H,1,9,1
      01 09 01
6F2D 8B         00600          DB      8BH,1,0BFH,0
      01 BF 00
6F31 0F         00610          DB      0FH,2,88H,0
      02 88 00
6F35 C0         00620          DB      0C0H,2,5EH,0
      02 5E 00
6F39 84         00630 DIETON   DB      84H,3,43H,0      ;FROG DYING TONE,REVERSE
      03 43 00
                00640 ;
                00650 ;
6F3D 53         00660 SCRMS1   DM      'Score '
      63 6F 72 65 20
6F43 30         00670 SCORE    DB      30H,30H,30H,30H,30H,30H
      30 30 30 30 30
6F49 48         00680 SCRMS2   DM      'HIGH SCORE '
      49 47 48 20 53 43 4F 52
      45 20
6F54 30         00690 HISCR    DB      30H,30H,30H,30H,30H
      30 30 30 30
                00700 ;
                00710 ;
0005            00720 IMAGE    DS      5          ;PRINTING IMAGE OF SCORE
6F5E 00         00730 UPDWN    DEFB    0          ;SET WHEN FROG MOVES UP OR DOWN
                00740 ;
                00750 ;
6F5F 00         00760 COLUMN   DB      0          ;VARIABLE STORING SHAPE COLUMN
6F60 00         00770 ROW      DB      0          ;VARIABLE STORING SHAPE ROW
6F61 00         00780 SKIP     DEFB    0          ;CHAR SKIPPING DURING DRAW
6F62 00         00790 FILL     DEFB    0          ;CHAR DRAWN
6F63 0000       00800 ATTPOS   DEFW    0          ;HOLDING THE ATTRIBUTE FILE PTR
6F65 00         00810 ATTR     DB      0          ;ATTR OF CHARACTER BLOCK DRAWN
6F66 0000       00820 DRWPOS   DEFW    0          ;DRAW POSITION
6F68 0000       00830 STRPOS   DEFW    0          ;STORE POSITION
                00840 ;
                00850 ;
6F6A 0000       00860 ATTPTR   DEFW    0
6F6C 0000       00870 NEWPOS   DEFW    0          ;NEW TRAFFIC OBJJECT POSITION
6F6E 0000       00880 POSPTR   DEFW    0          ;TRAFFIC POSITION DATABASE PTR
6F70 00         00890 GENFLG   DEFB    0          ;TRAFFIC REGENERATION FLAG
                00900 ;
                00910 ;
6F71 00         00920 JAMFLG   DEFB    0          ;SET TO 1 AS TRAFFIC MOVE JAM
                00930 ;
                00940 ;
6F72 00         00950 CHASE    DEFB    0          ;SET WHEN POLICE CAR APPEARS
6F73 00         00960 SOUNDF   DEFB    0          ;SET WHEN USER WANT SIREN SOUND
6F74 00         00970 TONFLG   DEFB    0          ;DETERMINE WHICH SIREN TONE
6F75 0000       00980 RND      DEFW    0          ;POINTER TO ROM FOR RANDOM NO
                00990 ;
                01000 ;
6F77 01         01010 GAMFLG   DEFB    1          ;END IF ZERO
6F78 0000       01020 OLDFRG   DEFW    0          ;OLD FROG POS
6F7A 0000       01030 NEWFRG   DEFW    0          ;NEW FROG POS
```

```
6F7C 00         01040 CRHFLG  DEFB    0         ;SET TO 1 WHEN FROG WAS CRASH
6F7D 00         01050 TEMDIR  DEFB    0         ;FROG TEMPORARY NEW DIRECTION
6F7E 0000       01060 TEMPOS  DEFW    0         ;FROG TEMPORARY NEW POSITION
6F80 0000       01070 TEMSHP  DEFW    0         ;FROG TEMPORARY NEW SHAPE
                01080 ;
                01090 ;
5020            01100 BOTHY1  EQU     5020H     ;0,38. 0,39
5120            01110 BOTHY2  EQU     5120H
46A0            01120 TOPHY1  EQU     46A0H     ;0,128. 0,129
47A0            01130 TOPHY2  EQU     47A0H
4B60            01140 MIDHY1  EQU     4B60H     ;x,83. x,84
4C60            01150 MIDHY2  EQU     4C60H
                01160 ;
                01170 ;
3C00            01180 CHRSET  EQU     3C00H     ;FIRST 256 BYTES NOTHING
                01190 ;
                01200 ;
6F82 05         01210 NUMFRG  DEFB    5         ;NUMBER OF FROG
                01220 ;
                01230 ;
6F83 AF         01240 INIT    XOR     A                   ;000 FOR D2 D1 D0
6F84 D3FE       01250         OUT     (0FEH),A            ;SET BORDER COLOUR
6F86 32485C     01260         LD      (23624),A           ;TO BLACK
6F89 327C6F     01270         LD      (CRHFLG),A
6F8C 32796E     01280         LD      (FRGEXT),A          ;SET FROG NON EXIST
6F8F 3C         01290         INC     A
6F90 32776F     01300         LD      (GAMFLG),A          ;SET GAME FLAG
6F93 3E05       01310         LD      A,5                 ;INITIALISE FROG NO
6F95 32826F     01320         LD      (NUMFRG),A
6F98 ED5F       01330         LD      A,R                 ;GENERATE RANDOM PTR
6F9A E63F       01340         AND     3FH                 ;FOR THIS CYCLE
6F9C 67         01350         LD      H,A                 ;PTR POINTS TO ROM
6F9D ED5F       01360         LD      A,R
6F9F 6F         01370         LD      L,A
6FA0 22756F     01380         LD      (RND),HL
6FA3 21AC50     01390         LD      HL,50ACH            ;INIT FROG STATION
6FA6 22846E     01400         LD      (FRGSTN),HL
6FA9 CDD772     01410         CALL    CLRSCR              ;CLEAR SCREEN ROUTINE
6FAC CD0B70     01420         CALL    DRWHWY              ;DRAW HIGHWAY
6FAF CD5570     01430         CALL    LINEUP              ;LINE UP ALL EXIST FROGS
6FB2 210040     01440         LD      HL,4000H            ;MESSAGE LOCATION
6FB5 113D6F     01450         LD      DE,SCRMS1           ;LOAD SCORE MESSAGE
6FB8 0606       01460         LD      B,6
6FBA CD2873     01470         CALL    DISASC              ;DISPLAY ASCII CHARACTER
6FBD 21446F     01480         LD      HL,SCORE+1          ;PRINT SCORE
6FC0 CD6F77     01490         CALL    SCRIMG              ;CONVERT TO PRINTABLE IMAGE
MG
6FC3 210640     01500         LD      HL,4006H
6FC6 11596F     01510         LD      DE,IMAGE
6FC9 0605       01520         LD      B,5
6FCB CD2873     01530         CALL    DISASC
6FCE 210E40     01540         LD      HL,400EH            ;HIGH SCORE MESSAGE
6FD1 11496F     01550         LD      DE,SCRMS2
6FD4 060B       01560         LD      B,11
6FD6 CD2873     01570         CALL    DISASC
6FD9 21546F     01580         LD      HL,HISCR
6FDC CD6F77     01590         CALL    SCRIMG
```

```
6FDF 211940                LD      HL,4019H
6FE2 11596F                LD      DE,IMAGE
6FE5 0605                  LD      B,5
6FE7 CD2873                CALL    DISASC
6FEA 21256E                LD      HL,OB1EXT       ;SET ALL OBJ NONEXIST
6FED 110C00                LD      DE,12
6FF0 0607                  LD      B,7
6FF2 AF                    XOR     A
6FF3 77            INTLP1  LD      (HL),A
6FF4 19                    ADD     HL,DE
6FF5 10FC                  DJNZ    INTLP1
6FF7 32726F                LD      (CHASE),A       ;SET NO POLICE CAR CHASE
6FFA 3C                    INC     A
6FFB 32736F                LD      (SOUNDF),A      ;SET SIREN ON
6FFE 21436F                LD      HL,SCORE        ;INITIALISE SCORE TO
7001 11446F                LD      DE,SCORE+1      ;ASCII ZERO ie 30H
7004 0E05                  LD      C,5
7006 3630                  LD      (HL),30H
7008 EDB0                  LDIR                    ;INIT SCORE TO 30H
700A C9                    RET
                   ;
                   ;
700B 21A040        DRWHWY  LD      HL,40A0H        ;FILL TOP HWY
700E CD4170                CALL    FILHWY
7011 216048                LD      HL,4860H        ;FILL MIDDLE HWY
7014 CD4170                CALL    FILHWY
7017 212050                LD      HL,5020H        ;FILL BOTTOM HWY
701A CD4170                CALL    FILHWY
701D 21A046                LD      HL,TOPHY1       ;REVERSE BUILT HIGHWAY
7020 11A047                LD      DE,TOPHY2
7023 AF                    XOR     A
7024 CD3870                CALL    HIGHWY
7027 212050                LD      HL,BOTHY1
702A 112051                LD      DE,BOTHY2
702D CD3870                CALL    HIGHWY
7030 21604B                LD      HL,MIDHY1
7033 11604C                LD      DE,MIDHY2
7036 3EC3                  LD      A,195           ;BIN 11000011
7038 0620          HIGHWY  LD      B,32            ;32*8 BITS
703A 77            HWYLOP  LD      (HL),A
703B 12                    LD      (DE),A
703C 23                    INC     HL
703D 13                    INC     DE
703E 10FA                  DJNZ    HWYLOP
7040 C9                    RET
                   ;
                   ;
7041 3EFF          FILHWY  LD      A,0FFH
7043 D9                    EXX
7044 0620                  LD      B,32
7046 D9            FILHYL  EXX
7047 E5                    PUSH    HL
7048 0608                  LD      B,8
704A 77            FILCHR  LD      (HL),A
704B 24                    INC     H
704C 10FC                  DJNZ    FILCHR
```

```
704E E1                   POP     HL
704F 23                   INC     HL
7050 D9                   EXX
7051 10F3                 DJNZ    FILHYL
7053 D9                   EXX
7054 C9                   RET
          ;
          ;
          ;********  LINEUP   *********
          ;
          ;               draw all frogs left on the screen
          ;
          ;
7055 3E01       LINEUP    LD      A,1                ;RIGHT FROG
7057 327B6E               LD      (FRGDIR),A
705A 11D769               LD      DE,FROG2           ;RIGHT FROG SHAPE
705D 2A846E               LD      HL,(FRGSTN)        ;FROG STATION
7060 3E04                 LD      A,4                ;(PAPER 0)*8+(INK 4)
7062 32656F               LD      (ATTR),A
7065 3A826F               LD      A,(NUMFRG)         ;NUMBER OF FROG
7068 A7                   AND     A                  ;TEST FOR NO FROG LEFT
7069 C8                   RET     Z
706A 47                   LD      B,A                ;NUMBER OF FROG TIMES
706B C5         DRAWLN    PUSH    BC
706C D5                   PUSH    DE
706D E5                   PUSH    HL
706E CD7A70               CALL    DRWFRG             ;DRAW FROG ROUTINE
7071 E1                   POP     HL
7072 D1                   POP     DE
7073 2B                   DEC     HL
7074 2B                   DEC     HL
7075 2B                   DEC     HL
7076 C1                   POP     BC
7077 10F2                 DJNZ    DRAWLN
7079 C9                   RET
          ;
          ;
          ;********  DRWFRG   ********
          ;
          ;               similar to DRAW routine
          ;
707A 3E02       DRWFRG    LD      A,2                ;TWO ROW FROG SHAPE
707C 08                   EX      AF,AF'
707D E5                   PUSH    HL                 ;STORE POS PTR
707E E5         FRGLP0    PUSH    HL
707F 0E02                 LD      C,2                ;COLUMN COUNT
7081 E5         FRGLP1    PUSH    HL
7082 0608                 LD      B,8                ;DRAW CHARACTER
7084 1A         FRGLP2    LD      A,(DE)
7085 77                   LD      (HL),A
7086 13                   INC     DE
7087 24                   INC     H                  ;NEXT BYTE OF THE CHAR
7088 10FA                 DJNZ    FRGLP2
708A E1                   POP     HL                 ;CURRENT POINTER
708B 23                   INC     HL                 ;MOVE TO NEXT CHAR POS
708C 0D                   DEC     C                  ;DECR COLUMN COUNT
```

```
708D 20F2     02720        JR      NZ,FRGLP1
708F E1       02730        POP     HL           ;ROW PTR
7090 08       02740        EX      AF,AF'
7091 3D       02750        DEC     A            ;DEC LINES OF CHAR
7092 0E20     02760        LD      C,32
7094 280E     02770        JR      Z,FRGATT     ;LOAD FROG ATTRIBUTE
7096 08       02780        EX      AF,AF'
7097 A7       02790        AND     A
7098 ED42     02800        SBC     HL,BC        ;MOVE 32 CHAR/1 LINE UP
709A CB44     02810        BIT     0,H          ;TEST CROSS SCR SECTION
709C 28E0     02820        JR      Z,FRGLP0
709E 7C       02830        LD      A,H
709F D607     02840        SUB     7            ;UP ONE SCREEN SECTION
70A1 67       02850        LD      H,A
70A2 18DA     02860        JR      FRGLP0
70A4 E1       02870 FRGATT POP     HL           ;POS PTR
70A5 7C       02880        LD      A,H          ;CONVERT TO ATTRIBUTE PTR
70A6 E618     02890        AND     18H
70A8 CB2F     02900        SRA     A
70AA CB2F     02910        SRA     A
70AC CB2F     02920        SRA     A
70AE C658     02930        ADD     A,58H
70B0 67       02940        LD      H,A
70B1 3A656F   02950        LD      A,(ATTR)     ;FILL FROG SHAPE ATTR
70B4 77       02960        LD      (HL),A
70B5 23       02970        INC     HL           ;NEXT CHARACTER
70B6 77       02980        LD      (HL),A
70B7 ED42     02990        SBC     HL,BC        ;ONE LINE UP
70B9 77       03000        LD      (HL),A
70BA 2B       03010        DEC     HL           ;NEXT CHAR LEFT
70BB 77       03020        LD      (HL),A
70BC C9       03030        RET
              03040 ;
              03050 ;********  TFCTRL  ********
              03060 ;
              03070 ;          Traffic control routine
              03080 ;
70BD 21706F   03090 TFCTRL LD      HL,GENFLG    ;CHECK REGENERATION FLAG
70C0 AF       03100        XOR     A
70C1 BE       03110        CP      (HL)
70C2 2802     03120        JR      Z,GENER      ;IF ZERO, TEST GENERATE
70C4 35       03130        DEC     (HL)         ;DECR GENERATION FLAG
70C5 C9       03140        RET
70C6 21256E   03150 GENER  LD      HL,OB1EXT    ;START OF TRAFFIC DB
70C9 110C00   03160        LD      DE,12        ;12 BYTE DATABASE
70CC 0606     03170        LD      B,6          ;6 DB PAIRS
70CE BE       03180 TCTRLP CP      (HL)         ;TEST EXISTENCE
70CF 2004     03190        JR      NZ,NSPACE
70D1 CDD970   03200        CALL    REGEN        ;REGENERATION ROUTINE
70D4 C9       03210        RET
70D5 19       03220 NSPACE ADD     HL,DE
70D6 10F6     03230        DJNZ    TCTRLP
70D8 C9       03240        RET
              03250 ;
              03260 ;
              03270 ;********  REGEN  ********
```

```
                 03280 ;
                 03290 ;          regeneration of TRAFFIC
                 03300 ;          INPUT:  HL=>DB PAIRS
                 03310 ;
70D9 E5          03320 REGEN    PUSH    HL
70DA CDCC77      03330 RAND1    CALL    RANDNO          ;RANDOM NUMBER ROUTINE
70DD E607        03340          AND     7               ;GENERATE RANDOM NUMBER
70DF FE06        03350          CP      6               ;FROM 0 TO 5
70E1 30F7        03360          JR      NC,RAND1
70E3 012159      03370          LD      BC,5921H        ;TWO CHAR TEST
70E6 212059      03380          LD      HL,5920H        ;TEST JAM
70E9 CB47        03390          BIT     0,A             ;ODD NUMBER IS LEFT
70EB 2804        03400          JR      Z,RTRAF         ;RIGHT TRAFFIC
70ED 2EDF        03410          LD      L,0DFH
70EF 0EDE        03420          LD      C,0DEH
70F1 87          03430 RTRAF    ADD     A,A             ;GET DBINDEX PTR IN DE
70F2 5F          03440          LD      E,A
70F3 0A          03450          LD      A,(BC)          ;TEST 2 CHAR AHEAD
70F4 86          03460          ADD     A,(HL)
70F5 A7          03470          AND     A               ;ZERO PAPER, ZERO INK
70F6 2802        03480          JR      Z,LOADDB        ;IF 0, INITIALISE NEW OBJ
70F8 E1          03490          POP     HL              ;IF JAM, RETURN
70F9 C9          03500          RET
70FA 57          03510 LOADDB   LD      D,A             ;A=0
70FB 21896E      03520          LD      HL,DBINDEX      ;GET DB
70FE 19          03530          ADD     HL,DE
70FF 5E          03540          LD      E,(HL)          ;GET CORR DATABASE
7100 23          03550          INC     HL
7101 56          03560          LD      D,(HL)
7102 EB          03570          EX      DE,HL           ;SOURCE
7103 D1          03580          POP     DE              ;DESTINATION
7104 010C00      03590          LD      BC,12
7107 EDB0        03600          LDIR
7109 3E02        03610          LD      A,2             ;SET REGENRATION FLAG
710B 32706F      03620          LD      (GENFLG),A      ;SKIP FOR 2 CYCLES
710E C9          03630          RET
                 03640 ;
                 03650 ;
                 03660 ;********  MOVTRF  ********
                 03670 ;
                 03680 ;          MOVE TRAFFIC ROUTINE
                 03690 ;
710F D9          03700 MOVTRF   EXX
7110 21256E      03710          LD      HL,OB1EXT
7113 110C00      03720          LD      DE,12
7116 0606        03730          LD      B,6
7118 E5          03740 MTRFLP   PUSH    HL
7119 D9          03750          EXX
711A E1          03760          POP     HL              ;EXISTENCE
711B 7E          03770          LD      A,(HL)          ;SKIP WHEN NO EXIST
711C A7          03780          AND     A
711D CAA771      03790          JP      Z,NXTMOV
7120 23          03800          INC     HL              ;CYCLE COUNT
7121 35          03810          DEC     (HL)            ;DECR CYCLE COUNT
7122 C2A771      03820          JP      NZ,NXTMOV
7125 23          03830          INC     HL              ;DIRECTION
```

```
7126 7E               LD    A,(HL)         ;0 L TO R, 1 R TO L
7127 23               INC   HL
7128 23               INC   HL
7129 226E6F           LD    (POSPTR),HL    ;POS PTR
712C 5E               LD    E,(HL)         ;RESTORE POS
712D 23               INC   HL
712E 56               LD    D,(HL)
712F 1C               INC   E              ;MOVE RIGHT
7130 A7               AND   A
7131 2802             JR    Z,LDPOS
7133 1D               DEC   E              ;MOVE LEFT
7134 1D               DEC   E              ;MOVE LEFT
7135 ED536C6F LDPOS   LD    (NEWPOS),DE
7139 08               EX    AF,AF'
713A 010500           LD    BC,5           ;RESTORE OBJ LENGHT
713D 09               ADD   HL,BC
713E 7E               LD    A,(HL)         ;ROW
713F 32606F           LD    (ROW),A
7142 23               INC   HL
7143 7E               LD    A,(HL)         ;COLUMN
7144 325F6F           LD    (COLUMN),A
7147 3D               DEC   A
7148 4F               LD    C,A
7149 08               EX    AF,AF'
714A A7               AND   A              ;TEST DIRECTION
714B EB               EX    DE,HL
714C 2008             JR    NZ,RTOL        ;RIGHT TO LEFT
714E 09               ADD   HL,BC          ;FIND HEAD OF TRUCK
714F 7D               LD    A,L            ;LOB
7150 FE40             CP    40H            ;TEST RIGHT EDGE
7152 3046             JR    NC,MOVEOK      ;SKIP TEST AHEAD IF OFF
7154 1805             JR    TESTAH         ;TEST AHEAD
7156 7D       RTOL    LD    A,L            ;NEW POS, AHEAD AS WELL
7157 FEC0             CP    0C0H           ;TEST LEFT EDGE
7159 383F             JR    C,MOVEOK       ;SKIP TEST AHEAD
715B 7C       TESTAH  LD    A,H            ;COVERT TO ATTR
715C E618             AND   18H
715E CB2F             SRA   A
7160 CB2F             SRA   A
7162 CB2F             SRA   A
7164 C658             ADD   A,58H
7166 67               LD    H,A
7167 012000           LD    BC,32
716A AF               XOR   A
716B 32716F           LD    (JAMFLG),A     ;INITIALISE JAM FLAG
716E 3A606F           LD    A,(ROW)
7171 08       TAHLOP  EX    AF,AF'
7172 7E               LD    A,(HL)         ;RETRIEVE ATTR
7173 E607             AND   7
7175 280E             JR    Z,TFROG1       ;JUMP IF BLACK INK
7177 FE04             CP    4              ;TEST FOR GREEN,FROG
7179 2007             JR    NZ,JAM1        ;JAM IF NOT A FROG
717B 3E01             LD    A,1            ;MOVE IF IT IS FROG
717D 327C6F           LD    (CRHFLG),A     ;SET FROG CRASH
7180 1803             JR    TFROG1
7182 32716F   JAM1    LD    (JAMFLG),A     ;SET JAMFLG NON ZERO
```

```
7185 A7         04400 TFROG1  AND     A
7186 ED42       04410         SBC     HL,BC
7188 08         04420         EX      AF,AF'
7189 3D         04430         DEC     A               ;UPDATE ROW
718A 20E5       04440         JR      NZ,TAHLOP
718C 3A716F     04450         LD      A,(JAMFLG)      ;TEST TRAFFIC JAM
718F A7         04460         AND     A
7190 2808       04470         JR      Z,MOVEOK        ;MOVE IF NO JAM
7192 D9         04480         EXX                     ;ELSE STOP MOVE ONE CYCLE
7193 23         04490         INC     HL
7194 34         04500         INC     (HL)            ;LOAD 2 TO CYCLE COUNT
7195 34         04510         INC     (HL)
7196 2B         04520         DEC     HL
7197 D9         04530         EXX
7198 180D       04540         JR      NXTMOV
719A 2A6E6F     04550 MOVEOK  LD      HL,(POSPTR)     ;RETRIEVE PTR TO POS
719D ED5B6C6F   04560         LD      DE,(NEWPOS)
71A1 73         04570         LD      (HL),E          ;STORE NEWPOS IN DB
71A2 23         04580         INC     HL
71A3 72         04590         LD      (HL),D
71A4 CDAF71     04600         CALL    MVCTRL          ;MOVEMENT CONTROL
71A7 D9         04610 NXTMOV  EXX
71A8 19         04620         ADD     HL,DE
71A9 05         04630         DEC     B
71AA C21871     04640         JP      NZ,MTRFLP
71AD D9         04650         EXX
71AE C9         04660         RET
                04670 ;
                04680 ;********  MVCTRL   ********
                04690 ;
                04700 ;       Traffic movement control routine
                04710 ;
71AF 2B         04720 MVCTRL  DEC     HL
71B0 2B         04730         DEC     HL              ;DE=>NEWPOS, HL=>DB PTR
71B1 7B         04740         LD      A,E             ;LOB POS
71B2 E61F       04750         AND     1FH             ;TEST EDGE
71B4 2005       04760         JR      NZ,CHGRAF       ;CHANGE REAL ABS FLAG
71B6 7E         04770         LD      A,(HL)
71B7 3C         04780         INC     A
71B8 E601       04790         AND     1
71BA 77         04800         LD      (HL),A
71BB 2B         04810 CHGRAF  DEC     HL              ;PT DIR
71BC 7E         04820         LD      A,(HL)
71BD A7         04830         AND     A
71BE 200F       04840         JR      NZ,TOLEFT       ;RIGHT TO LEFT
71C0 7B         04850         LD      A,E
71C1 E61F       04860         AND     1FH             ;IF TO RIGHT AND ABS
71C3 201B       04870         JR      NZ,DRWOBJ
71C5 23         04880         INC     HL              ;GET RAF
71C6 7E         04890         LD      A,(HL)
71C7 2B         04900         DEC     HL              ;PT TO DIR
71C8 A7         04910         AND     A               ;IF ABSTRACT, DIES
71C9 2015       04920         JR      NZ,DRWOBJ
71CB D9         04930         EXX
71CC 77         04940         LD      (HL),A          ;SET NON EXISTENCE
71CD D9         04950         EXX
```

```
71CE C9                    RET
71CF 3A5F6F        TOLEFT  LD      A,(COLUMN)
71D2 4F                    LD      C,A
71D3 EB                    EX      DE,HL           ;TEST END OF OBJECT
71D4 09                    ADD     HL,BC           ;TOUCHES LEFT EDGE
71D5 7D                    LD      A,L
71D6 FEC0                  CP      0C0H
71D8 EB                    EX      DE,HL
71D9 2005                  JR      NZ,DRWOBJ
71DB D9                    EXX                     ;OBJECT NONEXIST AS
71DC 3600                  LD      (HL),0          ;IT MOVES OFF SCREEN
71DE D9                    EXX
71DF C9                    RET
71E0 D9            DRWOBJ  EXX
71E1 7E                    LD      A,(HL)
71E2 23                    INC     HL
71E3 77                    LD      (HL),A          ;REFILL CYCLE COUNT
71E4 2B                    DEC     HL
71E5 D9                    EXX
71E6 23                    INC     HL
71E7 E5                    PUSH    HL              ;PT TO RAF
71E8 23                    INC     HL
71E9 23                    INC     HL
71EA 23                    INC     HL
71EB 5E                    LD      E,(HL)          ;RETRIEVE SHAPE PTR
71EC 23                    INC     HL
71ED 56                    LD      D,(HL)
71EE 23                    INC     HL
71EF 4E                    LD      C,(HL)          ;RETRIEVE ATTR PTR
71F0 23                    INC     HL
71F1 46                    LD      B,(HL)
71F2 ED436A6F              LD      (ATTPTR),BC
71F6 23                    INC     HL
71F7 7E                    LD      A,(HL)
71F8 32606F                LD      (ROW),A
71FB 23                    INC     HL
71FC 7E                    LD      A,(HL)
71FD 325F6F                LD      (COLUMN),A
7200 E1                    POP     HL
7201 7E                    LD      A,(HL)          ;RAFLAG
7202 2A6C6F                LD      HL,(NEWPOS)
7205 CD0972                CALL    DRAW
7208 C9                    RET
                   ;
                   ;
                   ;
                   ;********  DRAW  ********
                   ;
                   ;       INPUT : HL=>START OF DISPLAY POS
                   ;               DE=>PTR TO SHAPE DB
                   ;               A =>POSITION REAL/ABSTRACT FLAG
                   ;               C =>NO. OF COL TO BE DISPLAY
                   ;               COL PASS AS VAR
                   ;
                   ;       VAR     COLUMN, ROW, ATTR, DRWPOS
                   ;               SKIP, FILL
```

```
                05520 ;
                05530 ;
                05540 ;         REG    : A,BC,DE,HL,A'
                05550 ;
7209 CD9672     05560 DRAW      CALL     RSHAPE          ;RETURN ROW/COL ATTPTR
720C 3A606F     05570           LD       A,(ROW)
720F 08         05580           EX       AF,AF'
7210 D5         05590 LPO       PUSH     DE
7211 E5         05600           PUSH     HL              ;STORE LINE PTR
7212 3A616F     05610           LD       A,(SKIP)
7215 4F         05620           LD       C,A
7216 0600       05630           LD       B,0
7218 09         05640           ADD      HL,BC           ;SKIP POS PTR
7219 87         05650           ADD      A,A             ;MULTIPLE OF 8 BYTES
721A 87         05660           ADD      A,A
721B 87         05670           ADD      A,A
721C 4F         05680           LD       C,A             ;SKIP SHAPE PTR
721D EB         05690           EX       DE,HL
721E 09         05700           ADD      HL,BC
721F EB         05710           EX       DE,HL
7220 CB44       05720           BIT      0,H             ;CROSS SCREEN SECTION?
7222 2804       05730           JR       Z,NOSKIP
7224 3E07       05740           LD       A,7             ;IF YES, MOVE UP
7226 84         05750           ADD      A,H
7227 67         05760           LD       H,A
7228 3A626F     05770 NOSKIP    LD       A,(FILL)
722B A7         05780           AND      A
722C 2811       05790           JR       Z,NXT
722E 4F         05800           LD       C,A             ;COLUMN TO BE FILLED
722F E5         05810 LP1       PUSH     HL              ;FILL CHARACTER
7230 0608       05820           LD       B,8
7232 1A         05830 LP2       LD       A,(DE)          ;FILL CHARACTER BYTES
7233 77         05840           LD       (HL),A
7234 13         05850           INC      DE
7235 24         05860           INC      H
7236 10FA       05870           DJNZ     LP2
7238 E1         05880           POP      HL
7239 0D         05890           DEC      C
723A 2803       05900           JR       Z,NXT
723C 23         05910           INC      HL              ;NEXT CHARACTER
723D 18F0       05920           JR       LP1
723F 08         05930 NXT       EX       AF,AF'
7240 E1         05940           POP      HL              ;RESTORE LINE PTR
7241 D1         05950           POP      DE              ;SHAPE DB PTR
7242 3D         05960           DEC      A               ;UPDATE ROW COUNT
7243 281A       05970           JR       Z,LDATTR
7245 08         05980           EX       AF,AF'
7246 A7         05990           AND      A               ;CLEAR CARRY
7247 0E20       06000           LD       C,20H
7249 ED42       06010           SBC      HL,BC           ;ONE LINE UP
724B CB44       06020           BIT      0,H             ;CROSS SCREEN SECTION?
724D 2804       06030           JR       Z,MODDB
724F 7C         06040           LD       A,H
7250 D607       06050           SUB      7
7252 67         06060           LD       H,A
7253 3A5F6F     06070 MODDB     LD       A,(COLUMN)
```

```
7256 87                    ADD     A,A
7257 87                    ADD     A,A
7258 87                    ADD     A,A              ;UPDATE SHAPE DB
7259 4F                    LD      C,A
725A EB                    EX      DE,HL
725B 09                    ADD     HL,BC
725C EB                    EX      DE,HL
725D 18B1                  JR      LPO
725F 2A636F       LDATTR   LD      HL,(ATTPOS)
7262 ED5B6A6F              LD      DE,(ATTPTR)
7266 3A606F                LD      A,(ROW)
7269 08           ATROW    EX      AF,AF'
726A D5                    PUSH    DE
726B E5                    PUSH    HL
726C 3A616F                LD      A,(SKIP)
726F 4F                    LD      C,A
7270 0600                  LD      B,0
7272 09                    ADD     HL,BC            ;SKIP ATTRIBUTE FILE
7273 EB                    EX      DE,HL
7274 09                    ADD     HL,BC            ;SKIP ATTRIBUTE DATABASE
7275 EB                    EX      DE,HL
7276 3A626F                LD      A,(FILL)
7279 A7                    AND     A
727A 2807                  JR      Z,SKIPAT         ;SKIP ATTRIBUTE
727C 47                    LD      B,A              ;FILL ATTRIBUTES
727D 1A           ATTR2    LD      A,(DE)
727E 77                    LD      (HL),A
727F 23                    INC     HL
7280 13                    INC     DE
7281 10FA                  DJNZ    ATTR2
7283 E1           SKIPAT   POP     HL
7284 D1                    POP     DE
7285 3A5F6F                LD      A,(COLUMN)
7288 A7                    AND     A                ;CLEAR CARRY
7289 0E20                  LD      C,20H
728B ED42                  SBC     HL,BC            ;NEXT ATTRIBUTE LINE UP
728D 4F                    LD      C,A
728E EB                    EX      DE,HL
728F 09                    ADD     HL,BC            ;UPDATE ATTRIBUTE DB
7290 EB                    EX      DE,HL
7291 08                    EX      AF,AF'
7292 3D                    DEC     A
7293 20D4                  JR      NZ,ATROW
7295 C9                    RET
                  ;
                  ;
                  ;********  RSHAPE  ********
                  ;
                  ;        INPUT:  HL=>POSITION
                  ;                A =>REAL/ABSTRACT FLAG
                  ;                DE=>SHAPE PTR
                  ;                COLUMN
                  ;
                  ;        OUTPUT: SKIP, FILL, ATTPOS
                  ;
7296 E5           RSHAPE   PUSH    HL
```

```
7297 08        06640        EX    AF,AF'        ;REAL SHAPE
7298 261F      06650        LD    H,1FH
729A 7C        06660        LD    A,H
729B A5        06670        AND   L             ;TRAP LOWER 5 BITS
729C 6F        06680        LD    L,A
729D 7C        06690        LD    A,H
729E 95        06700        SUB   L             ;SUBTRACT FROM 1FH
729F 3C        06710        INC   A
72A0 A4        06720        AND   H             ;ADJUST FOR ZERO DIFF
72A1 6F        06730        LD    L,A
72A2 08        06740        EX    AF,AF'
72A3 A7        06750        AND   A             ;0=>ABSTRACT, 1=>REAL
72A4 3A5F6F    06760        LD    A,(COLUMN)
72A7 200A      06770        JR    NZ,REAL
72A9 95        06780        SUB   L
72AA 32626F    06790        LD    (FILL),A
72AD 7D        06800        LD    A,L           ;RELOAD ABS DIFF
72AE 32616F    06810        LD    (SKIP),A
72B1 1811      06820        JR    CALATT
72B3 BD        06830 REAL   CP    L             ;TAKE MIN OF COL/FILL
72B4 3807      06840        JR    C,TOOBIG      ;FILL MORE THAN COL
72B6 7D        06850        LD    A,L
72B7 A7        06860        AND   A
72B8 2003      06870        JR    NZ,TOOBIG
72BA 3A5F6F    06880        LD    A,(COLUMN)
72BD 32626F    06890 TOOBIG LD    (FILL),A
72C0 AF        06900        XOR   A
72C1 32616F    06910        LD    (SKIP),A
72C4 E1        06920 CALATT POP   HL            ;CALCULATE ATT PTR
72C5 E5        06930        PUSH  HL
72C6 7C        06940        LD    A,H
72C7 E618      06950        AND   18H
72C9 CB2F      06960        SRA   A
72CB CB2F      06970        SRA   A
72CD CB2F      06980        SRA   A
72CF C658      06990        ADD   A,58H
72D1 67        07000        LD    H,A
72D2 22636F    07010        LD    (ATTPOS),HL
72D5 E1        07020        POP   HL
72D6 C9        07030        RET
               07040 ;
               07050 ;
72D7 210040    07060 CLRSCR LD    HL,4000H      ;HL=>START OF SCREEN
72DA 110140    07070        LD    DE,4001H
72DD 01FF17    07080        LD    BC,6143       ;SIZE OF SCREEN 17FFH
72E0 AF        07090        XOR   A             ;BLANK ACREEN
72E1 77        07100        LD    (HL),A
72E2 EDB0      07110        LDIR
72E4 210058    07120        LD    HL,5800H      ;SET FIRST LINE FOR SCORE
72E7 110158    07130        LD    DE,5801H      ;OF ATTRIBUTE FILE
72EA 011F00    07140        LD    BC,31
72ED 3607      07150        LD    (HL),7        ;INK SEVEN
72EF EDB0      07160        LDIR
72F1 212058    07170        LD    HL,5820H      ;SET ATTRIBUTE
72F4 112158    07180        LD    DE,5821H      ;START FROM SECOND LINE
72F7 01DF02    07190        LD    BC,735
```

```
72FA 77         07200             LD      (HL),A          ;(PAPER 0)*8 + (INK 0)
72FB EDB0       07210             LDIR
72FD 21A058     07220             LD      HL,58A0H        ;SET HIGHWAY
7300 116059     07230             LD      DE,5960H        ;HIGH, MIDDLE, BOTTOM
7303 01205A     07240             LD      BC,5A20H
7306 3E38       07250             LD      A,56            ;(PAPER 7)*8 + (INK 0)
7308 D9         07260             EXX
7309 0620       07270             LD      B,32            ;FILL ONE LINE
730B D9         07280 HWYATT      EXX
730C 77         07290             LD      (HL),A
730D 12         07300             LD      (DE),A
730E 02         07310             LD      (BC),A
730F 23         07320             INC     HL
7310 13         07330             INC     DE
7311 03         07340             INC     BC
7312 D9         07350             EXX
7313 10F6       07360             DJNZ    HWYATT
7315 D9         07370             EXX
7316 C9         07380             RET
                07390 ;
                07400 ;
7317 E5         07410 SHAPE       PUSH    HL              ;SAVE HL PTR
7318 3A7B6E     07420             LD      A,(FRGDIR)
731B 87         07430             ADD     A,A
731C 21AF69     07440             LD      HL,FRGSHP
731F 1600       07450             LD      D,0
7321 5F         07460             LD      E,A
7322 19         07470             ADD     HL,DE           ;PTR TO POS OF SHAPE
7323 5E         07480             LD      E,(HL)          ;DE RETURN SHAPE PTR
7324 23         07490             INC     HL
7325 56         07500             LD      D,(HL)
7326 E1         07510             POP     HL
7327 C9         07520             RET
                07530 ;
                07540 ;
                07550 ;********   DISASC   ********
                07560 ;
                07570 ;           display ASCII value from character set
                07580 ;           NB:----  store DE, the message pointer
                07590 ;                    HL stays the same after display
                07600 ;                    used BC register as well
                07610 ;
                07620 ;
7328 C5         07630 DISASC      PUSH    BC
7329 D5         07640             PUSH    DE
732A E5         07650             PUSH    HL
732B 1A         07660             LD      A,(DE)          ;LOAD ASCII CHAR
732C 6F         07670             LD      L,A
732D 2600       07680             LD      H,0
732F 29         07690             ADD     HL,HL           ;MULTIPLE OF 8 BYTES
7330 29         07700             ADD     HL,HL
7331 29         07710             ADD     HL,HL
7332 EB         07720             EX      DE,HL
7333 21003C     07730             LD      HL,CHRSET       ;START OF CHARACTER SET
7336 19         07740             ADD     HL,DE
7337 EB         07750             EX      DE,HL
```

```
7338 E1       07760          POP    HL
7339 0608     07770 DRWCHR   LD     B,8            ;DRAW CHARACTER
733B E5       07780          PUSH   HL
733C 1A       07790 CHARLP   LD     A,(DE)
733D 77       07800          LD     (HL),A
733E 13       07810          INC    DE
733F 24       07820          INC    H
7340 10FA     07830          DJNZ   CHARLP
7342 E1       07840          POP    HL
7343 D1       07850          POP    DE
7344 23       07860          INC    HL             ;POS PTR
7345 13       07870          INC    DE             ;MESSAGE PTR
7346 C1       07880          POP    BC
7347 10DF     07890          DJNZ   DISASC
7349 C9       07900          RET
              07910 ;
              07920 ;
734A D9       07930 POLICE   EXX
734B 216D6E   07940          LD     HL,PCAREXT
734E 7E       07950          LD     A,(HL)         ;TEST POLICE CAR EXIST
734F E5       07960          PUSH   HL
7350 D9       07970          EXX
7351 A7       07980          AND    A
7352 2023     07990          JR     NZ,MOVPC       ;MOVE POLICE CAR
7354 D1       08000          POP    DE             ;DB EXT PTR
7355 CDCC77   08010          CALL   RANDNO         ;MOVE WHEN MULTIPLE OF
7358 E61F     08020          AND    1FH            ;31
735A FE1F     08030          CP     1FH
735C C0       08040          RET    NZ
735D 3E01     08050          LD     A,1            ;SET CHASE FLAG
735F 32726F   08060          LD     (CHASE),A
7362 21F56E   08070          LD     HL,RPCDB       ;RIGHT PC
7365 CDCC77   08080          CALL   RANDNO
7368 E601     08090          AND    1
736A 2803     08100          JR     Z,RHTPC
736C 21DD6E   08110          LD     HL,LPCDB
736F 010C00   08120 RHTPC    LD     BC,12
7372 EDB0     08130          LDIR
7374 D9       08140          EXX
7375 E5       08150          PUSH   HL
7376 D9       08160          EXX
7377 E1       08170 MOVPC    POP    HL             ;EXISTENCE PTR
7378 23       08180          INC    HL
7379 23       08190          INC    HL             ;DIRECTION
737A 7E       08200          LD     A,(HL)
737B 47       08210          LD     B,A            ;STORE DIR
737C 23       08220          INC    HL
737D 23       08230          INC    HL             ;POSPTR
737E 226E6F   08240          LD     (POSPTR),HL
7381 5E       08250          LD     E,(HL)
7382 23       08260          INC    HL
7383 56       08270          LD     D,(HL)
7384 1C       08280          INC    E              ;ASSUME MOVE RIGHT
7385 A7       08290          AND    A
7386 2802     08300          JR     Z,PCMRHT       ;POLICE CAR MOVE RIGHT
7388 1D       08310          DEC    E
```

```
7389 1D         08320         DEC    E
738A ED536C6F   08330 PCMRHT  LD     (NEWPOS),DE
738E 3E02       08340         LD     A,2              ;TWO ROW
7390 32606F     08350         LD     (ROW),A
7393 3E06       08360         LD     A,6
7395 325F6F     08370         LD     (COLUMN),A
7398 C5         08380         PUSH   BC               ;DIRECTION
7399 3A706E     08390         LD     A,(PCARRAP)      ;REAL/ABS FLAG
739C EB         08400         EX     DE,HL
739D CD9672     08410         CALL   RSHAPE           ;RET SKIP/FILL,ATTR
73A0 2A636F     08420         LD     HL,(ATTPOS)
73A3 F1         08430         POP    AF
73A4 A7         08440         AND    A                ;IF 1,OK
73A5 2004       08450         JR     NZ,PCTAH         ;POLICE CAR TEST AHEAD
73A7 010500     08460         LD     BC,5
73AA 09         08470         ADD    HL,BC
73AB 7E         08480 PCTAH   LD     A,(HL)
73AC E607       08490         AND    7
73AE 012000     08500         LD     BC,32
73B1 A7         08510         AND    A
73B2 ED42       08520         SBC    HL,BC
73B4 FE04       08530         CP     4
73B6 2807       08540         JR     Z,ISFRG2
73B8 7E         08550         LD     A,(HL)
73B9 E607       08560         AND    7
73BB FE04       08570         CP     4
73BD 2009       08580         JR     NZ,NFROG2
73BF 3E01       08590 ISFRG2  LD     A,1
73C1 327C6F     08600         LD     (CRHFLG),A       ;SET CRASH FLAG
73C4 3D         08610         DEC    A                ;BLANK COLOUR
73C5 77         08620         LD     (HL),A           ;BLANK FRONT OF PC
73C6 09         08630         ADD    HL,BC
73C7 77         08640         LD     (HL),A           ;** SHOULD BLANK FRONT*
73C8 CDDF73     08650 NFROG2  CALL   STRPC            ;STORE NEW UNDERNEATH
73CB 2A6E6F     08660         LD     HL,(POSPTR)
73CE ED5B6C6F   08670         LD     DE,(NEWPOS)
73D2 73         08680         LD     (HL),E
73D3 23         08690         INC    HL
73D4 72         08700         LD     (HL),D
73D5 CDAF71     08710         CALL   MVCTRL
73D8 D9         08720         EXX                     ;IF NON-EXIST
73D9 7E         08730         LD     A,(HL)
73DA 32726F     08740         LD     (CHASE),A
73DD D9         08750         EXX
73DE C9         08760         RET
                08770 ;
                08780 ;
                08790 ;********  STRPC  ********
                08800 ;
                08810 ;       STORE UNDERNEATH POLICE CAR
                08820 ;
73DF 2A6C6F     08830 STRPC   LD     HL,(NEWPOS)      ;POS PTR
73E2 11AD6D     08840         LD     DE,PCSTR         ;STORAGE LOC
73E5 EB         08850         EX     DE,HL
73E6 73         08860         LD     (HL),E           ;STORE POSITION
73E7 23         08870         INC    HL
```

```
73E8 72         08880         LD     (HL),D
73E9 23         08890         INC    HL
73EA EB         08900         EX     DE,HL
73EB 21606F     08910         LD     HL,ROW         ;LOAD 5 BYTES OF INFO
73EE 7E         08920         LD     A,(HL)
73EF 010500     08930         LD     BC,5
73F2 EDB0       08940         LDIR
73F4 08         08950         EX     AF,AF'
73F5 2A6C6F     08960         LD     HL,(NEWPOS)
73F8 E5         08970 SPCLP1  PUSH   HL
73F9 3A616F     08980         LD     A,(SKIP)
73FC 4F         08990         LD     C,A
73FD 09         09000         ADD    HL,BC
73FE CB44       09010         BIT    0,H
7400 2804       09020         JR     Z,NSSPS
7402 7C         09030         LD     A,H
7403 C607       09040         ADD    A,7
7405 67         09050         LD     H,A
7406 3A626F     09060 NSSPS   LD     A,(FILL)
7409 A7         09070         AND    A
740A 280F       09080         JR     Z,NXTSPC
740C 4F         09090         LD     C,A
740D E5         09100 SPCLP2  PUSH   HL             ;RESTORE CHAR
740E 0608       09110         LD     B,8
7410 7E         09120 SPCLP3  LD     A,(HL)         ;STORE SCREEN FIRST
7411 12         09130         LD     (DE),A
7412 13         09140         INC    DE
7413 24         09150         INC    H
7414 10FA       09160         DJNZ   SPCLP3
7416 E1         09170         POP    HL
7417 23         09180         INC    HL             ;NEXT CHAR
7418 0D         09190         DEC    C
7419 20F2       09200         JR     NZ,SPCLP2
741B E1         09210 NXTSPC  POP    HL
741C 08         09220         EX     AF,AF'         ;UPD ROW COUNT
741D 3D         09230         DEC    A
741E 280F       09240         JR     Z,SPCATR       ;RESTORE POLICE ATTR
7420 08         09250         EX     AF,AF'
7421 0E20       09260         LD     C,32
7423 ED42       09270         SBC    HL,BC          ;UP ONE LINE
7425 CB44       09280         BIT    0,H            ;CROSS SCREEN SECTION?
7427 28CF       09290         JR     Z,SPCLP1
7429 7C         09300         LD     A,H
742A D607       09310         SUB    7
742C 67         09320         LD     H,A
742D 18C9       09330         JR     SPCLP1
742F 2A636F     09340 SPCATR  LD     HL,(ATTPOS)    ;ATTRIBUTE START POS
7432 3A606F     09350         LD     A,(ROW)
7435 08         09360         EX     AF,AF'
7436 E5         09370 SPCAT1  PUSH   HL
7437 3A616F     09380         LD     A,(SKIP)
743A 4F         09390         LD     C,A
743B 09         09400         ADD    HL,BC
743C 3A626F     09410         LD     A,(FILL)
743F A7         09420         AND    A
7440 2803       09430         JR     Z,NXTSPA
```

```
7442 4F         09440          LD      C,A
7443 EDB0       09450          LDIR
7445 E1         09460 NXTSPA   POP     HL
7446 08         09470          EX      AF,AF'
7447 3D         09480          DEC     A
7448 C8         09490          RET     Z
7449 08         09500          EX      AF,AF'
744A 0E20       09510          LD      C,32
744C ED42       09520          SBC     HL,BC
744E 18E6       09530          JR      SPCAT1
                09540 ;
                09550 ;
7450 3A6D6E     09560 RESPC    LD      A,(PCAREXT)      ;TEST PC EXIST
7453 A7         09570          AND     A
7454 C8         09580          RET     Z
7455 11606F     09590          LD      DE,ROW
7458 21AF6D     09600          LD      HL,PCSTR+2
745B 010500     09610          LD      BC,5
745E EDB0       09620          LDIR                     ;RETRIEVE 5 INFO
7460 EB         09630          EX      DE,HL            ;DE STORAGE PTR
7461 2AAD6D     09640          LD      HL,(PCSTR)       ;LOAD POS
7464 3A606F     09650          LD      A,(ROW)
7467 08         09660          EX      AF,AF'
7468 E5         09670 RPCLP1   PUSH    HL               ;SAVE POS
7469 3A616F     09680          LD      A,(SKIP)
746C 4F         09690          LD      C,A
746D 09         09700          ADD     HL,BC
746E CB44       09710          BIT     0,H
7470 2804       09720          JR      Z,NSRPS
7472 3E07       09730          LD      A,7
7474 84         09740          ADD     A,H
7475 67         09750          LD      H,A
7476 3A626F     09760 NSRPS    LD      A,(FILL)
7479 A7         09770          AND     A
747A 280F       09780          JR      Z,NXTRPC
747C 4F         09790          LD      C,A
747D E5         09800 RPCLP2   PUSH    HL
747E 0608       09810          LD      B,8
7480 1A         09820 RPCLP3   LD      A,(DE)           ;RESTORE CHAR
7481 77         09830          LD      (HL),A
7482 13         09840          INC     DE
7483 24         09850          INC     H
7484 10FA       09860          DJNZ    RPCLP3
7486 E1         09870          POP     HL
7487 23         09880          INC     HL
7488 0D         09890          DEC     C
7489 20F2       09900          JR      NZ,RPCLP2
748B E1         09910 NXTRPC   POP     HL
748C 08         09920          EX      AF,AF'
748D 3D         09930          DEC     A                ;UPD ROW COUNT
748E 280F       09940          JR      Z,RPCATR         ;RETORE POLICE CAR
7490 08         09950          EX      AF,AF'
7491 0E20       09960          LD      C,32
7493 ED42       09970          SBC     HL,BC            ;MOVE UP ONE LINE
7495 CB44       09980          BIT     0,H
7497 28CF       09990          JR      Z,RPCLP1
```

```
7499 7C        10000         LD     A,H
749A D607      10010         SUB    7                ;CROSS BOUNDARY
749C 67        10020         LD     H,A
749D 18C9      10030         JR     RPCLP1
749F 2A636F    10040 RPCATR  LD     HL,(ATTPOS)      ;ATTR START LOADING POS
74A2 3A606F    10050         LD     A,(ROW)
74A5 08        10060         EX     AF,AF'
74A6 E5        10070 RPCAT1  PUSH   HL
74A7 3A616F    10080         LD     A,(SKIP)
74AA 4F        10090         LD     C,A
74AB 09        10100         ADD    HL,BC
74AC 3A626F    10110         LD     A,(FILL)
74AF A7        10120         AND    A
74B0 2805      10130         JR     Z,NXTRPA
74B2 EB        10140         EX     DE,HL
74B3 4F        10150         LD     C,A
74B4 EDB0      10160         LDIR
74B6 EB        10170         EX     DE,HL
74B7 E1        10180 NXTRPA  POP    HL
74B8 08        10190         EX     AF,AF'
74B9 3D        10200         DEC    A
74BA C8        10210         RET    Z
74BB 08        10220         EX     AF,AF'
74BC 0E20      10230         LD     C,32
74BE ED42      10240         SBC    HL,BC
74C0 18E4      10250         JR     RPCAT1
               10260 ;
               10270 ;
74C2 3A7C6F    10280 FROG    LD     A,(CRHFLG)       ;CRASH FLAG
74C5 A7        10290         AND    A
74C6 2017      10300         JR     NZ,FRGCRH        ;FROG CRASH
74C8 325E6F    10310         LD     (UPDWN),A        ;SET NO SCORE
74CB CDE374    10320         CALL   REGFRG           ;REGENERATE FROG
74CE 217A6E    10330         LD     HL,FRGCYC        ;TEST MOVE
74D1 35        10340         DEC    (HL)
74D2 C0        10350         RET    NZ
74D3 2B        10360         DEC    HL
74D4 7E        10370         LD     A,(HL)           ;RESET CYCLE COUNT
74D5 23        10380         INC    HL
74D6 77        10390         LD     (HL),A
74D7 CD1075    10400         CALL   MOVFRG
74DA 3A7C6F    10410         LD     A,(CRHFLG)
74DD A7        10420         AND    A
74DE C8        10430         RET    Z
74DF CD9176    10440 FRGCRH  CALL   CRASH
74E2 C9        10450         RET
               10460 ;
               10470 ;********  REGFRG  ********
               10480 ;
               10490 ;         Regenerate frog if any left
               10500 ;         Set GAMFLG to 0 if none left
               10510 ;
74E3 3A796E    10520 REGFRG  LD     A,(FRGEXT)
74E6 A7        10530         AND    A
74E7 C0        10540         RET    NZ               ;RETURN IF EXIST
74E8 21816E    10550         LD     HL,FRGDB
```

```
74EB 11796E     10560            LD      DE,FRGEXT
74EE 010800     10570            LD      BC,8
74F1 EDB0       10580            LDIR
74F3 21846E     10590            LD      HL,FRGSTN        ;UPDATE FROG STATION
74F6 35         10600            DEC     (HL)             ;MOVE 3 CHARACTER LEFT
74F7 35         10610            DEC     (HL)
74F8 35         10620            DEC     (HL)
74F9 2A7C6E     10630            LD      HL,(FRGPOS)
74FC 22786F     10640            LD      (OLDFRG),HL
74FF 227A6F     10650            LD      (NEWFRG),HL
7502 21896D     10660            LD      HL,FRGSTR        ;INIT FRG STR FOR RES
7505 118A6D     10670            LD      DE,FRGSTR+1      ;BLANK FROG STORE
7508 012300     10680            LD      BC,35
750B 3600       10690            LD      (HL),0
750D EDB0       10700            LDIR
750F C9         10710            RET
                10720 ;
                10730 ;********  MOVFRG  ********
                10740 ;
                10750 ;          Move frog, store and restore
                10760 ;
7510 AF         10770 MOVFRG     XOR     A
7511 2120E0     10780            LD      HL,0E020H        ;H=-32, L=32
7514 4F         10790            LD      C,A              ;C=>ABS MOVEMENT
7515 08         10800            EX      AF,AF'
7516 3EDF       10810            LD      A,0DFH           ;TEST RIGHT
7518 DBFE       10820            IN      A,(0FEH)
751A E601       10830            AND     1
751C 2006       10840            JR      NZ,LEFT
751E 0C         10850            INC     C
751F 11D769     10860            LD      DE,FROG2
7522 0601       10870            LD      B,1
7524 3EDF       10880 LEFT       LD      A,0DFH           ;TEST LEFT
7526 DBFE       10890            IN      A,(0FEH)
7528 E604       10900            AND     4
752A 2006       10910            JR      NZ,DOWN
752C 0D         10920            DEC     C
752D 11176A     10930            LD      DE,FROG4
7530 0603       10940            LD      B,3
7532 3EFD       10950 DOWN       LD      A,0FDH           ;TEST DOWN
7534 DBFE       10960            IN      A,(0FEH)
7536 E601       10970            AND     1
7538 200B       10980            JR      NZ,UP
753A 79         10990            LD      A,C
753B 85         11000            ADD     A,L              ;ADD 32
753C 4F         11010            LD      C,A
753D 08         11020            EX      AF,AF'
753E 3D         11030            DEC     A
753F 08         11040            EX      AF,AF'           ;DEC UP/DWN FLG
7540 11F769     11050            LD      DE,FROG3
7543 0602       11060            LD      B,2
7545 3EF7       11070 UP         LD      A,0F7H           ;TEST UP
7547 DBFE       11080            IN      A,(0FEH)
7549 E601       11090            AND     1
754B 200B       11100            JR      NZ,VALID
754D 79         11110            LD      A,C
```

```
754E 84                    ADD     A,H             ;ADD -32
754F 4F                    LD      C,A
7550 08                    EX      AF,AF'
7551 3C                    INC     A
7552 08                    EX      AF,AF'
7553 11B769                LD      DE,FROG1
7556 0600                  LD      B,0
7558 78           VALID    LD      A,B             ;STORE TEMP DIR
7559 327D6F                LD      (TEMDIR),A
755C ED53806F              LD      (TEMSHP),DE     ;STORE TEMP SHAPE
7560 AF                    XOR     A
7561 B9                    CP      C
7562 C8                    RET     Z               ;IF NO MOVE GO BACK
7563 2A786F                LD      HL,(OLDFRG)
7566 CB79                  BIT     7,C             ;TEST -VE
7568 47                    LD      B,A
7569 1E07                  LD      E,7             ;FOR BOUNDARY ADJ
756B 2803                  JR      Z,NETDWN        ;NET MOVE RHT,DWN
756D 05                    DEC     B
756E 1EF9                  LD      E,-7
7570 09           NETDWN   ADD     HL,BC
7571 CB44                  BIT     0,H
7573 2803                  JR      Z,VALID1        ;NO CROSS BOUNDARY
7575 7C                    LD      A,H
7576 83                    ADD     A,E
7577 67                    LD      H,A             ;ADJ HOB
7578 227E6F       VALID1   LD      (TEMPOS),HL
757B EB                    EX      DE,HL
757C 3E40                  LD      A,40H           ;TEST UPSCR
757E BA                    CP      D
757F 7B                    LD      A,E
7580 2004                  JR      NZ,VALID2
7582 FE20                  CP      20H
7584 382F                  JR      C,NVALID
7586 E61F         VALID2   AND     1FH             ;TEST RIGHT BOUNDARY
7588 FE1F                  CP      1FH
758A 2829                  JR      Z,NVALID
758C 21BE50                LD      HL,50BEH        ;TEST BOT BOUNDARY
758F A7                    AND     A
7590 ED52                  SBC     HL,DE
7592 3821                  JR      C,NVALID
7594 217E50                LD      HL,507EH        ;TEST FROG STATION
7597 ED52                  SBC     HL,DE
7599 3011                  JR      NC,YVALID
759B 7B                    LD      A,E             ;TEST WITHIN BOX
759C E61F                  AND     1FH
759E 67                    LD      H,A
759F 3A846E                LD      A,(FRGSTN)
75A2 FEA0                  CP      0A0H            ;TEST LAST FROG
75A4 3806                  JR      C,YVALID        ;NO MORE FROG STATION
75A6 3C                    INC     A               ;WHEN NO FROG LEFT
75A7 E61F                  AND     1FH
75A9 94                    SUB     H
75AA 3009                  JR      NC,NVALID
75AC ED537A6F     YVALID   LD      (NEWFRG),DE     ;STORE NEW POS
75B0 08                    EX      AF,AF'
```

```
75B1 325E6F               LD      (UPDWN),A
75B4 08                   EX      AF,AF'
75B5 2A786F      NVALID   LD      HL,(OLDFRG)     ;TEST OLDFRG=NEWFRG
75B8 A7                   AND     A
75B9 ED52                 SBC     HL,DE
75BB 7D                   LD      A,L
75BC B4                   OR      H
75BD C8                   RET     Z               ;RETURN IF SAME
75BE CDD675               CALL    RESFRG          ;RESTORE FROG
75C1 2A7A6F               LD      HL,(NEWFRG)     ;UPDATE OLD FROG POS
75C4 22786F               LD      (OLDFRG),HL
75C7 217D6F               LD      HL,TEMDIR
75CA 117B6E               LD      DE,FRGDIR
75CD 010500               LD      BC,5
75D0 EDB0                 LDIR
75D2 CD2876               CALL    STRFRG
75D5 C9                   RET
                 ;
                 ;
75D6 11896D      RESFRG   LD      DE,FRGSTR       ;STORAGE PTR
75D9 2A786F               LD      HL,(OLDFRG)     ;RESTORE FROM OLDPOS
75DC E5                   PUSH    HL
75DD 3E02                 LD      A,2             ;ROW COUNTER
75DF 08                   EX      AF,AF'
75E0 E5          RFRLP1   PUSH    HL
75E1 0E02                 LD      C,2             ;COLUMN COUNTER
75E3 E5          RFRLP2   PUSH    HL
75E4 0608                 LD      B,8
75E6 1A          RFRLP3   LD      A,(DE)          ;RESTORE FROM DB
75E7 77                   LD      (HL),A          ;ONTO SCREEN
75E8 13                   INC     DE
75E9 24                   INC     H               ;NEXT CHAR BYTE
75EA 10FA                 DJNZ    RFRLP3
75EC E1                   POP     HL
75ED 23                   INC     HL
75EE 0D                   DEC     C               ;COLUMN COUNT
75EF 20F2                 JR      NZ,RFRLP2
75F1 E1                   POP     HL
75F2 08                   EX      AF,AF'
75F3 3D                   DEC     A               ;ROW COUNT
75F4 2810                 JR      Z,RFRATR
75F6 08                   EX      AF,AF'
75F7 A7                   AND     A
75F8 0E20                 LD      C,32            ;UP ONE LINE
75FA ED42                 SBC     HL,BC
75FC CB44                 BIT     0,H
75FE 28E0                 JR      Z,RFRLP1
7600 7C                   LD      A,H
7601 D607                 SUB     7
7603 67                   LD      H,A
7604 18DA                 JR      RFRLP1
7606 E1          RFRATR   POP     HL
7607 7C                   LD      A,H
7608 E618                 AND     18H
760A CB2F                 SRA     A
760C CB2F                 SRA     A
```

```
760E CB2F            SRA     A
7610 C658            ADD     A,58H
7612 67              LD      H,A
7613 3E02            LD      A,2           ;ROW COUNTER
7615 08              EX      AF,AF'
7616 E5      RFRAT1  PUSH    HL
7617 EB              EX      DE,HL
7618 0E02            LD      C,2           ;RESTORE ATTR
761A EDB0            LDIR
761C EB              EX      DE,HL
761D E1              POP     HL
761E 08              EX      AF,AF'
761F 3D              DEC     A             ;UPDATE ROW COUNTER
7620 C8              RET     Z
7621 08              EX      AF,AF'
7622 0E20            LD      C,32
7624 ED42            SBC     HL,BC
7626 18EE            JR      RFRAT1
             ;
             ;
7628 11896D  STRFRG  LD      DE,FRGSTR
762B 2A7A6F          LD      HL,(NEWFRG)   ;STORE BASE ON NEWPOS
762E D9              EXX
762F 2A7E6E          LD      HL,(FROGSH)   ;LOAD SHAPE AS WELL
7632 D9              EXX
7633 E5              PUSH    HL
7634 3E02            LD      A,2
7636 08              EX      AF,AF'
7637 E5      SFRLP1  PUSH    HL
7638 0E02            LD      C,2
763A E5      SFRLP2  PUSH    HL
763B 0608            LD      B,8           ;STORE AND LOAD A CHAR
763D 7E      SFRLP3  LD      A,(HL)
763E 12              LD      (DE),A
763F D9              EXX
7640 7E              LD      A,(HL)
7641 23              INC     HL
7642 D9              EXX
7643 77              LD      (HL),A
7644 13              INC     DE
7645 24              INC     H
7646 10F5            DJNZ    SFRLP3
7648 E1              POP     HL
7649 23              INC     HL            ;NEXT CHAR
764A 0D              DEC     C
764B 20ED            JR      NZ,SFRLP2
764D E1              POP     HL
764E 08              EX      AF,AF'
764F 3D              DEC     A
7650 2810            JR      Z,SFRATR
7652 08              EX      AF,AF'
7653 A7              AND     A
7654 0E20            LD      C,32
7656 ED42            SBC     HL,BC         ;NEXT ROW
7658 CB44            BIT     0,H
765A 28DB            JR      Z,SFRLP1
```

```
765C 7C       12800          LD     A,H
765D D607     12810          SUB    7
765F 67       12820          LD     H,A
7660 18D5     12830          JR     SFRLP1
7662 E1       12840 SFRATR   POP    HL
7663 7C       12850          LD     A,H             ;CALCULATE ATTR POS
7664 E618     12860          AND    18H
7666 CB2F     12870          SRA    A
7668 CB2F     12880          SRA    A
766A CB2F     12890          SRA    A
766C C658     12900          ADD    A,58H
766E 67       12910          LD     H,A
766F 3E02     12920          LD     A,2
7671 08       12930          EX     AF,AF'
7672 0602     12940 SFRAT1   LD     B,2
7674 E5       12950          PUSH   HL
7675 7E       12960 SFRATLP  LD     A,(HL)
7676 12       12970          LD     (DE),A
7677 3604     12980          LD     (HL),4          ;FILL FROG ATTR
7679 23       12990          INC    HL
767A 13       13000          INC    DE
767B E607     13010          AND    7               ;TEST CRASH
767D 2805     13020          JR     Z,NFROG3
767F 3E01     13030          LD     A,1
7681 327C6F   13040          LD     (CRHFLG),A
7684 10EF     13050 NFROG3   DJNZ   SFRATLP
7686 E1       13060          POP    HL
7687 08       13070          EX     AF,AF'
7688 3D       13080          DEC    A
7689 C8       13090          RET    Z
768A 08       13100          EX     AF,AF'
768B 0E20     13110          LD     C,32
768D ED42     13120          SBC    HL,BC
768F 18E1     13130          JR     SFRAT1
              13140 ;
              13150 ;
7691 AF       13160 CRASH    XOR    A
7692 327C6F   13170          LD     (CRHFLG),A      ;RESET CRASH FLAG
7695 32796E   13180          LD     (FRGEXT),A      ;SET FROG NONEXIST
7698 CDA776   13190          CALL   FRGDIE          ;FROG DYING ROUTINE
769B CDD675   13200          CALL   RESFRG
769E 21826F   13210          LD     HL,NUMFRG
76A1 35       13220          DEC    (HL)            ;DECREASE FROG NUMBER
76A2 C0       13230          RET    NZ
76A3 32776F   13240          LD     (GAMFLG),A      ;ZEROISE GAME FLAG
76A6 C9       13250          RET                    ;WHEN NO FROG LEFT
              13260 ;
              13270 ;
76A7 2A786F   13280 FRGDIE   LD     HL,(OLDFRG)     ;OLD POS OF FRG
76AA 010240   13290          LD     BC,4002H        ;RED COLOUR
76AD D9       13300          EXX
76AE 21396F   13310          LD     HL,DIETON       ;SET DIE TONE
76B1 D9       13320          EXX
76B2 7C       13330          LD     A,H             ;TEST END OF JOURNEY
76B3 B8       13340          CP     B
76B4 2016     13350          JR     NZ,NOTEND
```

```
76B6 7D         13360             LD       A,L
76B7 B8         13370             CP       B
76B8 3012       13380             JR       NC,NOTEND
76BA 11466F     13390             LD       DE,SCORE+3        ;100 PTS BONUS
76BD EB         13400             EX       DE,HL
76BE 34         13410             INC      (HL)
76BF 21476F     13420             LD       HL,SCORE+4
76C2 CD4B77     13430             CALL     DISSCR
76C5 0E06       13440             LD       C,6               ;YELLOW
76C7 D9         13450             EXX
76C8 21156F     13460             LD       HL,HOMTON
76CB D9         13470             EXX
76CC 79         13480 NOTEND      LD       A,C
76CD 32656F     13490             LD       (ATTR),A
76D0 2A786F     13500             LD       HL,(OLDFRG)
76D3 ED5B7E6E   13510             LD       DE,(FROGSH)
76D7 CD7A70     13520             CALL     DRWFRG
76DA 112000     13530             LD       DE,32             ;LINE ADJUST
76DD 19         13540             ADD      HL,DE
76DE 08         13550             EX       AF,AF'
76DF 3A656F     13560             LD       A,(ATTR)
76E2 08         13570             EX       AF,AF'
76E3 0605       13580             LD       B,5
76E5 C5         13590 FLASLP      PUSH     BC
76E6 E5         13600             PUSH     HL                ;ATTRIBUTE PTR
76E7 AF         13610             XOR      A                 ;BLACK INK BLACK PAPER
76E8 77         13620             LD       (HL),A
76E9 23         13630             INC      HL
76EA 77         13640             LD       (HL),A
76EB ED52       13650             SBC      HL,DE
76ED 77         13660             LD       (HL),A
76EE 2B         13670             DEC      HL
76EF 77         13680             LD       (HL),A
76F0 CD0877     13690             CALL     FRGTON            ;GENERATE FROG TONE
76F3 E1         13700             POP      HL
76F4 E5         13710             PUSH     HL
76F5 08         13720             EX       AF,AF'
76F6 77         13730             LD       (HL),A            ;BLACK PAPER, RED OR
76F7 23         13740             INC      HL                ;YELLOW INK
76F8 77         13750             LD       (HL),A
76F9 A7         13760             AND      A
76FA ED52       13770             SBC      HL,DE
76FC 77         13780             LD       (HL),A
76FD 2B         13790             DEC      HL
76FE 77         13800             LD       (HL),A
76FF 08         13810             EX       AF,AF'
7700 CD0877     13820             CALL     FRGTON
7703 E1         13830             POP      HL
7704 C1         13840             POP      BC
7705 10DE       13850             DJNZ     FLASLP
7707 C9         13860             RET
                13870 ;
                13880 ;
7708 D9         13890 FRGTON      EXX
7709 E5         13900             PUSH     HL
770A CDB577     13910             CALL     TONE1
```

```
770D E1         13920            POP    HL
770E 010400     13930            LD     BC,4              ;MOVE DOWN DATABASE
7711 08         13940            EX     AF,AF'
7712 FE06       13950            CP     6
7714 2803       13960            JR     Z,HOME
7716 01FCFF     13970            LD     BC,-4             ;MOVE UP DATABASE
7719 09         13980 HOME       ADD    HL,BC
771A D9         13990            EXX
771B 08         14000            EX     AF,AF'
771C C9         14010            RET
                14020 ;
                14030 ;
771D 3A796E     14040 CALSCR     LD     A,(FRGEXT)        ;TEST EXISTENCE
7720 A7         14050            AND    A
7721 C8         14060            RET    Z                 ;NO UPDATE OF SCORE
7722 3A5E6F     14070            LD     A,(UPDWN)         ;TEST UP/DOWN MOVEMENT
7725 A7         14080            AND    A                 ;TEST ANY SCORE
7726 C8         14090            RET    Z
7727 21476F     14100            LD     HL,SCORE+4        ;ADD 10 TO SCORE
772A CB7F       14110            BIT    7,A               ;TEST MOVE DOWN
772C 2003       14120            JR     NZ,DWNSCR         ;DOWN SCORE
772E 34         14130            INC    (HL)
772F 181A       14140            JR     DISSCR            ;DIS SCORE
7731 3A796F     14150 DWNSCR     LD     A,(OLDFRG+1)      ;TEST HOB
7734 FE40       14160            CP     40H               ;TEST FIRST BLOCK
7736 2009       14170            JR     NZ,TLHWY          ;TEST LOW HIGHWAY
7738 3A786F     14180            LD     A,(OLDFRG)
773B FEC0       14190            CP     0C0H              ;NOT EVEN STEP ON HWY
773D D8         14200            RET    C
773E 34         14210            INC    (HL)
773F 180A       14220            JR     DISSCR
7741 FE50       14230 TLHWY      CP     50H               ;TEST IN LOW HWY
7743 C0         14240            RET    NZ
7744 3A786F     14250            LD     A,(OLDFRG)
7747 FE20       14260            CP     20H
7749 D0         14270            RET    NC                ;NO SCORE IF STEP HWY
774A 34         14280            INC    (HL)
774B 0604       14290 DISSCR     LD     B,4               ;HL => TENTH'S POS
774D 7E         14300 ADDLOP     LD     A,(HL)
774E FE3A       14310 CRYLOP     CP     3AH               ;CARRY LOOP
7750 3807       14320            JR     C,UPDDIG          ;UPDATE DIGIT
7752 D60A       14330            SUB    10
7754 2B         14340            DEC    HL
7755 34         14350            INC    (HL)              ;CARRY
7756 23         14360            INC    HL
7757 18F5       14370            JR     CRYLOP
7759 77         14380 UPDDIG     LD     (HL),A
775A 2B         14390            DEC    HL
775B 10F0       14400            DJNZ   ADDLOP
775D 21446F     14410            LD     HL,SCORE+1
7760 CD6F77     14420            CALL   SCRIMG            ;SCORE IMAGE
7763 210640     14430            LD     HL,4006H
7766 11596F     14440            LD     DE,IMAGE
7769 0605       14450            LD     B,5
776B CD2873     14460            CALL   DISASC
776E C9         14470            RET
```

```
                 14480 ;
                 14490 ;
776F 11596F      14500 SCRIMG   LD      DE,IMAGE
7772 010500      14510          LD      BC,5
7775 EDB0        14520          LDIR
7777 21596F      14530          LD      HL,IMAGE
777A 013004      14540          LD      BC,0430H
777D 79          14550 PREZER   LD      A,C
777E BE          14560          CP      (HL)            ;TEST 30H
777F 2005        14570          JR      NZ,PREZEX
7781 3620        14580          LD      (HL),20H        ;SPACE FILL
7783 23          14590          INC     HL
7784 10F7        14600          DJNZ    PREZER
7786 C9          14610 PREZEX   RET
                 14620 ;
                 14630 ;
7787 3EBF        14640 SIREN    LD      A,0BFH
7789 DBFE        14650          IN      A,(0FEH)
778B E601        14660          AND     1
778D 2009        14670          JR      NZ,NSOUND
778F 3A736F      14680          LD      A,(SOUNDF)      ;RESET SOUND CONDITION
7792 3C          14690          INC     A
7793 E601        14700          AND     1
7795 32736F      14710          LD      (SOUNDF),A
7798 3A736F      14720 NSOUND   LD      A,(SOUNDF)
779B A7          14730          AND     A
779C 2825        14740          JR      Z,DELAY
779E 3A726F      14750          LD      A,(CHASE)       ;IS POLICE CAR ON
77A1 A7          14760          AND     A
77A2 281F        14770          JR      Z,DELAY
77A4 3A746F      14780          LD      A,(TONFLG)
77A7 3C          14790          INC     A
77A8 E601        14800          AND     1
77AA 32746F      14810          LD      (TONFLG),A
77AD 210D6F      14820          LD      HL,PCTON1
77B0 2803        14830          JR      Z,TONE1
77B2 21116F      14840          LD      HL,PCTON2
77B5 5E          14850 TONE1    LD      E,(HL)          ;DE=DURATION*FREQUENCY
77B6 23          14860          INC     HL
77B7 56          14870          LD      D,(HL)
77B8 23          14880          INC     HL
77B9 4E          14890          LD      C,(HL)
77BA 23          14900          INC     HL
77BB 46          14910          LD      B,(HL)
77BC C5          14920          PUSH    BC
77BD E1          14930          POP     HL              ;HL=437500/FREQ-30.125
77BE CDB503      14940          CALL    03B5H
77C1 F3          14950          DI                      ;03B5H ENABLE INTERRUPT
77C2 C9          14960          RET
77C3 010018      14970 DELAY    LD      BC,6144
77C6 0B          14980 WAIT     DEC     BC
77C7 78          14990          LD      A,B
77C8 B1          15000          OR      C
77C9 20FB        15010          JR      NZ,WAIT
77CB C9          15020          RET
                 15030 ;
```

```
                 15040 ;
77CC E5          15050 RANDNO  PUSH    HL
77CD C5          15060         PUSH    BC
77CE 2A756F      15070         LD      HL,(RND)
77D1 46          15080         LD      B,(HL)
77D2 23          15090         INC     HL
77D3 3E3F        15100         LD      A,3FH          ;BOUND POINTER WITHIN ROM
77D5 A4          15110         AND     H
77D6 67          15120         LD      H,A
77D7 78          15130         LD      A,B
77D8 22756F      15140         LD      (RND),HL
77DB C1          15150         POP     BC
77DC E1          15160         POP     HL
77DD C9          15170         RET
                 15180 ;
                 15190 ;
77DE 21446F      15200 OVER    LD      HL,SCORE+1     ;HIGH SCORE MANAGE
77E1 11546F      15210         LD      DE,HISCR
77E4 0605        15220         LD      B,5
77E6 1A          15230 SORTLP  LD      A,(DE)
77E7 BE          15240         CP      (HL)
77E8 2803        15250         JR      Z,SAMSCR       ;TEST 1ST NE DIGIT
77EA D0          15260         RET     NC
77EB 1805        15270         JR      SCRGT          ;UPDATE HIGH SCORE
77ED 13          15280 SAMSCR  INC     DE
77EE 23          15290         INC     HL
77EF 10F5        15300         DJNZ    SORTLP
77F1 C9          15310         RET
77F2 21446F      15320 SCRGT   LD      HL,SCORE+1
77F5 11546F      15330         LD      DE,HISCR
77F8 010500      15340         LD      BC,5
77FB EDB0        15350         LDIR
77FD C9          15360         RET
                 15370 ;
                 15380 ;
77FE 3E38        15390 FINAL   LD      A,56           ;SET WHITE BORDER
7800 32485C      15400         LD      (23624),A
7803 210040      15410         LD      HL,4000H       ;START OF SCREEN
7806 110140      15420         LD      DE,4001H
7809 01FF17      15430         LD      BC,6143        ;SIZE OF SCREEN
780C 3600        15440         LD      (HL),0
780E EDB0        15450         LDIR
7810 210058      15460         LD      HL,5800H       ;START OF ATTRIBUTE FILE
7813 110158      15470         LD      DE,5801H
7816 01FF02      15480         LD      BC,767
7819 3638        15490         LD      (HL),56        ;WHITE PAPER BLACK INK
781B EDB0        15500         LDIR
781D C9          15510         RET
                 15520 ;
                 15530 ;
6978             15540         END     START
00000 Total errors
```

APPENDIX A

SPECTRUM KEY INPUT TABLE

Input Value in A for ØFE H	D4	D3	D2	D1	DØ
ØFE H	V	C	X	Z	CAP SHIFT
ØFD H	G	F	D	S	A
ØFB H	7	R	E	W	Q
ØF7 H	5	4	3	2	1
ØEF H	6	7	8	9	Ø
ØDF H	Y	U	I	O	P
ØBF H	H	J	K	L	ENTER
Ø7F H	B	N	M	SYM SHIFT	BREAK SPACE
χ:	16	8	4	2	1

```
NB: To trap a key
    i.  Load A with INPUT VALUE of the corresponding row.
                LD  A,  07FH         ;Bottom Row
   ii.  Fetch from input port OFEH.
                IN  A,  (OFEH)
  iii.  Test Dx set to low for desired key.
                AND 1                ;trap BREAK/SPACE key
   iv.  If zero, then key is set.
                JR  Z,keyset         ;normal state is always
                                     ;high
```

APPENDIX B

MEMORY IN HEX	ATTRIBUTE IN HEX	LINE		MEMORY IN HEX	ATTRIBUTE IN HEX
4000	5800	0		401F	581F
4020	5820	1		403F	583F
4040	5840	2		405F	585F
4060	5860	3		407F	587F
4080	5880	4		409F	589F
40A0	58A0	5		40BF	58BF
40C0	58C0	6		40DF	58DF
40E0	58E0	7		40FF	58FF
4800	5900	8		481F	591F
4820	5920	9		483F	593F
4840	5940	10		485F	595F
4860	5960	11		487F	597F
4880	5980	12		489F	599F
48A0	59A0	13		48BF	59BF
48C0	59C0	14		48DF	59DF
48E0	59E0	15		48FF	59FF
5000	5A00	16		501F	5A1F
5020	5A20	17		503F	5A3F
5040	5A40	18		505F	5A5F
5060	5A60	19		507F	5A7F
5080	5A80	20		509F	5A9F
50A0	5AA0	21		50BF	5ABF
50C0	5AC0	22		50DF	5ADF
50E0	5AE0	23		50FF	5AFF

APPENCIX C

SPECTRUM CHARACTER SET TABLE

HEX	H0B	0	1	2	3	4	5	6	7
L0B	BITS	000	001	010	011	100	101	110	111
0	0000	NU	INK ctrl	SPACE	Ø	@	P	£	p
/	0001	NU	PAPER ctrl	!	1	A	Q	a	q
2	0010	NU	FLASH ctrl	"	2	B	R	b	r
3	0011	NU	BRIGHT ctrl	#	3	C	S	c	s
4	0100	NU	INVERSE ctrl	$	4	D	T	d	t
5	0101	Nu	OVER ctrl	%	5	E	U	e	u
6	0110	PRINT	AT ctrl	&	6	F	V	f	v
7	0111	EDIT	TAB ctrl	'	7	G	W	g	w
8	1000	cursor left	NU	(	8	H	X	h	x
9	1001	cursor right	NU	)	9	I	Y	i	y
A	1010	cursor down	NU	*	:	J	Z	j	z
B	1011	cursor up	NU	+	;	K	[	k	{
C	1100	DELETE	NU	,	<	L	\	l	¦
D	1101	ENTER	NU	—	=	M	]	m	}
E	1110	number	NU	.	>	N	↑	n	~
F	1111	NU	NU	/	?	O	—	o	©
		← NON PRINTABLE →		← PRINTABLE →					

NB: NU = Not Used.

APPENDIX D

DECIMAL HEXADECIMAL CONVERSION TABLES

HEX	0	1	2	3	4	5	6	7	8	9	A	B	C	D	E	F	00XX	XX00
0	0	1	2	3	4	5	6	7	8	9	10	11	12	13	14	15	0	0
1	16	17	18	19	20	21	22	23	24	25	26	27	28	29	30	31	256	4096
2	32	33	34	35	36	37	38	39	40	41	42	43	44	45	46	47	512	8192
3	48	49	50	51	52	53	54	55	56	57	58	59	60	61	62	63	768	12288
4	64	65	66	67	68	69	70	71	72	73	74	75	76	77	78	79	1024	16384
5	80	81	82	83	84	85	86	87	88	89	90	91	92	93	94	95	1280	20480
6	96	97	98	99	100	101	102	103	104	105	106	107	108	109	110	111	1536	24576
7	112	113	114	115	116	117	118	119	120	121	122	123	124	135	126	127	1792	28672
8	128	129	130	131	132	133	134	135	136	137	138	139	140	141	142	143	2048	32768
9	144	145	146	147	148	149	150	151	152	153	154	155	156	157	158	159	2304	36864
A	160	161	162	163	164	165	166	167	168	169	170	171	172	273	174	175	2560	40960
B	176	177	178	179	180	181	182	183	184	185	186	187	188	189	190	191	2816	45056
C	192	193	194	195	196	197	198	199	200	201	202	203	204	205	206	207	3072	49152
D	208	209	210	211	212	213	214	215	216	217	218	219	220	221	222	223	3328	53248
E	224	225	226	227	228	229	230	231	232	233	234	235	236	237	238	239	3584	57344
F	240	241	242	243	244	245	246	247	248	249	250	251	252	253	254	255	3840	61440

We can demonstrate using this table by working through an example.

Let's find the Hexadecimal equivalent of the decimal number 6200. We have to determine the 16-bit binary number;

```
    ie  bbbbbbbb    bbbbbbbb
          HOB          LOB
```

i. From the leftmost column of the table under the heading xx00, we find that 6200 is between 4096 and 8192. So we choose the lower value 4096 and from the row value, we take the most significant four bits of the HOB (High Order Byte) to be 1 ie 01.

```
        0001bbbb    bbbbbbbb
          HOB          LOB
```

ii. The second step is to determine the less significant four bits of the HOB. We find the difference of 6200 and 4096 to be 2104. Since the difference is still greater than 255, we refer to the second leftmost column of the table under the column heading 00xx and find that 2104 is between 2048 and 2304. Again we take the lower value 2048 and arrive from the row value that the less significant four bytes of HOB is 8 ie 1000.

```
        00011000    bbbbbbbb
          HOB          LOB
```

iii.The third step is to determine the LOB (Low Order Byte) for the number. We find the difference between 2104 and 2048 as 56. From the large middle big sub-table we find that 56 is at the intersection of row 3 and column 8. So we take the LOB as 38H.

```
        00011000    00111000
          HOB          LOB
```

So the HEX-value of the number 6200 is 1838H.

APPENDIX E

2's COMPLEMENT DECIMAL HEXADECIMAL CONVERSION TABLE

HEX	0	1	2	3	4	5	6	7	8	9	A	B	C	D	E	F
8	−128	−127	−126	−125	−124	−123	−122	− 121	−120	−119	−118	−117	−116	−115	−114	−113
9	−112	−111	−110	−109	−108	−107	−106	−105	−104	−103	−102	−101	−100	− 99	− 98	− 97
A	− 96	− 95	− 94	− 93	− 92	− 91	− 90	− 89	− 88	− 87	− 86	− 85	− 84	− 83	− 82	− 81
B	− 80	− 79	− 78	− 77	− 76	− 75	− 74	− 73	− 72	− 71	− 70	− 69	− 68	− 67	− 66	− 65
C	− 64	− 63	− 62	− 61	− 60	− 59	− 58	− 57	− 56	− 55	− 54	− 53	− 52	− 51	− 50	− 49
D	− 48	− 47	− 46	− 45	− 44	− 43	− 42	− 41	− 40	− 39	− 38	− 37	− 36	− 35	− 34	− 33
E	− 32	− 31	− 30	− 29	− 28	− 27	− 26	− 25	− 24	− 23	− 22	− 21	− 20	− 19	− 18	− 17
F	− 16	− 15	− 14	− 13	− 12	− 11	− 10	− 9	− 8	− 7	− 6	− 5	− 4	− 3	− 2	− 1

APPENDIX F

HEXADECIMAL ADDITION TABLE

+	0	1	2	3	4	5	6	7	8	9	A	B	C	D	E	F
0	0	1	2	3	4	5	6	7	8	9	A	B	C	D	E	F
1	1	2	3	4	5	6	7	8	9	A	B	C	D	E	F	10
2	2	3	4	5	6	7	8	9	A	B	C	D	E	F	10	11
3	3	4	5	6	7	8	9	A	B	C	D	E	F	10	11	12
4	4	5	6	7	8	9	A	B	C	D	E	F	10	11	12	13
5	5	6	7	8	9	A	B	C	D	E	F	10	11	12	13	14
6	6	7	8	9	A	B	C	D	E	F	10	11	12	13	14	15
7	7	8	9	A	B	C	D	E	F	10	11	12	13	14	15	16
8	8	9	A	B	C	D	E	F	10	11	12	13	14	15	16	17
9	9	A	B	C	D	E	F	10	11	12	13	14	15	16	17	18
A	A	B	C	D	E	F	10	11	12	13	14	15	16	17	18	19
B	B	C	D	E	F	10	11	12	13	14	15	16	17	18	19	1A
C	C	D	E	F	10	11	12	13	14	15	16	17	18	19	1A	1B
D	D	E	F	10	11	12	13	14	15	16	17	18	19	1A	1B	1C
E	E	F	10	11	12	13	14	15	16	17	18	19	1A	1B	1C	1D
F	F	10	11	12	13	14	15	16	17	18	19	1A	1B	1C	1D	1E

APPENDIX G

FLAG OPERATION SUMMARY TABLE

INSTRUCTION	C	Z	P/V	S	N	H	COMMENTS
ADC HL, SS	#	#	V	#	Ø	X	16-bit add with carry
ADX s; ADD s	#	#	V	#	Ø	#	8-bit add or add with carry
ADD DD, SS	#	—	—	—	Ø	X	16-bit add
AND s	Ø	#	P	#	Ø	1	Logical operations
BIT b, s	—	#	X	X	Ø	1	State of bit b of location s is copied into the Z flag
CCF	#	—	—	—	Ø	X	Complement carry
CPD; CPDR; CPI; CPIR	—	#	#	X	1	X	Block search instruction Z=1 if A=(HL), else Z=Ø P/V=1 if BC≠Ø, otherwise P/V=Ø
CP s	#	#	V	#	1	#	Compare accumulator
CPL	—	—	—	—	1	1	Complement accumulator
DAA	#	#	P	#	—	#	Decimal adjust accumulator
DEC s	—	#	V	#	1	#	8-bit decrement
IN r, (C)	—	#	P	#	Ø	Ø	Input register indirect
INC s	—	#	V	#	Ø	#	8-bit increment
IND; INI	—	#	X	X	1	X	Block input Z=Ø if B≠Ø else Z=1
INDR:INIR	—	1	X	X	1	X	Block input Z=Ø if B≠Ø else Z=1
LD A,I ; LD A,R	—	#	IFF	#	Ø	Ø	Content of interrupt enable Flip-Flop is copied into the P/V flag
LDD; LDI	—	X	#	X	Ø	Ø	Block transfer instructions
LDDR; LDIR	—	X	Ø	X	Ø	Ø	P/V=1 if BC≠Ø, otherwise P/V=Ø
NEG	#	#	V	#	1	#	Negate accumulator
OR s	Ø	#	P	#	Ø	Ø	Logical OR accumulator
OTDR; OTIR	—	1	X	X	1	X	Block output; Z=Ø if B≠Ø otherwise Z=1
OUTD; OUTI	—	#	X	X	1	X	Block output; Z=Ø if B≠Ø otherwise Z=1
RLA; RLCA; RRA; RRCA	#	—	—	—	Ø	Ø	Rotate accumulator
RLD; RRD	—	#	P	#	Ø	/	Rotate digit left and right
RLS; RLC s; RR s; RRC s SLA s; SRA s; SRL s	#	#	P	#	Ø	Ø	Rotate and shift location s
SBC HL, SS	#	#	V	#	1	X	16-bit subtract with carry
SCF	1	—	—	—	Ø	Ø	Set carry
SBC s; SUB s			V		1		8-bit subtract with carry
XOR x	Ø		P		Ø	Ø	Exclusive OR accumulator

Appendix G

SYMBOL	OPERATION
C	Carry flag. C=1 if the operation produced a carry from the most significant bit of the operand or result.
Z	Zero flag. Z=1 if the result of the operation is zero.
S	Sign flag. S=1 if the most significant bit of the result is one, ie a negative number.
P/V	Parity or overflow flag. Parity (P) and overflow (O) share the same flag. Logical operations affect this flag with the parity of the result while arithmetic operations affect this flag with the overflow of the result. If P/V holds parity, P/V=1 if the result of the operation is even, P/V=0 if result is odd. If P/V holds overflow, P/V=1 if the result of the operation produced an overflow.
H	Half-carry flag. H=1 if the add or subtract operation produced a carry into or borrow from bit 4 of the accumulator.
N	Add/Subtract flag. N=1 if the previous operations was a subtract. H and N flags are used in conjunction with the decimal adjust instruction (DAA) to properly correct the result into packed BCD format following addition or subtractionusing operands with packed BCD format.
#	The flag is affected according to the result of the operation.
-	The flag is unchanged by the operation.
0	The flag is reset (=0) by the operation.
1	The flag is set (=1) by the operation.
X	The flag result is unknown.
V	The P/V flag is affected according to the overflow result of the operation.
P	P/V flag is affected according to the parity result of the operation.
r	Any one of the CPU registers A,B,C,D,E,H,L.
s	Any 8-bit location for all the addressing modes allowed for the particular instructions.
SS	Any 16-bit location for all the addressing modes allowed for that instruction.
R	Refresh register
n	8-bit value in range 0-255.
nn	16-bit value in range 0-65535.

APPENDIX H

Z80—CPU INSTRUCTIONS SORTED BY OP-CODE

HEXADECIMAL	MNEMONIC	HEXADECIMAL	MNEMONIC	HEXADECIMAL	MNEMONIC
00	NOP	49	LD C,C	92	SUB D
01 XXXX	LD BC,NN	4A	LD C,D	93	SUB E
02	LD (BC),A	4B	LD C,E	94	SUB H
03	INC BC	4C	LD C,H	95	SUB L
04	INC B	4D	LD C,L	96	SUB (HL)
05	DEC B	4E	LD C,(HL)	97	SUB A
06XX	LD B,N	4F	LD C,A	98	SBC A,B
07	RLCA	50	LD D,B	99	SBC A,C
08	EX AF, AF'	51	LD D,C	9A	SBC A,D
09	ADD HL,BC	52	LD D,D	9B	SBC A,E
0A	LD A, (BC)	53	LD D,E	9C	SBC A,H
0B	DEC BC	54	LD D,H	9D	SBC A,L
0C	INC C	55	LD D,L	9E	SBC A,(HL)
0D	DEC C	56	LD D,(HL)	9F	SBC A,A
0EXX	LD C,N	57	LD D,A	A0	AND B
0F	RRCA	58	LD E,B	A1	AND C
10XX	DJNZ DIS	59	LD E,C	A2	AND D
11XXXX	LD DE,NN	5A	LD E,D	A3	AND E
12	LD (DE),A	5B	LD E,E	A4	AND H
13	INC DE	5C	LD E,H	A5	AND L
14	INC D	5D	LD E,L	A6	AND (HL)
15	DEC D	5E	LD E,(HL)	A7	AND A
16XX	LD D,N	5F	LD E,A	A8	XOR B
17	RLA	60	LD H,B	A9	XOR C
18XX	JR DIS	61	LD H,C	AA	XOR D
19	ADD HL,DE	62	LD H,D	AB	XOR E
1A	LD A,(DE)	63	LD H,E	AC	XOR H
1B	DEC DE	64	LD H,H	AD	XOR L
1C	INC E	65	LD H,L	AE	XOR (HL)
1D	DEC E	66	LD H,(HL)	AF	XOR A
1EXX	LD E,N	67	LD H,A	B0	OR B
1F	RRA	68	LD L,B	B1	OR C
20XX	JR NZ,DIS	69	LD L,C	B2	OR D
21XXXX	LD HL,NN	6A	LD L,D	B3	OR E
22XXXX	LD (NN),HL	6B	LD L,E	B4	OR H
23	INC HL	6C	LD L,H	B5	OR L
24	INC H	6D	LD L,L	B6	OR (HL)
25	DEC H	6E	LD L,(HL)	B7	OR A
26XX	LD H,N	6F	LD L,A	B8	CP B
27	DAA	70	LD (HL),B	B9	CP C
28XX	JR Z,DIS	71	LD (HL),C	BA	CP D
29	ADD HL,HL	72	LD (HL),D	BB	CP E
2AXXXX	LD HL,(NN)	73	LD (HL),E	BC	CP H
2B	DEC HL	74	LD (HL),H	BD	CP L
2C	INC L	75	LD (HL),L	BE	CP (HL)
2D	DEC L	76	HALT	BF	CP A
2EXX	LD L,N	77	LD (HL),A	C0	RET NZ
2F	CPL	78	LD A,B	C1	POP BC
30XX	JR NC,DIS	79	LD A,C	C2XXXX	JP NZ,NN
31XXXX	LD SP,NN	7A	LD A,D	C3XXXX	JP NN
32XXXX	LD (NN),A	7B	LD A,E	C4XXXX	CALL NZ,NN
33	INC SP	7C	LD A,H	C5	PUSH BC
34	INC (HL)	7D	LD A,L	C6XX	ADD A,N
35	DEC (HL)	7E	LD A,(HL)	C7	RST 0
36XX	LD (HL),N	7F	LD A,A	C8	RET Z
37	SCF	80	ADD A,B	C9	RET
38XX	JR C,DIS	81	ADD A,C	CAXXXX	JP Z.NN
39	ADD HL,SP	82	ADD A,D	CCXXXX	CALL Z,NN
3AXXXX	LD A,(NN)	83	ADD A,E	CDXXXX	CALL NN
3B	DEC SP	84	ADD A,H	CEXX	ADC A,N
3C	INC A	85	ADD A,L	CF	RST 8
3D	DEC A	86	ADD A,(HL)	D0	RET NC
3EXX	LD A,N	87	ADD A,A	D1	POP DE
3F	CCF	88	ADC A,B	D2XXXX	JP NC,NN
40	LD B,B	89	ADC A,C	D3XX	OUT (N),A
41	LD B,C	8A	ADC A,D	D4XXXX	CALL NC,NN
42	LD B,D	8B	ADC A,E	D5	PUSH DE
43	LD B,E	8C	ADC A,H	D6XX	SUB N
44	LD B,H,	8D	ADC A,L	D7	RST 10H
45	LD B,L	8E	ADC A,(HL)	D8	RET C
46	LD B,(HL)	8F	ADC A,A	D9	EXX
47	LD B,A	90	SUB B	DAXXXX	JP C,NN
48	LD C,B	91	SUB C	DBXX	IN A,(N)

HEXADECIMAL	MNEMONIC	HEXADECIMAL	MNEMONIC	HEXADECIMAL	MNEMONIC
DCXXXX	CALL C,NN	CB28	SRA B	CB79	BIT 7,C
DEXX	SBC A,N	CB29	SRA C	CB7A	BIT 7,D
DF	RST 18H	CB2A	SRA D	CB7B	BIT 7,E
E0	RET PO	CB2B	SRA E	CB7C	BIT 7,H
E1	POP HL	CB2C	SRA H	CB7D	BIT 7,L
E2XXXX	JP PO,NN	CB2D	SRA L	CB7E	BIT 7,(HL)
E3	EX (SP),HL	CB2E	SRA (HL)	CB7F	BIT 7,A
E4XXXX	CALL PO,NN	CB2F	SRA A	CB80	RES 0,B
E5	PUSH HL	CB38	SRL B	CB81	RES 0,C
E6XX	AND N	CB39	SRL C	CB82	RES 0,D
E7	RST 20 H	CB3A	SRL D	CB83	RES 0,E
E8	RET PE	CB3B	SRL E	CB84	RES 0,H
E9	JP (HL)	CB3C	SRL H	CB85	RES 0,L
EAXXXX	JE PE NN	CB3D	SRL L	CB86	RES 0,(HL)
EB	EX DE,HL	CB3E	SRL (HL)	CB87	RES 0,A
ECXXXX	CALL PE,NN	CB3F	SRL A	CB88	RES 1,B
EEXX	XOR N	CB40	BIT 0,B	CB89	RES 1,C
EF	RST 28H	CB41	BIT 0,C	CB8A	RES 1,D
F0	RET P	CB42	BIT 0,D	CB8B	RES 1,E
F1	POP AF	CB43	BIT 0,E	CB8C	RES 1,H
F2XXXX	JR P,NN	CB44	bit 0,H	CB8D	RES 1,L
F3	DI	CB45	BIT 0,L	CB8E	RES 1,(HL)
F4XXXX	CALL P,NN	CB46	BIT 0,(HL)	CB8F	RES 1,A
F5	PUSH AF	CB47	BIT 0,A	CB90	RES 2,B
F620XX	OR N	CB48	Bit 1.B	CB91	RES 2,C
F7	RST 30H	CB49	BIT 1,C	CB92	RES 2,D
F8	RET M	CB4A	BIT 1,D	CB93	RES 2,E
F9	LD,SP,HL	CB4B	BIT 1,E	CB94	RES 2,H
FAXXXX	JPM,NN	CB4C	BIT 1,H	CB95	RES 2,L
FB	EI	CB4D	BIT 1,L	CB96	RES 2,(HL)
FCXXXX	CALL M,NN	CB4E	BIT 1,(HL)	CB97	RES 2,A
FE20XX	CP N	CB4F	BIT 1,A	CB98	RES 3,B
FF	RST 38H	CB50	BIT 2,B	CB99	RES 3,C
CB00	RLC B	CB51	BIT 2,C	CB9A	RES 3,D
CB01	RLC C	CB52	BIT 2,D	CB9B	RES 3,E
CB02	RLC D	CB53	BIT 2,E	CB9C	RES e,H
CB03	RLC E	CB54	BIT 2,H	CB9D	RES 3,L
CB04	RLC H	CB55	BIT 2,L	CB9E	RES 3,(HL)
CB05	RLC L	CB56	BIT 2,(HL)	CB9F	RES 3,A
CB06	RLC (HL)	CB57	BIT 2,A	CBA0	RES 4,B
CB07	RLC A	CB58	BIT 3,B	CBA1	RES 4,C
CB08	RRC B	CB59	BIT 3,C	CBA2	RES 4,D
CB09	RRC C	CB5A	BIT 3,D	CBA3	RES e,E
CB0A	RRC D	CB5B	BIT 3,E	CBA4	RES e,H
CB0B	RRC E	CB5C	BIT 3,H	CBA5	RES 4,L
CB0C	RRC H	CB5D	BIT 3,L	CBA6	RES 4,(HL)
CB0D	RRC L	CB5E	BIT 3,(HL)	CBA7	RES 4,A
CB0E	RRC (HL)	CB5F	BIT 3,A	CBA8	RES 5,B
CB0F	RRC A	CB60	BIT 4,B	CBA9	RES 5,C
CB10	RL B	CB61	BIT 4,C	CBAA	RES 5,D
CB11	RL C	CB62	BIT 4,D	CBAB	RES 5,E
CB12	RL D	CB63	BIT 4,E	CBAC	RES 5,H
CB13	RL E	CB64	BIT 4,H	CBAD	RES 5,L
CB14	RL H	CB65	BIT 4,L	CBAE	RES 5,(HL)
CB15	RL L	CB66	BIT 4,(HL)	CBAF	RES 5,A
CB16	RL (HL)	CB67	BIT 4,A	CBB0	RES 6,B
CB17	RL A	CB68	BIT 5,B	CBB1	RES 6,C
CB18	RR B	CB69	BIT 5,C	CBB2	RES 6,D
CB19	RR C	CB6A	BIT 5,D	CBB3	RES 6,E
CB1A	RR D	CB6B	BIT 5,E	CBB4	RES 6,H
CB1B	RR E	CB6C	BIT 5,H	CBB5	RES 6,L
CB1C	RR H	CB6D	BIT 5,L	CBB6	RES 6,(HL)
CB1D	RR L	CB6E	BIT 5,(HL)	CBB7	RES 7,A
CB1E	RR (HL)	CB6F	BIT 5,A	CBB8	RES 7,B
CB1F	RR A	CB70	BIT 6,B	CBB9	RES 7,C
CB20	SLA B	CB71	BIT 6,C	CBBA	RES 7,D
CB21	SLA C	CB72	BIT 6,D	CBBB	RES 7,E
CB22	SLA D	CB73	BIT 6,E	CBBC	RES 7,H
CB23	SLA E	CB74	BIT 6,H	CBBD	RES 7,L
CB24	SLA H	CB75	BIT 6,L	CBBE	RES 7,(HL)
CB25	SLA L	CB76	BIT 6,(HL)	CBBF	RES 7,A
CB26	SLA (HL)	CB77	BIT 6,A	CBC0	SET 0,B
CB27	SLA A	CB78	BIT 7,B	CBC1	SET 0,C
				CBC2	SET 0,D

HEXADECIMAL	MNEMONIC	HEXADECIMAL	MNEMONIC	HEXADECIMAL	MNEMONIC
CBC3	SET 0,E	DD4EXX	LD C,(IX+d)	ED53XXXX	LD(NN),DE
CBC4	SET 0,H	DD56XX	LD D,(IX+d)	ED56	IN 1
CBC5	SET 0,L	DD5EXX	LD E,(IX+d)	ED57	LD A,1
CBC6	SET 0,(HL)	DD66XX	LD H,(IX+d)	ED58	IN E,(C)
CBC7	SET 0,A	DD6EXX	LD L,(IX+d)	ED59	OUT (C),E
CBC8	SET 1,B	DD70XX	LD (IX+d),B	ED5A	ADC HL,DE
CBC9	SET 1,C	DD71XX	LD (IX+d),C	ED5BXXXX	LD DE,(NN)
CBCA	SET 1,D	DD72XX	LD (IX+d),D	ED5E	IM 2
CBCB	SET 1,E	DD73XX	LD (IX+d),E	ED5F	LD A,R
CBCC	SET 1,H	DD74XX	LD (IX+d),H	ED60	IN H,(C)
CBCD	SET 1,L	DD75XX	LD (IX+d),L	ED61	OUT(C),H
CBCE	SET 1,(HL)	DD77XX	LD (IX+d),A	ED62	SBC HL,HL
CBCF	SET 1,A	DD7EXX	LD A,(IX+d)	ED63XXXX	LD(NN),HL
CBD0	SET 2,B	DD86XX	ADD A,(IX+d)	ED67	RRD
CBD1	SET 2,C	DD8EXX	ADC A,(IX+d)	ED68	IN L,(C)
CBD2	SET 2,D	DD96XX	SUB(IX+d)	ED69	OUT(C),L
CBD3	SET 2,E	DD9EXX	SBC A,(IX+d)	ED6A	ADC HL,HL
CBD4	SET 2,H	DDA6XX	AND(IX+d)	ED6BXXXX	LDHL, (ADDR)
CBD5	SET 2,L	DDAEXX	XOR(IX+d)	ED6F	RLD
CBD6	SET 2,(HL)	DDB6XX	OR(IX+d)	ED72	SBC HL,SP
CBD7	SET 2,A	DDBEXX	CP(IX+d)	ED73XXXX	LD(NN),SP
CBD8	SET 3,B	DDE1	POP IX	ED78	IN A,(C)
CBD9	SET 3,C	DDE3	EX(SP),IX	ED79	OUT(C),A
CBDA	SET 3,D	DDE5	PUSH IX	ED7A	ADC HL,SP
CBDB	SET 3,E	DDE9	JP(IX)	ED7BXXXX	LD SP,(NN)
CBDC	SET 3,H	DDF9	LD SP,IX	EDA0	LDI
CBDD	SET 3,L	DDCBXX06	RLC(IX+d)	EDA1	CPI
CBDE	SET 3,(HL)	DDCBXX0E	RRC(IX+d)	EDA2	INI
CBDF	SET 3,A	DDCBXX16	RL(IX+d)	EDA3	OUTI
CBE0	SET 4,B	DDCBXX1E	RR(IX+d)	EDA8	LDD
CBE1	SET 4,C	DDCBXX26	SLA(IX+d)	EDA9	CPD
CBE2	SET 4,D	DDCBXX2E	SRA(IX+d)	EDAA	IND
CBE3	SET 4,E	DDCBXX3E	SRL(IX+d)	EDAB	OUTD
CBE4	SET 4,H	DDCBXX46	BIT 0,(IX+d)	EDB0	LDIR
CBE5	SET 4,L	DDCBXX4E	BIT 1,(IX+d)	EDB1	CPIR
CBE6	SET 4,(HL)	DDCBXX56	BIT 2,(IX+d)	EDB2	INIR
CBE7	SET 4,A	DDCBXX5E	BIT 3,(IX+d)	EDB3	OTIR
CBE8	SET 5,B	DDCBXX66	BIT 4,(IX+d)	EDB8	LDDR
CBE9	SET 5,C	DDCBXX6E	BIT 5,(IX+d)	EDB9	CPDR
CBEA	SET 5,D	DDCBXX76	BIT 6,(IX+d)	EDBA	INDR
CBEB	SET 5,E	DDCBXX7E	BIT 7,(IX+d)	EDBB	OTDR
CBEC	SET 5,H	DDCBXX86	RES 0,(IX+d)	ED09	ADD IY,BC
CBED	SET 5,L	DDCBXX8E	RES 1,(IX+d)	ED19	ADD IY,DE
CBEE	SET 5,(HL)	DDCBXX96	RES 2,(IX+d)	ED21XXXX	LD IY,NN
CBEF	SET 5,A	DDCBXX9E	RES 3,(IX+d)	FD22XXXX	LD(NN),IY
CBF0	SET 6,B	DDCBXXA6	RES 4,(IX+d)	FD23	INC IY
CBF1	SET 6,C	DDCBXXAE	RES 5,(IX+d)	FD29	ADD IY,IY
CBF2	SET 6,D	DDCBXXB6	RES 6,(IX+d)	FD2AXXXX	LD IY,(NN)
CBF3	SET 6,E	DDCBXXBE	RES 7,(IX+d)	FD2B	DEC IY
CBF4	SET 6,H	DDCBXXC6	SET 0,(IX+d)	FD34XX	INC(IY+d)
CBF5	SET 6,L	DDCBXXCE	SET 1,(IX+d)	FD35XX	DEC(IY+d)
CBF6	SET 6,(HL)	DDCBXXD6	SET 2,(IX+d)	FD36XX20	LD(IY+d),N
CBF7	SET 6,A	DDCBXXDE	SET 3,(IX+d)	FD39	ADD IY,SP
CBF8	SET 7,B	DDCBXXE6	SET 4,(IX+d)	FD46XX	LD B,(IY+d)
CBF9	SET 7,C	DDCBXXEE	SET 5,(IX+d)	FD3EXX	LD C,(IY+d)
CBFA	SET 7,D	DDCBXXF6	SET 6,(IX+d)	FD56XX	LD D,(IY+d)
CBFB	SET 7,E	DDCBXXFE	SET 7,(IX+d)	FD5EXX	LD E,(IY+d)
CBFC	SET 7,H	ED40	IN B,(C)	FD66XX	LD H,(IY+d)
CBFD	SET 7,L	ED41	OUT(C),B	FD6EXX	LD L,(IY+d)
CBFE	SET 7,(HL)	ED42	SBC HL,BC	FD70XX	LD (IY+d),B
CBFF	SET 7,A	ED43XXXX	LD(NN),BC	FD71XX	LD (IY+d),C
DD09	ADD IX,BC	ED44	NEG	FD72XX	LD (IY+d),D
DD19	ADD IX,DE	ED45	RETN	FD73XX	LD (IY+d),E
DD21XXXX	LD IX,NN	ED46	IM 0	FD74XX	LD (IY+d),H
DD22XXXX	LD(NN),IX	ED47	LD I,A	FD75XX	LD (IY+d),L
DD23	INC IX	ED48	IN C,(C)	FD77XX	LD (IY+d),A
DD29	ADD IX,IX	ED49	OUT(C) ,C	FD7EXX	LD A,(IY+d)
DD2AXXXX	LD IX,(NN)	ED4A	ADC HL,BC	FD86XX	ADD A,(IY+d)
DD2B	DEC IX	ED4BXXXX	LD BC,(NN)	FD8EXX	ADC A,(IY+d)
DD34XX	INC(IX+d)	ED4D	RET I	FD96XX	SUB(IY+d)
DD35XX	DEC(IX+d)	ED4F	LD R,A	FD9EXX	SBC A,(IY+d)
DD36XX20	LD(IX+d),N	ED50	IN D,(C)	FDA6XX	AND (IY+d)
DD39	ADD IX,SP	ED51	OUT(C),D	FDAEXX	XOR (IY+d)
DD46XX	LD B,(IX+d)	ED52	SBC HL,DE	FDB6XX	OR (IY+d)

HEXADECIMAL	MNEMONIC	HEXADECIMAL	MNEMONIC	HEXADECIMAL	MNEMONIC
FDBEXX	CP (IY+d)				
FDE1	POP IY				
FDE3	EX (SP), IY				
FDE5	PUSH IY				
FDE9	JP (IY)				
FDF9	LD SP,IY				
FDCBXX06	RLC(IY+d)				
FDCBXX0E	RRC(IY+d)				
FDCBXX16	RL(IY+d)				
FDCBXX1E	RR(IY+d)				
FDCBXX26	SLA(IY+d)				
FDCBXX2E	SRA(IY+d)				
FDCBXX3E	SRL(IY+d)				
FDCBXX46	BIT 0,(IY+d)				
FDCBXX4E	BIT 1,(IY+d)				
FDCBXX56	BIT 2,(IY+d)				
FDCBXX5E	BIT 3,(IY+d)				
FDCBXX66	BIT 4,(IY+d)				
FDCBXX6E	BIT 5,(IT+d)				
FDCBXX76	BIT 6,(IY+d)				
FDCBXX7E	BIT 7,(IY+d)				
FDCBXX86	RES 0,(IY+d)				
FDCBXX8E	RES 1,(IY+d)				
FDCBXX96	RES 2,(IY+d)				
FDCBXX9E	RES 3,(IY+d)				
FDCBXXA6	RES 4,(IY+d)				
FDCBXXAE	RES 5,(IY+d)				
FDCBXXB6	RES 6,(IY+d)				
FDCBXXBE	RES 7,(IY+d)				
FDCBXXC6	SET 0,(IY+d)				
FDCBXXCE	SET 1,(IY+d)				
FDCBXXD6	SET 2,(IY+d)				
FDCBXXDE	SET 3,(IY+d)				
FDCBXXE6	SET 4,(IY+d)				
FDCBXXEE	SET 5,(IY+d)				
FDCBXXF6	SET 6,(IY+d)				
FDCBXXFE	SET 7,(IY+d)				

APPENDIX I

Z80–CPU INSTRUCTIONS SORTED BY MNEMONIC

MNEMONIC	HEXADECIMAL	MNEMONIC	HEXADECIMAL	MNEMONIC	HEXADECIMAL
ADC A, (HL)	8E	BIT 2,B	CB 50	CP n	FE XX
ADC A, (IX+dis)	DD 8E XX	BIT 2,C	CB 51	CP E	BB
ADC A,(IY+dis)	FD 8E xx	BIT 2,D	CB 52	CP H	BC
ADC A,A	8F	BIT 2,E	CB 53	CP L	BD
ADC A,B	88	BIT 2,H	CB 54	CPD	ED A9
ADC A,C	89	BIT 2,L	CB 55	CPDR	ED B9
ADC A,D	8A	BIT 3,(HL)	CB 5E	CPI	ED A1
ADC A,n	CE XX	BIT 3,(IX+dis)	DD CB XX 5E	CPIR	ED B1
ADC A,E	8B	BIT 3,(IY+dis)	FD CB XX 5E	CPL	2F
ADC A,H	8C	BIT 3,A	CB 5F	DAA	27
ADC A,L	8D	BIT 3,B	CB 58	DEC (HL)	35
ADC HL,BC	ED 4A	BIT 3,C	CB 59	DEC (IX+dis)	DD 35 XX
ADC HL,DE	ED 5A	BIT 3,D	CB 5A	DEC (IY+dis)	FD 35 XX
ADC HL,HL	ED 6A	BIT 3,E	CB 5B	DEC A	3D
ADC HL,SP	ED 7A	BIT 3,H	CB 5C	DEC B	05
ADD A, (HL)	86	BIT 3,L	CB 5D	DEC BC	0B
ADD A,(IX+dis)	DD 86XX	BIT 4,(HL)	CB 66	DEC C	0D
ADD A,(IY+dis)	FD 86XX	BIT 4,(IX+dis)	DD CB XX 66	DEC D	15
ADD A,A	87	BIT 4,(IY+dis)	FD CB XX 66	DEC DE	1B
ADD A,B	80	BIT 4,A	CB 67	DEC E	1D
ADD A,C	81	BIT 4,B	CB 60	DEC H	25
ADD A,D	82	BIT 4,C	CB 61	DEC HL	2B
ADD A,n	C6 XX	BIT 4,D	CB 62	DEC IX	DD 2B
ADD A,E	83	BIT 4,E	CB 63	DEC IY	FD 2B
ADD A,H	84	BIT 4,H	CB 64	DEC L	2D
ADD A,L	85	BIT 4,L	CB 65	DEC SP	3B
ADD HL,BC	09	BIT 5,(HL)	CB 6E	DI	F3
ADD HL,DE	19	BIT 5,(IX+dis)	DD CB XX 6E	DJNZ,dis	10 XX
ADD HL,HL	29	BIT 5,(IY+dis)	FD CB XX 6E	EI	FB
ADD HL,SP	39	BIT 5,A	CB 6F	EX (SP) ,HL	E3
ADD IX,BC	DD 09	BIT 5,B	CB 68	EX (SP) ,IX	DD E3
ADD IX,DE	DD 19	BIT 5,C	CB 69	EX (SP) ,IY	FD E3
ADD IX,IX	DD 29	BIT 5,D	CB 6A	EX AF,AF'	08
ADD IX,SP	DD 39	BIT 5,E	CB 6B	EX DE,HL	EB
ADD IY,BC	FD 09	BIT 5,H	CB 6C	EXX	D9
ADD IY,DE	FD 19	BIT 5,L	CB 6D	HALT	76
ADD IY,IY	FD 29	BIT 6,(HL)	CB 76	IM 0	ED 46
ADD IY,SP	FD 39	BIT 6,(IX+dis)	DD CB XX 76	IM 1	ED 56
AND (HL)	A6	BIT 6,(IY+dis)	FD CB XX 76	IM 2	ED 5E
AND (IX+dis)	DD A6 XX	BIT 6,A	CB 77	IN A, (C)	ED 78
AND (IY+dis)	FD A6 XX	BIT 6,B	CB 70	IN A,port	DB XX
AND A	A7	BIT 6,C	CB 71	IN B, (C)	ED 40
AND B	A0	BIT 6,D	CB 72	IN C, (C)	ED 48
AND C	A1	BIT 6,E	CB 73	IN D, (C)	ED 50
AND D	A2	BIT 6,H	CB 74	IN E, (C)	ED 58
AND n	E6 XX	BIT 6,L	CB 75	IN H, (C)	ED 60
AND E	A3	BIT 7,(HL)	CB 7E	IN L, (C)	ED 68
AND H	A4	BIT 7,(IX+dis)	DD CB XX 7E	INC (HL)	34
AND L	A5	BIT 7,(IY+dis)	FD CB XX 7E	INC (IX+dis)	DD 34 XX
BIT 0,(HL)	CB 46	BIT 7,A	CB 7F	INC (IY+dis)	FD 34 XX
BIT 0,(IX+dis)	DD CB XX 46	BIT 7,B	CB 78	INC A	3C
BIT 0,(IY+dis)	FD CB XX 46	BIT 7,C	CB 79	INC B	04
BIT 0,A	CB 47	BIT 7,D	CB 7A	INC BC	03
BIT o,B	CB 40	BIT 7,E	CB 7B	INC C	0C
BIT 0,C	CB 41	BIT 7,H	CB 7C	INC D	14
BIT 0,D	CB 42	BIT 7,L	CB 7D	INC DE	13
BIT 0,E	CB 43	CALL ADDR	CD XX XX	INC E	1C
BIT 0,H	CB 44	CALL C,ADDR	DC XX XX	INC H	24
BIT 0,L	CB 45	CALL M,ADDR	FC XX XX	INC HL	23
BIT 1,(HL)	CB 4E	CALL NC,ADDR	D4 XX XX	INC IX	DD 23
BIT 1,(IX+dis)	DD CB XX 4E	CALL NZ,ADDR	C4 XX XX	INC IY	FD 23
BIT 1,(IY+dis)	FD CB XX 4E	CALL P,ADDR	F4 XX XX	INC L	2C
BIT 1,A	CB 4F	CALL PE,ADDR	EC XX XX	INC SP	33
BIT 1,B	CB 48	CALL PO,ADDR	E4 XX XX	IND	ED AA
BIT 1,C	CB 49	CALL Z,ADDR	CC XX XX	INDR	ED BA
BIT 1,D	CB 4A	CCF	3F	INI	ED A2
BIT 1,E	CB 4B	CP (HL)	BE	INIR	ED B2
BIT 1,H	CB 4C	CP (IX+dis)	DD BE XX	JP (HL)	E9
BIT 1,L	CB 4D	CP (IY+dis)	FD BE XX	JP (IX)	DD E9
BIT 2,(HL)	CB 56	CP A	BF	JP (IY)	FD E9
BIT 2,(IX+dis)	DD CB XX 56	CP B	B8	JP ADDR	C3 XX XX
BIT 2,(IY+dis)	FD CB XX 56	CP C	B9	JP C,ADDR	DA XX XX
BIT 2,A	CB 57	CP D	BA	JP M,ADDR	FA XX XX

MNEMONIC	HEXADECIMAL
JP NC,ADDR	D2 XX XX
JP NZ,ADDR	C2 XX XX
JP P,ADDR	F2 XX XX
JP PE,ADDR	EA XX XX
JP PO,ADDR	E2 XX XX
JP Z,ADDR	CA XX XX
JR C,dis	38 XX
JR dis	18 XX
JR NC,dis	30 XX
JR NZ,dis	20 XX
JR Z,dis	28 XX
LD (ADDR) ,A	32 XX XX
LD(ADDR) ,BC	ED 43 XX XX
LD (ADDR) ,DE	ED 53 XX XX
LD(ADDR) ,HL	ED 63 XX XX
LD (ADDR) ,HL	22 XX XX
LD (ADDR) ,IX	DD 22 XX XX
LD (ADDR) , IY	FD 22 XX XX
LD (ADDR) ,SP	ED 73 XX XX
LD (BC) ,A	02
LD (DE) ,A	12
LD (HL) ,A	77
LD (HL) ,B	70
LD (HL), C	71
LD (HL) ,D	72
LD (HL) ,n	36 XX
LD (HL) ,E	73
LD (HL) ,H	74
LD (HL) ,L	75
LD (IX+dis) ,A	DD 77 XX
LD (IX+dis) ,B	DD 70 XX
LD (IX+dis) ,C	DD 71 XX
LD (IX+dis) ,D	DD 72 XX
LD (IX+dis) ,n	DD 36 XX XX
LD (IX+dis) ,E	DD 73 XX
LD (IX+dis) ,H	DD 74 XX
LD (IX+dis) ,L	DD 75 XX
LD (IY+dis) ,A	FD 77 XX
LD (IY+dis) ,B	FD 70 XX
LD (IY+dis) ,C	FD 71 XX
LD (IY+dis) ,D	FD 72 XX
LD (IY+dis) ,n	FD 36 XX XX
LD (IY+dis) ,E	FD 73 XX
LD (IY+dis) ,H	FD 74 XX
LD (IY+dis) ,L	FD 75 XX
LD A, (ADDR)	3A XX XX
LD A, (BC)	0A
LD A, (DE)	1A
LD A, (HL)	7E
LD A, (IX+dis)	DD 7E XX
LD A, (IY+dis)	FD 7E XX
LD A,A	7F
LD A,B	78
LD A,C	79
LD A,D	7A
LD A,n	3E XX
LD A,E	7B
LD A,H	7C
LD A,I	ED 57
LD A,L	7D
LD A,R	ED 5F
LD B, (HL)	46
LD B, (IX+dis)	DD 46 XX
LD B, (IY+dis)	FD 46 XX
LD B,A	47
LD B,B	40
LD B,C	41
LD B,D	42
LD B,n	06 XX
LD B,E	43
LD B,H	44
LD B,L	45
LD BC, (ADDR)	ED 4B XX XX

MNEMONIC	HEXADECIMAL
LD BC,nn	01 XX XX
LD C, (HL)	4E
LD C, (IX+dis)	DD 4E xx
LD C, (IY+dis)	FD 4E XX
LD C,A	4F
LD C,B	48
LD C,C	49
LD C,D	4A
LD C,n	0E XX
LD C,E	4B
LD C,H	4C
LD C,L	4D
LD D, (HL)	56
LD D, (IX+dis)	DD 56 XX
LD D, (IY+dis)	FD 56 XX
LD D,A	57
LD D,B	50
LD D,C	51
LD D,D	52
LD D,n	16 XX
LD D,E	53
LD D,H	54
LD D,L	55
LD DE, (ADDR)	ED 5B XX XX
LD DE,nn	11 XX XX
LD E, (HL)	5E
LD E, (IX+dis)	DD 5E XX
LD E, (IY+dis)	FD 5E XX
LD E,A	5F
LD E,B	58
LD E,C	59
LD E,D	5A
LD E,n	1E XX
LD E,E	5B
LD E,H	5C
LD E,L	5D
LD H, (HL)	66
LD H, (IX+dis)	DD 66 XX
LD H, (IY+dis)	FD 66 XX
LD H,A	67
LD H,B	60
LD H,C	61
LD H,D	62
LD H,n	26 XX
LD H,E	63
LD H,H	64
LD H,L	65
LD HL, (ADDR)	ED 6B XX XX
LD HL,(ADDR)	2A XX XX
LD HL,nn	21 XX XX
LD I,A	ED 47
LD IX, (ADDR)	DD 2A XX XX
LD IX,nn	DD 21 XX XX
LD IY (ADDR)	FD 2A XX XX
LD IY,nn	FD 21 XX XX
LD L,A	6F
LD L,B	68
LD L,C	69
LD L,D	6A
LD L,n	2E XX
LD L,E	6B
LD L, (HL)	6E
LD L,(IX+dis)	DD 6E XX
LD L, (IY+dis)	FD 6E XX
LD L,H	6C
LD L,L	6D
LD R,A	ED 4F
LD SP, (ADDR)	ED 7B XX XX
LD SP,nn	31 XX XX
LD SP,HL	F9
LD SP,IX	DD F9
LD SP,IY	FD F9
LDD	ED A8

MNEMONIC	HEXADECIMAL
LDDR	ED B8
LDI	ED A0
LDIR	ED B0
NEG	ED 44
NOP	00
OR (HL)	B6
OR (IX+dis)	DD B6 XX
OR (IY+dis)	FD B6 xx
OR A	B7
OR B	B0
OR C	B1
OR D	B2
OR n	F6 XX
OR E	B3
OR H	B4
OR L	B5
OTDR	ED BB
OTIR	ED B3
OUT (C) ,A	ED 79
OUT (C) ,B	ED 41
OUT (C) ,C	ED 49
OUT (C) ,D	ED 51
OUT (C) ,E	ED 59
OUT (C) ,H	ED 61
OUT (C) ,L	ED 69
OUT part,A	D3 port
OUTD	ED AB
OUTI	ED A3
POP AF	F1
POP BC	C1
POP DE	D1
POP HL	E1
POP IX	DD E1
POP IY	FD E1
PUSH AF	F5
PUSH BC	C5
PUSH DE	D5
PUSH HL	E5
PUSH IX	DD E5
PUSH IY	FD E5
RES 0, (HL)	CB 86
RES 0, (IX+dis)	DD CB XX 86
RES 0, (IY+dis)	FD CB XX 86
RES 0,A	CB 87
RES 0,B	CB 80
RES 0,C	CB 81
RES 0,D	CB 82
RES 0,E	CB 83
RES 0,H	CB 84
RES 0,L	CB 85
RES 1, (HL)	CB 8E
RES 1, (IX+dis)	DD CB XX 8E
RES 1, (IY+dis)	FD CB XX 8E
RES 1,A	CB 8F
RES 1,B	CB 88
RES 1,C	CB 89
RES 1,D	CB 8A
RES 1,E	CB 8B
RES 1,H	CB 8C
RES 1,L	CB 8D
RES 2, (HL)	CB 96
RES 2, (IX+dis)	DD CB XX 96
RES 2, (IY+dis)	FD CB XX 96
RES 2,A	CB 97
RES 2,B	CB 90
RES 2,C	CB 91
RES 2,D	CB 92
RES 2,E	CB 93
RES 2,H	CB 94
RES 2,L	CB 95
RES 3, (HL)	CB 9E
RES 3, (IX+dis)	DD CB XX 9E
RES 3, (IY+dis)	FD CB XX 9E
RES 3,A	CB 9F

MNEMONIC	HEXADECIMAL
RES 3,B	CB 98
RES 3,C	CB 99
RES 3,D	CB 9A
RES 3,E	CB 9B
RES 3,H	CB 9C
RES 3,L	CB 9D
RES 4, (HL)	CB A6
RES 4, (IX+dis)	DD CB XX A6
RES 4, (IY+dis)	FD CB XX A6
RES 4,A	CB A7
RES 4,B	CB A0
RES 4,C	CB A1
RES 4,D	CB A2
RES 4,E	CB A3
RES 4,H	CB A4
RES 4,L	CB A5
RES 5 (HL)	CB AE
RES 5, (IX+dis)	DD CB XX AE
RES 5, (IY+dis)	FD CB XX AE
RES 5,A	CB AF
RES 5,B	CB A8
RES 5,C	CB A9
RES 5,D	CB AA
RES 5,E	CB AB
RES 5,H	CB AC
RES 5,L	CB AD
RES 6, (HL)	CB B6
RES 6, (IX+dis)	DD CB XX B6
RES 6, (IY+dis)	FD CB XX B6
RES 6,A	CB B7
RES 6,B	CB B0
RES 6,C	CB B1
RES 6,D	CB B2
RES 6,E	CB B3
RES 6,H	CB B4
RES 6,L	CB B5
RES 7, (HL)	CB BE
RES 7, (IX+dis)	DD CB XX BE
RES 7, (IY+dis)	FD CB XX BE
RES 7,A	CB BF
RES 7,B	CB B8
RES 7,C	CB B9
RES 7,D	CB BA
RES 7,E	CB BB
RES 7,H	CB BC
RES 7,L	CB BD
RET	C9
RET C	D8
RET M	F8
RET NC	D0
RET NZ	C0
RET P	F0
RET PE	E8
RET PO	E0
RET Z	C8
RETI	ED 4D
RETN	ED 45
RL (HL)	CB 16
RL (IX+dis)	DD CB XX 16
RL (IY+dis)	FD CB XX 16
RL A	CB 17
RL B	CB 10
RL C	CB 11
RL D	CB 12
RL E	CB 13
RL H	CB 14
RL L	CB 15
RLA	17
RLC (HL)	CB 06
RLC (IX+dis)	DD CB XX 06
RLC (IY+dis)	FD CB XX 06
RLC A	CB 07
RLC B	CB 00
RLC C	CB 01
RLC D	CB 02
RLC E	CB 03
RLC H	CB 04
RLC L	CB 05
RLCA	07
RLD	ED 6F
RR (HL)	CB 1E
RR (IX+dis)	DD CB XX 1E
RR (IY+dis)	FD CB XX 1E
RR A	CB 1F
RR B	CB 18
RR C	CB 19
RR D	CB 1A
RR E	CB 1B
RR H	CB 1C
RR L	CB 1D
RRA	1F
RRC (HL)	CB 0E
RRC (IX+dis)	DD CB XX 0E
RRC (IY+dis)	FD CB XX 0E
RRC A	CB 0F
RRC B	CB 08
RRC C	CB 09
RRC D	CB 0A
RRC E	CH 0B
RRC H	CB 0C
RRC L	CB 0D
RRCA	0F
RRD	ED 67
RST 00	C7
RST 08	CF
RST 10	D7
RST 18	DF
RST 20	E7
RST 28	EF
RST 30	F7
RST 38	FF
SBC A, (HL)	9E
SBC A, (IX+dis)	DD 9E XX
SBC A, (IY+dis)	FD 9E XX
SBC A,A	9F
SBC A,B	98
SBC A,C	99
SBC A,D	9A
SBC A,n	DE XX
SBC A,E	9B
SBC A,H	9C
SBC A,L	9D
SBC HL,BC	ED 42
SBC HL,DE	ED 52
SBC HL,HL	ED 62
SBC HL,SP	ED 72
SCF	37
SET 0, (HL)	CB C6
SET 0, (IX+dis)	DD CB XX C6
SET 0, (IY+dis)	FD CB XX C6
SET 0,A	CB C7
SET 0,B	CB C0
SET 0,C	CB C1
SET 0,D	CB C2
SET 0,E	CB C3
SET 0,H	CB C4
SET 0,L	CB C5
SET 1, (HL)	CB CE
SET 1, (IX+dis)	DD CB XX CE
SET 1, (IY+dis)	FD CB XX CE
SET 1,A	CB CF
SET 1,B	CB C8
SET 1,C	CB C9
SET 1,D	CB CA
SET 1,E	CB CB
SET 1,H	CB CC
SET 1,L	CB CD
SET 2, (HL)	CB D6
SET 2, (IX+dis)	DD CB XX D6
SET 2, (IY+dis)	FD CB XX D6
SET 2,A	CB D7
SET 2,B	CB D0
SET 2,C	CB D1
SET 2,D	CB D2
SET 2,E	CB D3
SET 2,H	CB D4
SET 2,L	CB D5
SET 3, (HL)	CB DE
SET 3, (IX+dis)	DD CB XX DE
SET 3, (IY+dis)	FD CB XX DE
SET 3,A	CB DF
SET 3,B	CB D8
SET 3,C	CB D9
SET 3,D	CB DA
SET 3,E	CB DB
SET 3,H	CB DC
SET 3,L	CB DD
SET 4, (HL)	CBE6
SET 4, (IX+dis)	DD CB XX E6
SET 4, (IY+dis)	FD CB XX E6
SET 4,A	CB E7
SET 4,B	CB E0
SET 4,C	CB E1
SET 4,D	CB E2
SET 4,E	CB E3
SET 4,H	CB E4
SET 4,L	CB E5
SET 5, (HL)	CB EE
SET 5, (IX+dis)	DD CB XX EE
SET 5, (IY+dis)	FD CB XX EE
SET 5,A	CB EF
SET 5,B	CB E8
SET 5,C	CB E9
SET 5,D	CB EA
SET 5,E	CB EB
SET 5,H	CB EC
SET 5,L	CB ED
SET 6, (HL)	CB F6
SET 6, (IX+dis)	DD CB XX F6
SET 6, (IY+dis)	FD CB XX F6
SET 6,A	CB F7
SET 6,B	CB F0
SET 6,C	CB F1
SET 6,D	CB F2
SET 6,E	CB F3
SET 6,H	CB F4
SET 6,L	CB F5
SET 7, (HL)	CB FE
SET 7, (IX+dis)	DD CB XX FE
SET 7,(IY+dis)	FD CB XX FE
SET 7,A	CB FF
SET 7,B	CB F8
SET 7,C	CB F9
SET 7,D	CB FA
SET 7,E	CB FB
SET 7,H	CB FC
SET 7,L	CB FD
SLA (HL)	CB 26
SLA (IX+dis)	DD CB XX 26
SLA (IY+dis)	FD CB XX 26
SLA A	CB 27
SLA B	CB 20
SLA C	CB 21
SLA D	CB 22
SLA E	CB 23
SLA H	CB 24
SLA L	CB 25
SRA (HL)	CB 2E
SRA (IX+dis)	DD CB XX 2E

MNEMONIC	HEXADECIMAL	MNEMONIC	HEXADECIMAL	MNEMONIC	HEXADECIMAL
SRA (IY+dis)	FD CB XX 2E				
SRA A	CB 2F				
SRA B	CB 28				
SRA C	CB 29				
SRA D	CB 2A				
SRA E	CB 2B				
SRA H	CB 2C				
SRA L	CB 2D				
SRL (HL)	CB 3E				
SRL (IX+dis)	DD CB XX 3E				
SRL (IY+dis)	FD CB XX 3E				
SRL A	CB 3F				
SRL B	CB 38				
SRL C	CB 39				
SRL D	CB 3A				
SRL E	CB 3B				
SRL H	CB 3C				
SRL L	CB 3D				
SUB (HL)	96				
SUB (IX+dis)	DD 96 XX				
SUB (IY+dis)	FD 96 XX				
SUB A	97				
SUB B	90				
SUB C	91				
SUB D	92				
SUB E	93				
SUB n	D6 XX				
SUB H	94				
SUB L	95				
XOR (HL)	AE				
XOR (IX+dis)	DD AE XX				
XOR (IY+dis)	FD AE XX				
XOR A	AF				
XOR B	A8				
XOR C	A9				
XOR D	AA				
XOR n	EE XX				
XOR E	AB				
XSOR H	AC				
XOR L	AD				

INDEX

SPECTRUM
MACHINE LANGUAGE FOR THE ABSOLUTE BEGINNER

========================

R E G I S T R A T I O N
C A R D

Please fill out this page and return it promptly in order that we may keep you informed of new software and special offers that arise. Simply cut along the dotted line and return it to the correct address selected from those overleaf.

Where did you learn of this product?

☐ Magazine. If so, which one?.......................

☐ Through a friend

☐ Saw it in a Retail Store

☐ Other. Please specify.............................

Which Magazines do you purchase?

Regularly:...

Occassionally:.....................................

What Age are you?

☐ 10-15 ☐ 16-19 ☐ 20-24 ☐ Over 25

We are continually writing new material and would appreciate receiving your comments on our product.

How would you rate this book?

☐ Excellent ☐ Value for money

☐ Good ☐ Priced right

☐ Poor ☐ Overpriced

Please tell us what software you would like to see produced for your computer.

____

____

____

Name...

Address..

.................................Code...................

PUT THIS IN A STAMPED ENVELOPE AND SEND TO:

In the United States of America return page to:
Melbourne House Software Inc., 347 Reedwood Drive,
Nashville TN 37217.

In the United Kingdom return page to:
Melbourne House (Publishers) Ltd., Melbourne House, Church Yard,
Tring, Hertfordshire, HP23 5LU

In Australia & New Zealand return page to:
Melbourne House (Australia) Pty. Ltd., Suite 4, 75 Palmerston Crescent,
South Melbourne, Victoria, 3205.